CONFIRM

THEN AND

Mark
6. Oct. 1982

ALCUIN CLUB COLLECTIONS
No. 60

The Committee of the Alcuin Club

Confirmation

THEN AND NOW

by J. D. C. Fisher

ALCUIN CLUB/S.P.C.K.

First published in 1978
for the Alcuin Club
by S.P.C.K.
Holy Trinity Church
Marylebone Road
London NW1 4DU

ISBN 0 281 03666 7

Printed in Great Britain by
William Clowes & Sons Limited
London, Beccles and Colchester

Contents

Abbreviations

Bénoit	A. Bénoit, *Le Baptême Chrétien au Second Siècle*, Paris 1953
CQR	*Church Quarterly Review*
JTS	*Journal of Theological Studies*
Lampe	G. W. H. Lampe, *The Seal of the Spirit*, London [2]1967
Mason	A. J. Mason, *The Relation of Confirmation to Baptism*, London 1893
Mitchell	L. L. Mitchell, *Baptismal Anointing*, London 1966
RHE	*Révue d'Histoire Ecclésiastique*
RSR	*Recherches de Science Religieuse*
SC	*Sources Chrétiennes*
van Buchem	L. A. van Buchem, *L'Homélie Pseudo-Eusébienne de Pentecôte*, Nijmegen 1967
Whitaker	E. C. Whitaker, *Documents of the Baptismal Liturgy*, London [2]1970
Wirgman	*The Doctrine of Confirmation*, London 1897

Preface

My indebtedness to others more expert in the field of liturgy and theology can be gauged from the bibliography. In particular I am bound to mention three books which deal with the early evidence for confirmation with a thoroughness which I could not emulate in the space allotted to me. First, there is A. J. Mason's *The Relation of Confirmation to Baptism*, first published in 1891, which, although it dates somewhat now, is still valuable for its many excerpts from the Fathers. Secondly, there is A. T. Wirgman's *Doctrine of Confirmation*, a full-scale reply to Mason which goes over the same ground, but also dates somewhat. Thirdly, there is Professor G. W. H. Lampe's *Seal of the Spirit*, first published in 1951, a masterly treatment of the subject expressing a point of view diametrically opposed to that of Mason. For myself I have tried to steer a course between that of Dr Mason and of Professor Lampe, believing with the old Roman historian that in this instance *media simillima veris*. In my chapter on the emergence of confirmation in southern Gaul I have relied entirely on L. A. van Buchem's brilliantly thorough work on Pseudo-Eusebius, which is written in French and deserves to be more widely known in England.

The student of the early history of Christian Initiation is now greatly helped by a number of English translations of Greek and Latin texts. I have myself derived much assistance from Dom Gregory Dix's *Apostolic Tradition of St Hippolytus*, Dr Edward Yarnold's *Awe-Inspiring Rites of Initiation*, R. McL. Wilson's translations of the New Testament *Apocrypha*, P. W. Harkins' translation of Chrysostom's *Baptismal Instructions*, and from E. Evans' editions of the works of Tertullian, especially his *de Baptismo*, while I am only one of many who has found Canon E. C. Whitaker's *Documents of the Baptismal Liturgy* invaluable.

Lack of space has prevented me from considering the case for or against confirmation in the apostolic age. I do not believe that this disputed subject will be settled in the foreseeable future, a factor which of course complicates the ecumenical situation. In this book I have tried to show in what the rite of confirmation consisted, and what grace it was believed to confer, in the period when there is the first undisputed evidence of the rite's existence. I have shown how the rite developed during the middle ages in my *Christian Initiation: Baptism in the Medieval West*, which logically is a sequel to this book.

Every parish priest is deeply concerned about the practice of confirmation. If, like St Peter's first converts, we ask, 'What shall we do?', it is necessary to clear up our minds what confirmation is; and if we want to know where to go next, it is not unprofitable to know how we came to be where we are. So this volume is offered as a small contribution to the continuing debate about Christian Initiation.

Finally, I must offer my thanks to the Alcuin Club Committee for its interest in my work, and for accepting it as the Club's Collection for 1978.

J. D. C. FISHER

Cuckfield Vicarage,
West Sussex

P.S. Since parting with my manuscript, I have read J. A. T. Robinson's *Redating the New Testament*, and consider it possible that some of the documents mentioned in chapter 1 may belong to the first century.

1 *The Early Non-biblical Evidence*

In 1909 F. H. Chase, Bishop of Ely, published a book with the title *Confirmation in the Apostolic Age.* In 1951 Professor G. W. H. Lampe published his *Seal of the Spirit*, the fifth Chapter of which carries the heading, 'Confirmation in the Apostolic Age?' The question mark introduced by Professor Lampe is an indication, eloquent and succinct, of a problem very much under discussion at the present time, especially in Anglican circles, namely, whether the rite now known in the West as confirmation can be found, even if only in germ, in the New Testament. To answer this question it is necessary to consider by what means those who responded to the missionary preaching of the apostolic church received the Holy Spirit. That converts did in fact receive the Holy Spirit at their initiation into the Christian fellowship is clearly shown in the New Testament. But was the Holy Spirit normally imparted by means of a rite? And if so, in what did the rite consist? Did it include a simple confession of faith in Jesus as Lord, followed by a dipping in water, and no more than that? Or did it include further ceremonies, directly connected with the giving of the Spirit, namely, hand-laying and anointing, such as are attested by Tertullian at the end of the second century and by Hippolytus about twenty years later? For it is this hand-laying and anointing out of which has sprung the rite called confirmation.

The answer given to these questions depends largely upon the view taken of the laying on of hands in Acts 8.17 and 19.6 and Heb. 6.2; secondly, of the anointing mentioned in 2 Cor. 1.21 and in 1 John 2.20 and 27; and thirdly, of the sealing in 2 Cor. 1.22 and Eph. 1.13 and 4.30. Whether these biblical references to hand-laying, anointing, and sealing are, or are not, in fact allusions to a rite of baptism which included, at any rate in some churches, a hand-laying, an anointing and a signing with the cross—any or all of these—has long been disputed, is still disputed, and the end of the dispute is not in sight.

Limitation of space prevents a full discussion of this topic here. Suffice it to say that the New Testament evidence about confirmation is plainly patient of more than one interpretation; and this being so, it is legitimate to turn to the earliest non-biblical Christian literature in the hope that it may throw light on what is obscure. For the liturgical practices of the second century grew out of those of the first; and when allowance has been made for that which at first was fluid to assume in time a more fixed form, and that which was simple to become more complex, it might still be hoped that the known baptismal practices of the second century would help to solve some of the mysteries which surround the practice of the first. But to turn with this hope to the early extra-biblical writings is to experience a sense of frustration, and for three reasons. First, the extant literature is not plentiful, and much of it is totally irrelevant to the subject of initiation. Nobody now knows how many letters, homilies, or tracts which would have brought certainty where now there is only conjecture perished in the persecution of Diocletian when Christians were ordered to surrender their sacred writings. Secondly, so far as our knowledge goes, no second century writers except Melito of Sardis, whose work on baptism is lost except for one fragment, Justin Martyr, and the anonymous author of the *Didache* attempted to describe the rite of initiation which they knew; at best we have allusions, more or less explicit, to the subject. Thirdly, while the *Didache* and Justin's first *Apology* are invaluable for the information which they give about the rite of baptism, these documents leave room for speculation as to how much of the rite they may have passed over in silence. It is not till the very end of the second century that the fog of uncertainty is dispersed by the appearance of Tertullian's *de Baptismo* and, a little later, Hippolytus' *Apostolic Tradition*.

The *Didache*, or *Teaching of the Twelve Apostles*, has one short section on baptism, the value of which would be greatly enhanced if its date and provenance could be determined with some degree of accuracy. Whether or not Audet is right in dating it between 50 and 70 A.D., it is not likely to have been written later than the beginning of the second century, because the ecclesiastical ministry of which it shows knowledge is in a primitive and undeveloped state, inasmuch as there are still apostles and prophets as in Eph. 2.20 and 4.11, practising an itinerant ministry, and taking precedence over the local ministry, which, as in Phil. 1.1 and 1 Tim. 3.1–13, consists in bishops and deacons. Its subject matter suggests that the *Didache* was addressed to a Jewish-Christian church in a district, possibly of Syria or Palestine, where shortage of water might necessitate baptism by affusion.

Section 7 deals with the administration of baptism:

> With regard to baptism ye shall baptize as follows: after first reciting all these things (i.e. the matters mentioned in the previous chapters concerning the Two Ways, the way of life and the way of death), ye

shall baptize in the name of the Father and of the Son and of the Holy Spirit in living (i.e. running) water. But if thou dost not have living water, thou shalt baptize in other water; and if thou art not able in cold, then in warm water. But if thou hast neither, pour water on the head three times in the name of the Father, Son, and Holy Spirit. But before the baptism let him who baptizes and him who is baptized fast, and also others who are able: and thou shalt order him who is baptized to fast for one or two days beforehand.

From the fact that the first sentence uses the second person plural, and the following sentences use the second person singular, which we have made clearer by the use of 'ye' and 'thou', Audet[1] concluded that the first sentence was original and the remainder a later addition, inserted because the requirements of the first sentence led to practical difficulties.

In its original form this set of instructions could hardly have been briefer, being no more than an instruction to use the Trinitarian formula and running water. From this and from the fact that only one candidate seems to be envisaged it could be that the author is telling presbyters, deacons, or laymen how to baptize in emergency. Even in its enlarged form this section says very little about the rite of baptism.

The point of importance here is that there is no mention of an anointing before or after baptism, or of a hand-laying. Various suggestions have been offered to explain this omission. On the ground that the *Didache* was an elementary manual for priests and deacons Wirgman (p. 102) and Gore[2] did not expect to find in it any reference to liturgical acts which the local ministry was not allowed to perform. In Dix's[3] opinion the *Didache* was published for the guidance of the laity, giving detailed instructions only about those rites which they could perform in the absence of the clergy. But whether the silence of the *Didache* concerning hand-laying or unction is to be explained along these lines or not, Oulton[4] must surely be wrong in his assertion that the rite of baptism in the *Didache* is complete in itself and regarded by its author as such.

Bénoit (pp. 5f) drew attention to a Coptic fragment of the *Didache* which in section 10 has a sentence about thanksgiving over oil. It is, however, uncertain whether this interpolation is genuine, and, if it is, for what use this holy oil was destined.

In short, the information supplied by the *Didache* on the subject of initiation is of such a nature that we can only conclude with Lampe (p. 105) that it has little to our present purpose.

The writings of the Apostolic Fathers yield no firm evidence of a hand-laying or unction symbolical of the gift of the Holy Spirit. Clement of Rome[5] is aware that we have 'one God and one Christ and one Spirit of grace who was poured out on us.' The *Epistle of Barnabas* opens with a commendation of the readers for giving evidence of the Spirit poured out on them from the riches of the Lord's fount. There are in the *Shepherd of Hermas* six places where the readers are said to have received the Spirit—for example, *Mand.* 10.2.5: 'So put away sorrow from yourself and do not grieve the Holy Spirit who dwells in you.'[6] But in none of these instances is anything said about the occasion when the Holy Spirit was received.

The need to walk worthy of the vocation wherewith a Christian has been called is frequently stressed. In *2 Clement* 6.9 there is a warning of the difficulty of entering the kingdom of heaven 'if we fail to keep our baptism pure and undefiled.' In 7.6 the author refers to those who have not kept the seal, in 8.6 he exhorts to keep the flesh pure and the seal unspotted, and in 14.3 to guard the flesh so that you may share in the Spirit. Hermas commands to keep this flesh pure and undefiled so that the Spirit who dwells in it may bear witness to it.[7] Evidently baptism, the seal, and reception of the Spirit are interrelated. But the writers do not say that the Spirit is imparted by the act of baptism itself.

With regard to baptism 'Barnabas' says, 'Receiving forgiveness of our sins and hoping in the name we became new, created again from the beginning. Therefore God truly dwells within us in our habitation.'[8] But we cannot tell from a passage like this in what the rite of baptism consisted. 'Barnabas' also says that 'we go down into the water full of sins and filth, and we come up bearing fruit in our heart, having our fear and hope in Jesus in the spirit.'[9] By giving 'spirit' a capital letter Lampe (p. 104) was able to argue that remission of sins and the gift of the Spirit were both thought by the author to be conferred in the single act of baptism in water, an exegesis which would leave no room for any hand-laying or anointing by which the Spirit might be conferred. Lightfoot,[10] however, by not giving 'spirit' a capital letter, made the word refer not to the Holy Spirit but to the human spirit; and his rendering is preferable because it takes account of the parallelism between the phrase 'in the spirit' and the previous phrase 'in the heart'.

Whereas St Paul three times associated the seal with the Holy Spirit, the apostolic Fathers usually associated it with the Second Person of the Trinity and with the cross. Dealing with circumcision as a seal, 'Barnabas' saw significance in the fact that Abraham circumcised eighteen males and three hundred, and calculated that eighteen represented Jesus and three hundred the cross.[11] In *Sim.* 9.16.2ff Hermas says plainly that the seal is the water: 'they go down into the water dead and come up alive.' The seal is here called the seal of the Son of God, and he who receives the seal bears the name of the Son of God. This recalls Rev. 7.3 and 14.1, where the redeemed are said to be sealed in their foreheads and to have the Father's name written on

4

their foreheads. In *Sim.* 9.17.4, in a passage reminiscent of Rev. 21.24ff, Hermas writes of the twelve nations of the earth, each with its peculiar characteristics being of one understanding and one mind, having received the seal. Here, too, the seal enables those who receive it to bear the name of the Son of God. The spirits of the virgins whom these nations have received seem to stand for certain impersonal Christian virtues. In *Sim.* 8.2.1–4, where the faithful receive a white robe and seals, the choice of imagery has been affected by Rev. 7, where the faithful are arrayed in white robes and have been sealed in their foreheads.

Hence if the seal is the water, and yet is closely associated with the cross and enables those who are sealed to bear the name of the Son of God, it could be that the seal was the sign of the cross imprinted on the foreheads of the baptized as they emerged from the water. It is clear, however, that the Apostolic Fathers do not say that the Holy Spirit is conferred upon the initiates either by the act of baptism itself or by the seal.

There is no mention at all of any hand-laying or unction in connection with baptism or the seal. If that which is not recorded in black and white did not happen, then certainly confirmation was unknown to the Apostolic Fathers. But since none of them attempted to describe the rite of initiation, this may not prove much; and in any case it is always difficult to be sure how much can be proved by the argument from silence. If, for instance, there is significance in the fact that 'Barnabas' does not mention confirmation, is there also significance in the fact that he does not mention the eucharist?

The Apocryphal Acts contain accounts of baptisms which, however legendary, may have some bearing on the content of the rite known to the authors. In the *Acts of Paul* Thecla asks for the seal in Christ, to which St Paul replies, 'Have patience, Thecla, and you will receive the water.'[12] The natural inference from this is that seal and water both refer to the act of baptism, unless this is the writer's quaint way of saying that the rite is twofold, consisting in baptism and sealing. Again it is to be noted that the seal is called the seal in Christ and not the seal of the Spirit.

Thecla's own self-baptism cannot have been accompanied by a hand-laying or anointing. But apart from the miraculous element the circumstances of this baptism are extraordinary in that there was no minister present to pronounce the baptismal formula or put the baptismal interrogations. So it can hardly be used to prove what was normal. When Thecla next met St Paul she told him that she had taken the bath, whereupon the apostle led her into the house of Hermias and heard everything from her.[13] From this Lampe (p. 106) concluded that her initiation was regarded as complete. Indeed, while St Paul could

5

have laid his hands on her or anointed her or given her communion when they were in the house, if that was customary, there is no suggestion that he did so. But if the author was silent about these things, he was equally silent about any giving of the Holy Spirit to Thecla.

Hermocrates and his wife received the grace of the Lord's seal.[14] St Paul promised Longus and Cestus that they would receive the seal in the Lord, and in due course with much joy they were given the seal in the Lord.[15] Thus three times the seal is associated not with the Holy Spirit but with the Lord.

On another occasion St Paul, loosed from his chains, went to the sea-shore where he initiated Eubula and Artemilla into holy baptism, after which he returned to his bonds.[16] This initiation, it seems, did not consist in anything more than baptism in water. In one version of these Acts St Paul prayed and laid his hands on Artemilla before baptizing her.[17] The writer does not say whether he believed this hand-laying to have any special significance, or whether such a hand-laying can be assumed in any of the other baptisms which he describes. Lampe (p. 107) was probably right in comparing it with the hand-laying in the Jewish rite of baptism.

In the *Acts of Peter*, while they were both on board ship, Theon invited St Peter to baptize him with the sign of the Lord, whereupon the apostle went down by a rope and baptized him in the name of the Father, the Son, and the Holy Spirit. Then a young man shining with brilliance appeared to them. Immediately 'Peter and Theon went up and entered the cabin; and Peter took bread and gave thanks to the Lord . . . And he said, Most excellent . . . in your name this man has been washed and signed with your holy sign. Therefore in your name I give to him your eucharist, that he may be your perfect servant for ever blameless.'[18] While initiation here evidently includes baptism and the eucharist, the question arises, what does the writer understand by 'signed with your holy sign'? Seeing that the phrase becomes excessively tautologous if it is treated as synonymous with the act of baptizing, the reference could be to a consignation at baptism. Once more the sign is called the sign of our Lord God, Jesus Christ; and, as Lampe (p. 108) observed, there is no suggestion that the writer regarded the sign as the seal of the Spirit.

In his work *On the Passover* Melito of Sardis drew an analogy between the Passover and Christian initiation:

> Then Moses, having slain the lamb and by night fulfilled the mystery with the sons of Israel, sealed the doors of the houses in order to protect the people and to frighten off the angel. When the lamb was slain and the passover eaten and the mystery fulfilled and

the people rejoiced and Israel was sealed, then the angel came to strike Egypt which was not initiated into the mystery, and had no part in the passover, and was not sealed with the blood, and was not guarded by the Spirit . . .[19]

The seal in this instance was the blood on the doorposts, a mark on the doors of the houses in which Israelites lived. The best sense would be obtained if we supposed that Melito was comparing the mark made on the doorposts with a mark made upon Christians during their initiation; and if this mark was the sign of the cross, the analogy with sealing with blood would be all the greater. It is noteworthy also that the words 'sealed with the blood' are followed at once by the words 'guarded by the Spirit'. While the two expressions may not be synonymous, there is evidently a fairly close connection between sealing and the Holy Spirit. This is borne out by what Melito wrote further on: 'In the Spirit he slew man-slaying death, because he . . . sealed our souls with his own Spirit and the members of his body with his own blood.'[20] This suggests that a physical sealing of the body, perhaps with the sign of the cross, was the outward sign of an inward sealing of the soul by the Spirit. There is no indication here as to the relationship between this sealing and the act of baptism in water.

There is one passage where Melito may possibly have let drop a hint that the sealing was performed with oil: 'After taking the blood of the lamb, anoint (*chrisate*) the front doors of your houses, placing on the door posts at the entry the sign of the blood . . .'[21] The reference is to Ex. 12.22, where, however, the word 'anoint' is not used. We may ask what caused Melito to use 'anoint' in this context when he did not find it in the relevant passage of scripture. Dix[22] believed that it was because Melito was aware that the sealing in initiation was performed with chrism. On the other hand Melito may have been influenced by 2 Cor. 1.21f, where St Paul had mentioned together anointing and sealing.[23]

Moreton has found possible evidence of confirmation in the D-text of Acts, where 19.5f reads thus: 'And when they heard this, they were baptized into the name of the Lord Jesus Christ for the forgiveness of sins. And when Paul had laid his hands on them the Holy Spirit at once fell on them.' Now AV, RSV, and NEB omit the words 'Christ for the forgiveness of sins', the presence of which in the D-text indicates a belief that the main purpose of baptism was to convey remission of sins, as it was the main purpose of the ensuing hand-laying to confer the gift of the Holy Spirit. Thus the D-text distinguishes more clearly between the moment of baptism for the remission of sins and the hand-laying for the giving of the Spirit.[24]

Similarly the usually preferred text of Acts 2.38 reads, '. . . be

baptized in the name of Jesus Christ for the remission of sins ...',
whereas the D-text has 'in the name of the Lord Jesus Christ'—exactly
the words used in the D-text of Acts 19.5. Whether or not the D-text is
to be preferred, the scribe who compiled it may have been influenced
by contemporary practice, knowing an initiatory rite which was
twofold, consisting in baptism for the forgiveness of sins and the laying
on of hands for the bestowal of the Spirit. If it does not belong to the
first, the D-text of Acts must belong to the second century, since it was
known to Marcion, Tatian, and Irenaeus.[25]

In 1945 at Nag Hammadi in Upper Egypt there was discovered
among the remains of the library of some Gnostic sect the *Gospel of
Philip*, a work which includes a number of references to initiation.
Baptism, it seems, conferred the gift of the Spirit: 'If any one goes
down to the water and comes up without receiving anything and says,
I am a Christian, he has taken the name at interest. But if he receives
the Holy Spirit, he has the gift of the name.'[26]

But the writer insists that there is something greater than baptism,
namely, anointing with chrism:

> So also they speak about baptism, saying that baptism is a great
> thing, because if (people) received it they will live ... The chrism is
> superior to baptism, for from the chrism we are called Christians,
> not because of the baptism: and Christ is so called because of the
> chrism. For the Father anointed the Son, and the Son anointed the
> apostles, and the apostles anointed us. He who is anointed possesses
> the All. He possesses the resurrection, the light, the Cross, the Holy
> Spirit.[27]

Here the reception of the Holy Spirit is linked with chrismation and
the cross in such a way as to suggest that in the earlier passage those
who take the name at interest are those who are only baptized in water,
while those who receive the gift of the Holy Spirit and possess the gift of
the name are those who also receive the chrismation.

Baptism and chrismation are two parts of an initiatory rite which
includes after them the eucharist: 'The Lord did everything in a
mystery, a baptism and a chrism and a eucharist and redemption and
a bridechamber.'[28] If the order of words is pressed, the chrismation
came after and not before the baptism.

The *Gospel of Philip* seems to belong to the Valentinian school of
Gnosticism described by Irenaeus.[29] Believing that it may have
originated in Syria, Whitaker[30] discounted the value of this document
for deducing the practice of the Syrian church at this time largely on
the ground that the Syrian evidence from the *Didache* onwards yields
no trace of a post-baptismal anointing such as we have here. He would

therefore dismiss the chrismation as a peculiarity of Gnosticism in no way representative of orthodox Syrian practice.

Although this Gospel is Gnostic, it contains a number of ideas which are found in other writings of whose orthodoxy there is no doubt, such as that of becoming a Christian or christ through chrismation. It may be that in the second century there was no very clear line of demarcation between orthodoxy and Gnostic heresy, and that the post-baptismal chrismation found in the *Gospel of Philip* was found in some more orthodox circles in the second century, perhaps in Egypt if not in Syria.

The evidence so far considered has provided no incontrovertible proof that confirmation existed in the second century. But it is of such a nature that those who hold that its existence has not been disproved beyond all doubt do not necessarily adopt an untenable position. More certain evidence, however, is found in Marcion, who used a rite of initiation which undoubtedly included more than baptism in water.

In *adv. Marcionem* 1.14, published in 207 after a first edition in 198,[31] Tertullian wrote:

> He certainly has not even yet rejected the Creator's water, for in it he washes his own, nor the oil with which he anoints them, nor the compound of milk and honey on which he weans them, nor the Creator's bread by which he makes manifest his own body. Even in his own rites and ceremonies he cannot do without things begged and borrowed from the Creator.[32]

This provides unmistakable evidence of an initiatory rite which consisted in baptism in water, anointing, the giving of milk and honey and the eucharist.

In 1.28 of the same work Tertullian asked a number of rhetorical questions arising out of Marcion's rite of baptism:

> For to what purpose, in his sight, is even baptism required? If there is remission of sins, how shall one be supposed to remit sins who is supposed not to retain them? . . . If there is a receiving of the Holy Spirit, how can one grant the Spirit who has not first supplied a soul? For soul is in some part that on which Spirit constructs its abode. Thus he sets his seal upon a man who has never to his mind been unsealed; he washes a man never to his mind defiled, and into this whole sacrament of salvation he plunges flesh which has no part or lot in salvation.[33]

In this passage, conspicuous for the orator's love of antithesis, Tertullian was trying to score debating points off Marcion for having in his sect a rite of initiation which contained features inconsistent with his dualistic theology. But amid much that is obscure the fact emerges that among the spiritual blessings which Marcion attributed to baptism were remission of sins, deliverance from death, regeneration, and the bestowal of the Holy Spirit. Furthermore the rite consisted in baptism in water and also sealing, although the unction and giving of milk and honey, mentioned in the former passage, are not alluded to here.

Much more information about the sealing is found in 3.22, where, after quoting Ezek. 9.4, Tertullian proceeds:

> For this same letter TAU of the Greeks, which is our T, has the appearance of the cross, which he foresaw we should have on our foreheads in the true and catholic Jerusalem, in which the twenty-first psalm, in the person of Christ himself addressing the Father, prophesies that Christ's brethren, the sons of God, will give glory to God the Father . . . And since all these are found in use with you also, the sign on the foreheads, and the sacraments of the churches, and the pureness of the sacrifices, you ought at once to break forth and affirm that it was for your Christ that the Creator's Spirit prophesied.'[34]

From this it becomes clear that the sealing mentioned further back is the sign of the cross made on the foreheads of the redeemed; and the reference to the catholic Jerusalem shows that the imagery of the seal is derived from the prophecy of Ezekiel.

When all this information is put together, the Marcionite rite of initiation is seen to consist in baptism in water, which conveys regeneration and remission of sins, anointing, signing with the cross, the giving of milk and honey, and finally the eucharist. This sequence of events corresponds very closely with that in Hippolytus' *Apostolic Tradition*.

Now the Marcionite rite is important for this reason that, although the Marcionites were a heretical and schismatic body, their liturgical practices, and not least their rite of initiation, seem to have been very similar to those of the Catholic church, so much so that Tertullian could say that the Marcionites, having their churches with bishops and presbyters, and their songs and martyrs, could be likened to a swarm of wasps building their combs in imitation of the bees.[35]

A very important question which arises here is, 'How old is Marcion's rite?' If it is correct that Marcion died in the pontificate of Eleutherius, his rite must have come into use before the year 189. But there are reasons for thinking that it may have been much older than that. According to Hippolytus Marcion was the son of the bishop of Sinope in Pontus, and grew up as an orthodox member of that church.[36] So it is possible to argue with Daniélou[37] that when Marcion left Sinope, now a heretic, and migrated to Rome, he retained for his sect the rite of initiation which he had used in Sinope. If this conjecture is sound, then unction, signing of the forehead, and the giving of milk and honey formed part of the baptismal liturgy used in Pontus as far back as the year 144. On the other hand of course it can be argued that the rite of Sinope at that time was more simple than this, and that Marcion, when he was no longer in communion with the Catholic Church, felt free to introduce into his rite of baptism ceremonies which were used in Gnostic circles. But the weakness of this argument has been exposed by Davis,[38] who has drawn attention to the well-known fact that Marcion believed matter to be evil, and that his dualistic outlook would have strongly dissuaded him from introducing into his rites the use of material things such as oil, milk, and honey. Indeed it is far more likely that Marcion's rite included anointing and the giving of milk and honey because these ceremonies were already included in the rite of the church to which he belonged, and that, since they had now become customary, he refrained from discontinuing them. Hence a persuasive, if not incontrovertible, case can be advanced for the use of anointing and consignation at baptism, at any rate in the church of Sinope, in the first half of the second century.

A much fuller account of the rite of baptism than anything we have encountered so far is found in the first *Apology* of Justin Martyr, who was put to death in Rome about the year 165. He wrote that catechumens were washed in the name of God, the Father of the universe, and of Jesus Christ our Saviour and of the Holy Spirit. Our main concern here lies with what Justin wrote a little further on:

> After thus washing him who has been persuaded and declared his assent we conduct him to those who are called brothers, in order to offer common prayers both for ourselves and for him who has been enlightened and all others everywhere earnestly, so that having learnt the things that are true we may be vouchsafed also by our works to be found good citizens and keepers of the commandments, so that we may obtain the everlasting salvation. We greet one another with a kiss when we have finished our prayers. Then there is brought to the president of the brothers bread and a cup of water and wine . . .[39]

That is to say, when he had been conducted into his place among the congregation, the newly baptized person shared for the first time in the church's intercessions and in the kiss of peace, and communicated for the first time with the faithful at the ensuing eucharist. The climax of initiation was thus the admission of the neophyte to communion. Whereas the personal aspect of initiation was emphasized at the baptism, necessarily for reasons of modesty administered in private, the final part of the rite, which took place in the presence of all the faithful, amongst other things emphasized the admission of the new member into the corporate life of the church, and, in particular, into its greatest act of fellowship, the eucharist.

But, great as is the value of Justin's all too brief account of initiation in Rome in the mid-second century, it raises one point of cardinal importance here, in that no other ceremonies are mentioned between the actual baptism and the beginning of the eucharist. Did Justin say nothing about hand-laying or unction because these were as yet not found in the Roman rite? Or did he know either or both of them but for reasons which seemed good to himself passed them over in silence? Conflicting answers have been given to these questions.

On the one hand Oulton alleged that Justin's account of baptism was complete in itself and regarded by the author as such,[40] a statement which Dix[41] rightly criticized as a precarious inference from the evidence. Turmel concluded that hand-laying and anointing were introduced into the baptismal liturgy after the death of Justin—hence his failure to mention them—and before the publication of Irenaeus' *Adversus Haereses*, and were a product of the Montanist movement, when a great effusion of the Spirit rolled like a wave over the Christian communities.[42] It is, however, not necessary to cite the influence of Montanism with its extravagances as the reason for the church's interest in the gift of the Holy Spirit in the later second century, because, unless the Acts of the Apostles and the Pauline Epistles have completely misrepresented the situation in the apostolic age, the church had this interest in the gift of the Holy Spirit from the very beginning. In R. P. C. Hanson's opinion Justin gave no indication whatever that initiation in his time consisted in any other ceremony except washing in water and invocation of the name,[43] while Lampe (p. 109) could not find any evidence that Justin knew of any second sacramental act, or second part of a single ceremony, by which Spirit-baptism was conferred. Since it is always possible to use the argument from silence in this way, this explanation of Justin's failure to mention anointing or hand-laying cannot be dismissed as untenable, and will never lack advocates.

Against this, however, Mason (p. 319) considered it probable that laying on of the hand was to be reckoned among those prayers which were, as Justin said, offered on behalf of the newly enlightened. Although he was opposed to Mason's viewpoint, Wirgman (p. 104) believed that Justin's account of baptism was made deliberately incomplete, possibly because he was writing about the rudiments of the faith to an unbeliever, and so concentrated his remarks on the two great sacraments of the gospel. Lowther Clarke suggested that Justin's silence was due to the fact that it would have been very difficult to explain the Christian conception of the Holy Spirit to pagans.[44] Wilson made the point that too much emphasis had sometimes been placed on Justin's failure to mention any other acts, and too little notice taken of his silence about the Holy Spirit in his account of baptism and its effects; hence he claimed with not a little justification that the argument from silence was a two-edged sword, which, if it was used to prove that Justin did not know of hand-laying or unction at baptism, could equally be used to prove that he did not know of a gift of the Spirit imparted in baptism.[45]

Now it cannot possibly be maintained that Justin's account of initiation is complete as the account in the *Apostolic Tradition* is complete. For instance Justin has not stated how the candidates confessed their faith, how many times they were dipped in the water, what was the rank of the officiant at baptism or of the president at the eucharist. Capelle has argued that the ritual of the catechumenate was richer than Justin's words actually suggest.[46] Bénoit (pp. 139f) detected in Justin a certain reluctance to speak about the sacred mysteries of Christianity to pagan readers. This he considered a fair inference from some words in *Apol.* 1.61: 'We will now expound to you how, renewed by Christ, we are consecrated to God. If we omitted this point in our exposition, we would appear to be at fault.' Justin, said Bénoit, would prefer not to speak of baptism at all: if he does so, it is solely in order to fulfil perfectly the task which he has assigned himself of describing the life and teaching of Christians, so as to prove their innocence of the crimes with which pagan calumny charged them. It is noteworthy, too, as Bénoit observed, that in the Apologies Justin refrained from using the words 'baptism' and 'baptize' at all.

There is also much to be said for the view expressed by Couratin,[47] that Justin was not so simple as he sounded. That is to say, being obliged to mention the matter of baptism, because it was common knowledge that people became Christians by taking a bath, and the bread and wine of the eucharist, because there were rumours that Christians ate the bodies and drank the blood of infants, Justin took care to reveal as much as that and no more; and he tried to dissuade the Emperor from making further enquiries by suggesting that Christianity was only one more oriental cult such as Mithraism. So, concluded Couratin, while Justin's evidence is good as far as it goes, no arguments can be placed upon his silence.

However, although Justin may be supposed to have deliberately refrained from divulging more than was necessary, Bénoit (pp. 140f) doubted whether his motive was simply a desire not to reveal to the uninitiated the most solemn mysteries of the church. For if he said little about sacramental practice, he was nevertheless ready enough to discuss Christian doctrine, his first *Apology* containing references to the virgin birth (1.33), the second advent (1.52) and the resurrection of the flesh (1.19). Hence Bénoit concluded that Justin intended in his *Apologies* not only to refute the slanders of the heathen but also to demonstrate to philosophical emperors (1.1) that Christianity was a philosophy. Consequently it would not have served his purpose to deal at length with the rite of initiation and the details of its administration.

It can, therefore, be argued persuasively, if not conclusively, that Justin's account of baptism contains some omissions, although it is only in the light of evidence from elsewhere that it can be maintained that the items omitted included hand-laying and anointing for the imparting of the Holy Spirit.

That Justin did in fact believe the Holy Spirit to be given in Christian initiation cannot be inferred from his *Apologies*; and yet the matter is not in doubt because in his *Dialogue with Trypho*,[48] a Jew to whom he could speak of sacred things with less reserve, Justin wrote, 'What have I, who have been witnessed to by God, to do with circumcision? What need do I have of that baptism (i.e. Jewish) who have been baptized with the Holy Spirit?' In that work, Justin did not describe the ritual of initiation.

This passage seemed to Dix to be sufficient evidence that Justin believed that the Holy Spirit was given by an anointing at baptism. To support his case he had to find a convincing reason why Justin failed to mention this anointing in his *Apology*. Dix claimed to have found such a reason, namely, that in that work Justin set out to answer the popular allegations against the Christians, including the dangerous charge of magic; the whole account of the Christian rites was cleverly adapted to show how harmless those rites were from the point of view of the pagan critics, and was less naive than it appears at first sight. To suggest that a Christian during his initiation was given what a pagan Roman examining magistrate would assume to be a familiar spirit was not the best way to achieve the desired end.[49] However, although this conjecture has been regarded sympathetically by Ratcliff[50] and Dewar,[51] it has been rejected by Bénoit (p. 175) on the ground that in other places in the *Apologies* Justin has not hesitated to develop an angelology and a demonology such as might well encourage in a pagan reader the notion that Christians were in league with familiar spirits. If, however, Dix's explanation is unacceptable, we may still reasonably hold with Couratin that Justin dealt only with that part of the initiatory rite of which pagans had heard, and refrained, perhaps gladly, from referring to other parts of the mystery of which they were ignorant.

An argument in favour of the presence in Justin's rite of a prayer similar to the confirmation prayer of the later Western church has been advanced on the strength of what Justin said happened immediately after the baptism. The candidate was conducted into the congregation, where prayers were offered 'for ourselves and for the person who has received illumination, and all others everywhere.' That no reference to anything analogous to confirmation should be read out of these words was urged by Oulton on the ground that the newly baptized person did not come first in the list of those prayed for, but simply took his place among the number of the brethren, being prayed for particularly only because he was now a member of the brotherhood.[52] Oulton's argument commended itself to Bénoit (p. 176), who considered that in Justin's account of initiation there was between the baptism and the eucharist no room for a special rite for conferring the Holy Spirit. Nevertheless, in a persuasive reply to Oulton, Ratcliff[53] observed that the common prayers evidently belonged to the initiatory setting: if they were to be interpreted as a general intercession appropriate to the regular Sunday congregation, violence would be done to the sense of the content and also to Justin's own account of the prayers, which were concerned with the meaning of initiation, their general tenor being petition for the graces of godliness and stability, that all the baptized might achieve the eternal salvation which was the purpose of their baptism. Hence, argued Ratcliff, there was nothing intrinsically improbable in the suggestion that the petitions for the person who had been enlightened should specially relate to his own initiation, and should include a prayer that the Holy Spirit, or the sevenfold gifts of Is. 11.2, should be given to the new member as they had been given to all the others. Moreover, as Ratcliff also pointed out, a further reason for believing that these prayers were related to the initiation of the new member lies in the fact that he did not share in the kiss of peace until they were finished.

Although too little is said in the *Apology* to indicate in any detail the content of these prayers, certain passages in the *Dialogue*, when taken together, in Ratcliff's view suggested that the prayers not only asked God to send the Holy Spirit upon the baptized, but possibly also made mention of the sevenfold gifts of the Spirit, enumerated in Is. 11.2.[54] Thus in *Dial*. 39 Justin wrote that God was deliberately deferring the punishment which the Jews deserved for their hardness of heart,

> because he knows that every day there will still be those who will forsake the error of their ways, and become disciples to the name of Christ. Those who are enlightened by the name of this Christ receive gifts such as they are worthy to receive, and such as are necessary and appropriate for them. For one receives the spirit of understanding, another the spirit of counsel, another the spirit of strength, another the spirit of healing, another the spirit of prophecy, another the spirit of doctrine, another the spirit of the fear of God.

Here Justin did not quote scripture accurately, but conflated Is. 11.2 with 1 Cor. 12.8, yet in such a way that the gifts in his list were still seven in number. Now seeing that for him enlightenment was a synonym for baptism, Justin was saying in effect that those who were baptized received the sevenfold gifts of the Holy Spirit, in fulfilment of the prophecy in Ps. 68. 18, quoted in Eph. 4.8. Since there was no word in the account of baptism in the *Apology* about spiritual gifts being bestowed upon those who were enlightened, this makes it reasonably certain that there are omissions in that account.

Rejecting the argument for a double rite of initiation, A. T. Hanson[55] maintained that the present tense of the participle, 'those who are enlightened', proves that the gifts of the Spirit are received while they are actually being enlightened, that is, being baptized in water: if they received the Spirit in a rite distinct from baptism, Justin would have used an aorist participle. But this is to read too much into the use of the present tense.[56] 'Those who are enlightened' does not have to be pressed to mean 'those who are in the process of being enlightened' or 'those who are at the moment in the font'. While enlightenment certainly includes baptism in water, it is a term wide enough to cover a rite which may have contained other ceremonies besides. Furthermore if Justin used a present participle and not an aorist, it is more probably because he did not think of the enlightenment of converts as something that happened once in the past, but as an event which was still happening from time to time.

Ratcliff also called attention to *Dial.* 87, where Justin returned to the theme of spiritual gifts, this time quoting Is. 11.2 accurately:

The scripture does not say that the powers of the Spirit above mentioned came upon him (i.e. our Lord) because he wanted them: but because they were to rest upon him, that is, cease in him, so that there were to be no more prophets of your nation, as there were formerly . . . (these gifts) by virtue of his spirit of power he bestows upon those who believe in him, as he judges them worthy of them.

Now although Justin did not say so, he must have regarded their initiation as the moment when Christians received these promised gifts.

This case that the prayers offered in church as soon as the newly baptized had been admitted into the congregation included a prayer invoking the sevenfold Spirit upon them cannot be said to be proved beyond doubt. Nothing short of an inclusion of the words of such a prayer within the text of Justin's *Apology* would disarm all Ratcliff's critics. At any rate it deserves a better fate than it has received at the hands of Lampe (p. 110), who dismissed it as a piece of pure speculation without any foundation in anything that Justin actually said.

Ratcliff found further support for his case in *Dial.* 88, where reference is made to the descent of the Holy Spirit upon our Lord at his baptism: 'Then Jesus came to the river Jordan, where John was baptizing: and while Jesus went into the water, a fire was lit in Jordan; and as he emerged from the water, the apostles of this Christ of ours have left on record that the Holy Spirit descended on him like a dove.'

16

In this chapter Justin has passed from the thought of Christians receiving the Holy Spirit to that of our Lord receiving the Holy Spirit at his baptism; the inference is that Justin believed that Christians received the Holy Spirit at their baptism. Hence Ratcliff claimed that in Justin's eyes the account of our Lord's baptism in the gospels was the rationale of, and provided the pattern for, the Christian's initiation.[57] That is to say, the Christian convert descends into the water, as if into the Jordan, there to be regenerated in the name of the Trinity, and to receive remission of all his sins; on emerging from the water he receives the Holy Spirit. There is, said Ratcliff, a distinction in Justin's mind between the actual moment of our Lord's baptism in the Jordan and the moment when he received the Spirit; and this latter moment could well be the moment when the person baptized has been led into the congregation and had the sevenfold Spirit invoked upon him.

Ratcliff's argument here does not carry conviction, because it is not certain that Justin meant that our Lord's baptism established the pattern of Christian baptism. Again, it is difficult to know how much to read into the clause, 'as he came out of the water'. These words could mean that Justin believed the baptism to be already over when the Spirit descended on our Lord, in which case it becomes possible to argue for a further ceremony after baptism itself to symbolize and effect the coming of the Spirit upon Christians at their initiation. Lampe (pp. 109f), however, maintained that Justin's words meant no more than that our Lord had emerged from the water in the sense that he was no longer actually under the water when the Spirit came down upon him, in which case the gift of the Spirit is so closely related with the act of baptism that any further ceremony to confer the Spirit would be unnecessary. So too Bénoit (p. 180) considered that in the account of our Lord's baptism the connection between baptism and the gift of the Spirit was so close that one could say that Christ received the Holy Spirit at the moment of his baptism.

However, while Justin's reference to our Lord's baptism can be interpreted in more than one way, so as to suggest the presence or absence of a hand-laying or anointing with prayer in his rite of baptism, this much can be said for certain, that Justin's words can be reconciled with the practice attested by the Western Fathers and the ancient baptismal liturgies, where anointing and hand-laying followed baptism immediately, being part of the same rite, but they lend no support whatever to the later Western practice of confirming people many years after their baptism. In Justin's rite either confirmation was an integral part of the baptism or there was no confirmation at all.

An examination of the typology in the *Dialogue with Trypho* led Couratin to the belief that Justin knew of an unction after baptism. For in *Dial.* 41 Justin said that the offering of fine flour was a type of

eucharistic bread which our Lord commanded us to offer in re-
membrance of his passion for those who cleanse their souls from sin.

The ritual for the cleansing of a leper, found in Lev. 14, is thus
summarized by Couratin:

> On the seventh day (verse 9) the leper bathes his flesh in water; and
> on the eighth day (verses 10 and following) he brings three lambs
> and fine wheat flour and oil to the priest who is responsible for his
> cleansing. The first lamb is sacrificed, and the leper is anointed with
> the blood. The oil is then offered, and with the remainder of the oil
> the leper is anointed. First, various parts of the body are smeared;
> and then apparently the oil is poured over him. And the rest of the
> oil that is in the priest's hand he shall put upon the head of him that
> is cleansed (verse 18, LXX). Finally, the two other lambs and the
> sacrifice (i.e. the fine flour) are offered, and the propitiation for the
> leper is completed (verses 19, 21, LXX).[58]

Now Couratin claimed that the reason why Justin thought of the rite
for the cleansing of the leper as a type of Christian initiation was not
only because the leper's bathing in water and offering of flour
corresponded with the baptism of a Christian and the eucharist to
which he was then admitted, but also because there was an even closer
similarity between the two rites:

> The cleansing of the leper concludes with a seventh/eighth day rite.
> So the initiation of the catechumen concluded with the
> Saturday/Sunday Paschal celebration. On the seventh day the leper
> bathes his flesh with water before coming to the Tent of Meeting. So
> on Saturday the catechumen was baptized, or baptized himself,
> before being introduced into the Christian assembly (*Apology* 65).
> On the eighth day the leper comes to the priest and makes his
> oblation of a fine wheaten loaf . . . The leper is then anointed with
> blood and with oil, first on various parts of the body and then
> generally by a pouring of oil over the head. So, if the pattern, with
> the obvious omission of the animal sacrifice, was worked out in the
> comparison, the newly baptized would be anointed with oil, with a
> thoroughness which reminds us of the post-baptismal unction
> described by Tertullian in *De Baptismo* 7. Finally the leper's
> cleansing reaches its climax in the making of the sin offering and the
> burnt-offering of fine wheat flour. So the newly baptized's initiation
> reached its climax in the offering of the eucharist, which is the
> antitype of the offering of fine wheat flour, and the only sacrifice
> which God accepts, now that he has rejected the sacrifices and
> priests of the Old Law (*Dialogue* 117).[59]

The two rituals are remarkably similar, and the case put forward by
Couratin is at the least plausible. Yet in the nature of things it cannot

be regarded as proven beyond doubt. The first purpose of *Dial.* 41 was to demonstrate that the offering of fine flour was a type of the eucharist. But even so Justin had in mind at the time more than the eucharist itself, because he almost at once referred to our Lord's sufferings for those who cleanse their souls from all iniquity, and later asserted that Jewish circumcision was a type of the true circumcision from sin and error—two clear allusions to baptism. But even allowing that in writing this chapter Justin had the contemporary rite of initiation in mind, the presence of anointing in that rite is not proved for certain, because baptism in water and the eucharist, without any anointing, could have seemed to Justin to constitute a sufficiently close parallel for the cleansing of the leper to be seen as a type of Christian initiation. It is a question of how close the parallel between the two rituals had to be before the one could be treated as the type of the other; and to that kind of question there can be no certain answer.

Couratin, however, strengthened his case by noticing the train of thought in *Dial.* 86, where Justin alleged that certain wooden objects mentioned in the Old Testament were types of the cross of Christ. With his rod Moses delivered Israel, divided the Red Sea and made water flow out of the rock; by throwing wood in the water of Mara he sweetened it; by putting rods in their water Jacob made Laban's sheep conceive; with his staff he passed over the river; he saw a ladder above which stood God. The wood and the water which are mentioned in most of these instances evidently seemed to Justin to be types of the cross and baptism, even if a clear allusion to baptism does not appear until the end of the chapter, where Justin wrote that 'our Christ by his sufferings on the cross, and purifying us with water, has redeemed us from those very heinous sins which we have committed . . .'

Now it is highly significant that in a passage where he certainly had baptism in mind Justin should at once pass to the subject of anointing, recalling how Jacob anointed the stone at Bethel, how our Lord was anointed with the oil of gladness, and how kings and also, it seems, priests were anointed. This led Justin to think about Aaron, and then the budding of Aaron's rod, and next the rod which Isaiah had prophesied would come forth out of the stem of Jesse, upon whom in the next chapter it is shown that the sevenfold Spirit was to 'rest'. Hence Couratin suggested that, when Justin's mind started running on Christian baptism, he began by thinking about water, producing Old Testament references of a more or less apposite kind, and then he went on to think about oil, producing similar references to pre-figurations of the anointing of Christ and of kings and priests, and finally proceeded to quote from Is. 11.1, with an implied reference to the sevenfold Spirit, imparted by Christ to those who believe in him. So the sequence of thought in Justin's mind may have been governed by his knowledge of an initiatory rite which consisted in baptism in water, anointing with oil and the giving of the sevenfold Spirit, such as is to be found in Tertullian's *De Baptismo*, which describes the African rite only one generation later. As Mitchell (p. 13) has concluded on this subject, the evidence is not sufficient to establish Couratin's thesis and to count Justin a witness to baptismal anointing; but there is no longer an all-compelling reason for counting him a witness against the anointing.

Thornton also argued from the typology in the *Dialogue with Trypho* that Justin knew an initiatory rite which included more than baptism in water. An analogy was drawn by Thornton between the events of Josh. 5.2–12 and Christian initiation. The Israelites (i) passed through the Jordan, (ii) were circumcised by Joshua (Jesus), (iii) entered the land flowing with milk and honey, (iv) had rest or peace until they were whole. Christians (i) are baptized, (ii) receive the seal of the new circumcision on their foreheads, (iii) are received into the congregation of the new Israel to lead a life of health and wholeness, (iv) receive the kiss of peace. Whether the parallelism is really as close as Thornton alleged is not self-evident. For, though it is possible, Justin has not made it clear that for him the new circumcision was a signing of the forehead during baptism. However, as evidence that the spiritual circumcision was at any rate not identical with baptism in water, as could be supposed, Thornton cited *Dial.* 18: '. . . God orders you to be washed in the laver, and to be circumcised with the true circumcision.' But although this passage could support Thornton's case, the washing and circumcision in this context, it can be argued, are not two different acts but an outward sign and its inner meaning.

Thornton also claimed that in the following chapter Justin repudiated Jewish circumcision and baptism in that order, because in the initiatory rite for proselytes circumcision preceded baptism, and then referred to Christian baptism and circumcision in that order, because in Christian initiation baptism preceded the new circumcision or consignation.[60] As Justin made a precise contrast between the two baptisms, so he distinguished the other two rites: therefore as Jewish baptism and circumcision were not identical, so Christian baptism and the true circumcision are not the same.

So far, even if he may be allowed to have shown that Justin may not have regarded the new circumcision as synonymous with baptism in water, Thornton has still not shown clearly in what Justin believed the new circumcision to consist. However, further on, accepting the case put forward by Couratin, he alleged that Justin's initiatory rite consisted in baptism in water, anointing, prayer for the descent of the Messianic Spirit and the eucharist, and that all that Justin wrote about the true circumcision referred to the anointing with oil which immediately followed baptism.

Thornton found further evidence to support his argument in *Dial.* 40, the chapter which immediately precedes that which is concerned with the cleansing of the leper. There Justin treated the paschal lamb as a type of our Lord, and said that those who believed in him anointed their own houses, that is, themselves, with his blood, and also that the plasm of which God moulded Adam became a house of the inbreathing which was from God. Thus Thornton inferred that the houses of Ex. 12 symbolize the bodies of Christian neophytes who anoint themselves and receive the Holy Spirit.[61] Furthermore in *Dial.* 86 Justin dealt with Old Testament events involving water, then with Old Testament reference to oil, and next to trees or wood as a type of the cross. Then in chapters 87 and 88 Justin considered the coming of the Spirit upon our Lord and his baptism in the Jordan and the descent of the dove. Next Justin passed to a consideration of types of the cross in the Old Testament. Finally Thornton cited the views expressed by Otto and Lukyn Williams in their editions of the *Dialogue*, that in chapter 111 Justin revealed a belief that in Ex. 12 the blood was sprinkled on the doorposts in the form of a cross, like the old form of Tau; hence it seemed reasonable to conclude that the sign of the Tau was for Justin the sign of the cross imprinted at baptism on the foreheads of Christian initiates.[62]

On the available evidence it must always remain an open question whether Justin knew of a baptismal ceremony answering to what is now called confirmation. For Ratcliff's case for the inclusion of a prayer invoking the sevenfold Spirit lacks certain proof, and does nothing to show whether that prayer was accompanied by any sacramental act. The cases advanced by Couratin and Thornton, if they are not dismissed as pure speculation, suggest that Justin may have known of a consignation of the forehead with oil, symbolizing the gift of the Spirit in initiation. But none of these authorities has produced any argument that Justin knew of an imposition of the hand at baptism. But even if it is not generally accepted that they have proved their case beyond reasonable doubt, they have at least shown that the question whether Justin knew confirmation or not remains wide open.

In the *Demonstration of the Apostolic Preaching* Irenaeus made several references to baptism, although none of them are explicit enough to permit a certainly correct reconstruction of the rite known to the author. In *Dem.* 3 he said that baptism administered in the name of the Trinity 'is the seal of eternal life, and is the new birth unto God that we should no longer be the sons of mortal men, but of the eternal and perpetual God.'[63] In calling this baptism the seal of eternal life Irenaeus applied the term 'seal' to the rite of baptism itself, and in particular to the naming of the three Persons of the Trinity over the candidates. Again, in *Dem.* 100 Irenaeus associated the seal with the Trinity: 'So then in respect of the three points of our seal error has strayed widely from the truth. For either they reject the Father, or they accept not the Son and speak against the dispensation of the incarnation: or else they receive not the Spirit, that is, they reject prophecy.'[64] The seal, then, is related to baptism, and especially to the Trinity, but not directly and exclusively with the Holy Spirit.

Nevertheless there is no doubt of Irenaeus' belief that Christians are people to whom the Spirit has been given. For in *Haer.* 3.17 he quoted Acts 2.38, while further back he wrote that the apostles were clothed with the power of the Holy Spirit, and those to whom they subsequently communicated the Spirit possessed the true gnosis, which the Gnostics lacked. Again in *Haer.* 5.9.1 we read: 'For since we cannot be saved without the Holy Spirit, the apostle commanded us through faith and holy conversation to guard the Spirit of God, lest not being partakers in the Spirit of God we should fail to obtain the kingdom of heaven.' Here the expression 'guard the Spirit of God' recalls the expressions 'guard your baptism' and 'guard the seal', found in the Apostolic Fathers. Hence for Irenaeus the Holy Spirit, baptism and the seal all belonged to the same complex of ideas.

There are, however, other passages which seem to imply that the Holy Spirit was imparted by baptism itself. For instance, in *Haer.* 3.18.1 Irenaeus wrote:

> For just as from dry wheat one lump cannot be made without moisture, nor one loaf, so neither could we who are many become one in Christ Jesus without the water which is from heaven . . . For our bodies entered into unity through that washing which is to incorruption, and our souls through the Spirit.

Again in *Haer.* 5.18.1 Irenaeus said that 'the Spirit is in us all, and he is the living water which the Lord grants to those who rightly believe in him and love him and know that there is one Father who is above all things and through all things and in us all.'

Further, in *Dem.* 42 Irenaeus wrote of believers that 'in them continually abides the Holy Spirit, who was given by him in baptism, and is retained by the receiver, if he walks in truth and holiness and righteousness and patient endurance.'[65] At first sight these words certainly imply that the Holy Spirit is received in baptism irrespective of any further ceremonies which might be included in the rite. But against this Crehan observed that the comparatively brief references to baptism in the *Demonstration* are quite indecisive about the parts or moments into which that rite was believed by Irenaeus to be divided.[66]

In the evidence so far considered there is no reason whatever for supposing that Irenaeus knew of any further baptismal ceremonies related with the giving of the Holy Spirit; and one could only conclude that for him baptism in water constituted a complete initiation. Reasons, however, have been advanced for believing that in Irenaeus' time the church's rite of baptism, at least in some areas, included anointing. For in a description in *Haer.* 1.14.2f of the initiatory rite used by the Marcosian Gnostics Irenaeus says that after baptism 'they anoint the initiated person with opo-balsamum. For this unguent they say is a symbol of the fragrance which is above all things.'[67]

Whence, then, did the Marcosians derive their custom of anointing at baptism? Mason (p. 111) thought that Irenaeus described this Gnostic form of baptism as if it were a profane improvement upon the catholic rites. Chase inferred that this unction was a custom in the church when the Marcosians broke away, and that consequently it must have been in use in the catholic church at least as early as the mid-second century.[68] Similarly Duchesne thought it difficult to believe that these very ancient sects had not borrowed this usage from the ritual already established at the time when they broke away, whatever may have been the modifications which they were able to introduce later.[69] This is a legitimate inference from the Marcosian practice of anointing at baptism. That it is, however, not the only possible inference has been shown by Lampe (p. 121) who, believing that unction had not yet made its way into the church's rite of initiation, was obliged to look for another source for this Marcosian usage. He argued that with their syncretistic outlook the heretical sects would naturally have been disposed to assimilate their rites to those of the pagan mysteries, and secondly that their love of elaboration would have induced them to embellish their initiatory rites by adding further ceremonies to the simple act of washing in water. Bénoit (pp. 203f) suggested that, as from the evidence of Jas. 5.14 it was evident that the apostolic church had used unction in the healing of the sick, so the Gnostics borrowed from the church the idea of using oil in their sacred rites and began to use it in their baptisms. If Lampe or Bénoit are right, as they could be, then the Marcosians' use of unction at baptism cannot be cited as firm evidence that the contemporary rite of the church included a similar unction. But the extent of our knowledge on this point is too limited for inferences to be drawn either way from the baptismal anointing practised by the Marcosians.

In *Haer.* 3.9.3 Irenaeus referred to our Lord's anointing with the Spirit: 'The Spirit of God therefore descended upon him—of that God who had promised through the prophets that he would anoint him, in order that we, obtaining of the abundance of his unction, might be saved.'[70] While, as Mason (p. 115) and Dix[71] observed, these words accord well with the hypothesis that Irenaeus knew of a physical unction at baptism, Lampe (p. 120) and Bénoit (p. 204) could reasonably claim that the unction in this context was metaphorical. The same comment is applicable to a passage in *Dem.* 47, where the

Son is said to receive from the Father the throne of the everlasting kingdom 'and the oil of anointing above his fellows. The oil of anointing is the Spirit, wherewith he has been anointed; and his fellows are the prophets and righteous men and apostles, and all who receive the fellowship of the kingdom.'[72] The question therefore whether Irenaeus knew of an anointing at baptism remains unproven.

The answer to the further question whether Irenaeus knew of a hand-laying at baptism depends upon the view taken of a single passage in *Haer.* 4.62f: 'And for this cause Paul says to the Corinthians, I gave you milk to drink, not meat; for ye were not able to bear it . . . As, therefore, it was in the power of the apostle to give the meat of which he speaks—for on whomsoever they laid their hands, they received the Holy Spirit, which is the meat of life . . .'[73] The important words here are those in the parenthesis. Clearly Irenaeus believed that the laying on of hands in Acts 8.17 and 19.6 represented the normal practice of the apostles. Whether he was in a position to know that this was so is a disputed point. Some would say that it was his reading of the text of Acts that led him to this opinion, which was probably erroneous. Pocknee, however, pointed out that he was an Easterner who came from Smyrna where he had been the disciple of Polycarp, who in turn had been the disciple of St John.[74] But whether or not Irenaeus had access to reliable sources of information denied to us, he does not say, or necessarily imply, that what he believed to be normal apostolic practice was also normal in his own time.

Hickinbotham considered that Irenaeus was not referring to hand-laying as a contemporary custom, and elsewhere habitually linked the gift of the Spirit with baptism.[75] Dix thought that this parenthesis about apostolic custom would have been superfluous if the rite had been well known in Irenaeus' own time,[76] an opinion with which Lampe (p. 119) agreed. But Dix differed from Lampe when he inferred from the parenthesis that Irenaeus despite his faulty history taught that the Holy Spirit was given not at the moment of baptism itself but at another moment, namely, the sealing with chrism.[77] Bénoit (p. 207) said that, according to Irenaeus, although this hand-laying imparted the Holy Spirit, it was not a ceremony of initiation; but he cannot be right, since Irenaeus must have had in mind Acts 8.17 and 19.6.

Yet it can be argued on the other side that the evidence of Acts, as the current debate shows, does not make it crystal clear whether the laying on of hands at Samaria and Ephesus was normal or not: and the more one school of thought tries to insist that it was abnormal, the more it becomes necessary to ask why Irenaeus thought it normal, in which case the answer could well be that he was encouraged in his allegedly false belief by the practice of his own day, as Coppens maintained.[78]

If Irenaeus knew of unction or hand-laying at baptism, these ceremonies were in his view that part of the rite of baptism which symbolized and imparted the baptismal gift of the Spirit. The regeneration and remission of sins conferred by baptism are separable in thought from the gift of the Spirit in the sense that the spiritual blessings associated with Good Friday and Easter are separable in thought from that associated with Pentecost; yet in the last resort they form an organic unity. If in the deepest sense the gift of the Spirit is not separable from baptism in water, as one school of thought strongly insists today, then, if there is a liturgical act which symbolizes the giving of the Spirit, that act is essentially inseparable from baptism. This is the conclusion to which we are led if we bear in mind all that Irenaeus has said about the work of the Holy Spirit in Christian initiation, and at the same time accept that he knew of an anointing or hand-laying for the imparting of the Spirit. If we take the view that on the evidence available he cannot have known either of these ceremonies, then in his time what we call confirmation did not exist at all. In short, either hand-laying and unction existed as integral parts of the rite of baptism with no very clear line of demarcation between them and baptism itself, or else confirmation did not exist at all in the churches known to Irenaeus.

If Bernard was right in saying that the *Odes of Solomon* are hymns of the baptized belonging to the later second century,[79] then these Odes contain a number of allusions to baptismal doctrine and practice in the East at that time. We may be inclined to agree with Lampe (p. 111) that Bernard was possibly right because he alone among the commentators on the Odes has found an intelligible and coherent elucidation of these extraordinary poems.

They contain three references to the seal: (i) 'For who is there that shall put on thy grace, and be hurt? For thy seal is known: and thy creatures know it.'[80] (ii) 8.16: 'for I knew them, and before they came into being I took knowledge of them, and on their faces I set my seal.' (iii) 42.25: 'And I heard their voice; and my name I sealed upon their heads.'

It is abundantly clear that in these contexts the seal is a mark placed on the faces of persons, by which they can be recognized. Although the author did not actually say so, the reference seems to be to the signing of the foreheads of Christians at their baptism. In none of these instances is there any suggestion of a specific relationship between the seal and the Holy Spirit, the author's use of the word being more akin to Ezek. 9.4 and Rev. 7.3 than to 2 Cor. 1.21f and Eph. 1.13 and 4.30.

In Ode 25.7f we read: 'Thou didst set me a lamp at my right hand and at my left: and in me there shall be nothing that is not light: and I was clothed with the covering of thy Spirit.' There may be here an allusion to the carrying of torches in processions by the newly baptized: and if the words are pressed, though they probably should not be pressed very far since they are poetry, the gift of the Spirit is apparently associated with the putting on of the baptismal robes. The words of Ode 28.7, 'and immortal life has come forth and has kissed me, and from that life is the Spirit within me, and it cannot die, for it lives,' reveal nothing about the moment when the Holy Spirit was given: but in Ode 36.3, 'I rested on the Spirit of the Lord: and she raised me on high . . . she brought me forth before the face of the Lord: and although a son of man, I was named the illuminated one, the son of God', there is a reference to the illumination, regeneration, and adoption conferred by the agency of the Spirit in baptism.

Twice the poet recounts the blessings conveyed by water. First, in Ode 6.7–17 we find:

> Blessed then are the ministers of that draught who are entrusted with that water of his: they have assuaged the dry lips, and the will that had fainted they have raised up . . . they gave strength for their coming and light to their eyes: for everyone knew them in the Lord, and they lived by the water of life for ever.

Secondly, in Ode 11.6–10 the author writes: 'and speaking waters touched my lips from the fountain of the Lord plenteously: and I drank and was inebriated with the living water that doth not die.' These two passages reveal a fervent belief that great spiritual blessings are conferred by means of water: and they show that Christian baptism in water is very far from being mere water-baptism. Here the writer's thought has been influenced by the Fourth Gospel rather than by the Pauline Epistles.

The custom of giving milk and honey to the newly baptized is alluded to in Ode 19.1: 'A cup of milk was offered to me: and I drank it in the sweetness of the delight of the Lord.' But nowhere in the Odes is there a clear reference to hand-laying at baptism, and only one, possibly, to a baptismal unction, in Ode 36.1: 'For according to the greatness of the Most High he renewed me; and he anointed me from his own perfection.' The anointing here could be, but does not have to be, understood figuratively. But if the anointing is taken figuratively, then by the same canons of criticism the water mentioned in Ode 6 must be understood figuratively.

The anonymous author of the *Odes of Solomon* knew an initiatory rite, it seems, which did not consist only in baptism in water, but included other significant ceremonies, the sealing of the forehead, the vesting in white robes and the giving of a draught of milk. If the rite of baptism had by this time become as complex as this, other meaningful ceremonies may also have been included, even if they are not mentioned.

The style of writing makes it difficult to decide with confidence in what liturgical context the author believed the Holy Spirit to be given; and since not all scholars are agreed that these Odes refer to Christian initiation at all, the support which they give to any theory about the content of the initiatory rite in the second century is at best precarious.

Writing about the year 180, Theophilus of Antioch made one reference to anointing which has been much quoted:

> When you laugh at me, calling me a Christian, you do not know what you are saying. First, that which is anointed is sweet and serviceable and not to be laughed at. What ship can be serviceable and seaworthy, unless it first be anointed? Or what man on entering this life, or when contending in the games, is not anointed with oil? What work can be comely and sightly, if it be not anointed and polished? Then, even the air and all that is under heaven is, in a kind of way, anointed with light and spirit, and do you wish to be anointed with the oil of God? We, therefore, are called Christians on this account, because we are anointed with the oil of God.[81]

The last sentence, although often quoted by itself, needs to be seen in its context. Once again the question arises whether this anointing is to be treated as a physical anointing or not. While Coppens[82] and Lampe (p. 114) have contended that this unction should be understood metaphorically, Mason (p. 330), Wirgman (p. 107), Sasse,[83] D'Alès,[84] Duchesne,[85] and Jalland[86] have all taken the opposite point of view.

When the last sentence only is quoted, out of its context, then it is easy enough to interpret the unction either way, or to assert that the anointing is figurative. But in the previous sentence reference has been made to the physical anointing of ships, towers, houses and athletes, although Theophilus then passed on to a different kind of anointing received by the air and all that is under heaven. Now it is difficult to know why Theophilus saw any point in citing these cases of physical anointing if the anointing received by Christians was purely spiritual. R. P. C. Hanson, however, found this argument unconvincing, because he thought it would be exceedingly odd if Theophilus, knowing full well that Christians were really so called because of their faith in Christ, should say that they owed their name to the fact that they were anointed with oil during their ceremony of initiation.[87] But, since the question which Theophilus was answering was, 'Why are we called anointed ones?', it is by no means impossible that this should have turned his mind to the anointing received at baptism. Secondly, Hanson expected that Theophilus would haven spoken of the oil of the Holy Spirit rather than the oil of God, if he had really been referring to a physical anointing received during initiation. This argument is not convincing, because in the circumstances Theophilus was not called upon to be precise. Thirdly, Hanson noted that Theophilus' argument worked up from physical anointings to a different kind of anointing by light and wind, and finally to an anointing by God which is entirely spiritual, the inference being that the anointing received by Christians was likewise entirely spiritual. But for all that the difficulty remains that, if the anointing was purely spiritual, there was no point in starting off by dealing with the physical anointing of houses and athletes.

Another reason for believing that the anointing in question was physical lies in the fact which Mitchell (p. 13) noticed, that Theophilus' words about Christians being so called from their anointing are very similar to some words of Tertullian in *de Baptismo* 7, 'called Christians from chrism', where physical anointing is not in doubt. But certainty on this point is unattainable, with the balance of probability in favour of the view that Theophilus showed knowledge of an actual anointing at baptism; and his previous words, 'anointed with light and spirit', strongly suggest that this anointing was related with the giving of the Holy Spirit.

So far our attention has been confined to Christian literature which is usually dated within the second century or earlier. There is, however, more to be said. Hand-laying and anointing at baptism are attested in some rites of the early third century, notably in the *de Baptismo* of Tertullian, published in Carthage *c.* A.D. 200, and in the *Apostolic Tradition* of Hippolytus, by the majority of scholars still believed to have first seen the light in Rome *c.* 217. They will be considered in detail later on. For the moment it is sufficient to observe that there is no reason to suppose that at the time of writing these further baptismal ceremonies were recent innovations. If they were established customs by the second decade of the third century, they must have had their origin back in the second century, although how far back is difficult to prove. But the clear existence of these ceremonies in the early third century has to be set against the failure of second century writers to supply evidence as unmistakable of their existence in the period between the end of the apostolic age and the time of Tertullian and Hippolytus.

In conclusion, the question in dispute is whether the rites of initiation in use in the second century were simple rites of baptism in water, or whether they were more complex rites, including amongst other things the imposition of the hand with prayer or unction or both, with which the gift of the Holy Spirit was specially linked. Those who believe that there was neither unction nor hand-laying at baptism in the New Testament will not easily be persuaded by the second-century evidence, such as it is, that this did not continue to be the case until the end of the century. For them the rite now known as confirmation is found neither in scripture nor in apostolic practice nor in the practice of the sub-apostolic age. On the other hand those who believe that confirmation can trace its pedigree back to the New Testament are not necessarily refuted by the failure of second-century writers to give conclusive proof that they are right. The evidence both from scripture and from the second century is of such a nature that each point of view is likely to have its staunch advocates throughout the foreseeable future.

2 *Africa*

Our knowledge of the church in the Roman province of Africa to all intents and purposes begins at the end of the second century, when Tertullian's works began to be published, revealing that an organized church had existed for some time in Carthage. On the subject of Christian initiation there is a fair amount of information in his writings, especially in his *de Baptismo*, dated *c.* 200. Like so much else that proceeded from its author's incisive pen, it had a strongly polemical purpose, to refute the false teaching of 'a certain viper of the Cainite sect who . . . carried off a good number with her exceptionally pestilential doctrine, making a particular point of demolishing baptism.'[1] Although little is known of the Gnostic sect to which this woman belonged, it probably so stressed the opposition between spirit and matter, soul and body, that it refused to admit that the material element of water could be the means of conveying spiritual blessings to the soul.[2] The occasion which evoked this tract required much to be said in defence of baptism in water: but it did not require, and Tertullian has not in fact produced, a balanced account of the initiatory rite as a whole. Hence, while he wrote much about baptism itself, he dealt very briefly with the catechumenate, omitted all mention of the consignation of which he showed knowledge in *de Res. Carnis* 8, and, more important still here, said comparatively little about the ceremonies which followed the actual baptism.

Baptism in water was immediately followed by an anointing:

> After that we come up from the washing and are anointed with the blessed unction, following that ancient practice by which, ever since Aaron was anointed by Moses, there was a custom of anointing them for priesthood with oil out of a horn. That is why (the high priest) is called a christ, from 'chrism' which is (the Greek for) 'anointing'. And from this also our Lord obtained his title, though it had become a spiritual anointing, in that he was anointed with the Spirit by God the Father . . . So also in our case, the unction flows upon the flesh, but turns to spiritual profit, just as in the baptism itself there is an act

that touches the flesh, that we are immersed in water, but a spiritual effect, that we are set free from sins.[3]

Although the word 'we are anointed' (*perungimur*) does not necessarily imply that the candidate's body was completely anointed, this is rather suggested by the words 'the unction flows', and also by the custom mentioned by Tertullian in *de Cor.* 3, that for seven days after their baptism the initiated refrained from taking a bath. In describing the unction as 'blessed' Tertullian shows that the oil was consecrated before use.

The meaning which Tertullian attached to this unction depends to a certain extent on the view taken of three variant readings in the second sentence of the passage quoted. While Evans and D'Alès[4] preferred the reading 'unde christus dicitur', other editors, including Borleffs[5] and Refoulé[6] have favoured another reading, 'unde christi dicti'. There is also a third variant, 'unde christiani dicti'. If the first reading is accepted, it is the high priest who is called a christ, or anointed one, from the chrism or unction which he received. In that case it is not so clear what effect Tertullian attributed to the unction received by Christians at their baptism; all that he will have said is that this anointing is copied from the Old Testament practice and 'turns to spiritual profit'. If preference is given to either of the other two readings, then Tertullian was saying that those who were anointed became christs, or anointed ones, at their baptism, from the chrism which they then received, so becoming members of Christ's priestly body. Many commentators have understood this to have been Tertullian's meaning, among the first being Didymus of Alexandria in the fourth century[7] and Isidore of Seville in the seventh.[8]

Although the gift of the Spirit was associated by Tertullian with the ensuing hand-laying and not with this unction, yet unction cannot be altogether separated from the giving of the Spirit, because it conferred membership in Christ, the anointed one, so called because he was anointed with the Holy Spirit. In a brief commentary in *de Res. Carnis* 8 on the principal symbolical acts in the rite of initiation Tertullian wrote that the flesh was anointed that the soul might be consecrated. But in view of the clear statement that the Holy Spirit was invoked upon the baptized at the subsequent imposition of the hand we may agree with Mitchell (p. 11) in approving the judgment of Galtier that it was with the person of Christ and not with the Holy Spirit that chrism and unction were placed in relation by Tertullian.[9] While Lampe (p. 159) was right in saying that Tertullian did not see this anointing as a sacramental sign of the gift of the Spirit, he was surely wrong in saying that Tertullian did not believe it to confer grace at all: 'it profits spiritually.'

If it be asked whether this anointing can be regarded as confirmation, a simple yes or no is not possible. Inasmuch as it confers membership in Christ, it is part of the Christian's christening, and cannot be divorced from baptism. On the other hand it cannot be completely separated from the hand-laying which, Tertullian says, conveys the Holy Spirit, seeing that it incorporates into him who was anointed with the Spirit. The plain truth is that the question cannot be answered in one word because it ought not to be asked. To apply the word 'confirmation', with the overtones which it has acquired in the West today, to this unction, or even to the ensuing hand-laying, is to introduce a dichotomy of which Tertullian was unconscious.

It is now necessary to discuss the hand-laying which followed the unction:

> Next follows the imposition of the hand in benediction, inviting and welcoming the Holy Spirit . . . At this point that most holy Spirit willingly comes down from the Father upon bodies cleansed and blessed, and comes to rest upon the waters of baptism as though revisiting his primal dwelling-place.[10]

In de Res, Carnis 8 Tertullian again emphasized the connection between the hand-laying and the Holy Spirit: 'the flesh is over-shadowed by the imposition of the hand that the soul may be illumined by the Spirit.' As scriptural precedent for this hand-laying Tertullian cited Gen. 48.14, where Jacob blessed Ephraim and Manasseh. Whether his thought was influenced by the laying on of hands in Acts 8.17 and 19.6 is open to conjecture: all that we know for certain is that he referred to the latter passage two chapters later. But the fact that the scriptural precedent which he quoted came from the Old Testament may be an indication that in this way justification was found for the post-baptismal hand-laying at a time when the Old Testament was the only sacred scripture of Christians.

With regard to the minister of initiation Tertullian wrote:

> To round off our slight treatment of this subject it remains for us to advise you of the rules to be observed in giving and receiving baptism. The supreme right of giving it belongs to the high priest, which is the bishop: after him, to the presbyters and deacons, yet not without commission from the bishop, on account of the church's dignity: for when this is safe, peace is safe. Except for that, even laymen have the right.[11]

Tertullian happens to have mentioned in *de Corona* 3 that the renunciation of Satan took place under the hand of the bishop. So at Paschal initiations it is likely that the bishop was present throughout the entire rite, and therefore probably himself performed the hand-laying. Whether presbyters, deacons, and laymen, when they baptized in the absence of a bishop, administered the entire rite including the hand-laying is a point on which Tertullian did not touch.

Although he did not mention it in *de Baptismo*, Tertullian knew also of a consignation, which apparently came between the unction and the hand-laying: 'the flesh is washed . . . the flesh is anointed . . . the flesh is signed (with the cross) that the soul too may be protected: the flesh is overshadowed by the imposition of the hand . . .'[12] We are not informed here on what part of the body the sign of the cross was made, nor what was its effect beyond that it was for the soul's protection. In Tertullian's time Christians were in the habit of signing themselves many times every day, at every going out or coming in and on numerous other occasions.[13] Evidently the sign of our Lord's victory was held to afford protection against demons and against misfortune; those who bore the sign of the cross were branded as the property of one who could be trusted to look after his own. Once Tertullian identified the sign of the cross with the mark set upon the foreheads of the faithful in Jerusalem in Ezek. 9.4–6 to preserve them from the doom that was to fall upon the wicked.[14] The quotation of this passage in the context of initiation justifies that assumption that the sign of the cross was in fact made upon the foreheads of the candidates.

Hence Tertullian's initiatory rite consisted in baptism in water, anointing, consignation and hand-laying, the purpose of the last act being to confer the Holy Spirit. In the last three acts can be clearly seen that out of which grew the rite later to be known as confirmation; but in Tertullian's time they were part and parcel of the rite of baptism.

The matter, however, is not so simple as this, because Tertullian said much about the activity of the Holy Spirit in baptism itself, so that it has been held that, despite what he said about the giving of the Spirit at the hand-laying, Tertullian really believed the Holy Spirit to be given at the moment of baptism itself, or else contradicted himself, not having thought the matter out clearly.

In the opening chapters of *de Baptismo* Tertullian sang the praises of water as a vehicle of grace, presumably because this was the chief target of Quintilla's attack. Referring to Gen. 1.1f, he noted the honour done to water in that it was the resting place of the Spirit of God. By Tertullian's time it had become customary to bless the water to be used for baptism. On this subject he wrote:

Therefore, in consequence of that ancient original privilege, all waters, when God is invoked, acquire the sacred significance of conveying sanctity: for at once the Spirit comes down from heaven and stays upon the waters, sanctifying them from within himself, and when thus sanctified they absorb the power of sanctifying . . . Thus when the waters have in some sense acquired healing power by an angel's intervention, the spirit is in those waters corporally washed, while the flesh is in those same waters spiritually cleansed.[15]

Tertullian believed the consecration to effect a kind of real presence of the Holy Spirit in the water of baptism: without the invocation of the Spirit upon the water the act of baptism would have been a mere physical washing: the blessing of the water ensured that the physical act of bathing the body in it was instrumental in procuring spiritual cleansing for the soul. The spiritual benefits conferred at the moment of baptism are said to be the washing away of sins and the gift of eternal life. Evidently, therefore, if the effect of consecration was as Tertullian said, these blessings were conferred by the agency of the Holy Spirit. Whatever he may have said about the ensuing hand-laying, Tertullian without doubt did not believe that baptism was a mere water-baptism, or that it was a kind of negative preparation for the positive gift bestowed by the subsequent imposition of the hand; on the contrary, by the agency of the Holy Spirit baptism conveyed the great positive gift of forgiveness of sins and eternal salvation. Yet clearly as he has said that the Holy Spirit is given to the water at the moment of consecration, he has not as clearly said that the Holy Spirit is given to the candidates themselves at the moment of baptism.

At the end of *de Baptismo* 5 comes a passage that seems to imply that the Holy Spirit is given and received at baptism itself. The important words are:

> In this way is man being restored to God, to the likeness of him who had aforetime been in God's image — the image had its actuality in the (man God) formed, the likeness (becomes actual) in eternity — for there is given back to him that spirit of God which of old he had received of God's breathing, but afterwards had lost through sin.[16]

Now it is not certain what Tertullian meant by the 'spirit of God', whether by this phrase he meant the Holy Spirit or the breath of life in Gen. 2.7, to which there is an allusion here, or whether he identified the breath of life with the Holy Spirit. If Tertullian did not make this identification,[17] then what he was saying is that by baptism in water man is restored to the state of innocence which was his before the Fall, and the breath which God breathed into him breathes in him freely once more. But the view has been widely held that Tertullian was here thinking of the Holy Spirit himself.[18] There would be no difficulty in accepting this view, if this were all that Tertullian had written on this subject. But this is not so because his very next words are:

> Not that the Holy Spirit is given to us in the water, but that in the water we are made clean by the action of the angel, and made ready for the Holy Spirit. Here also a type had come first. As John was our Lord's forerunner, preparing his ways, so also has the angel, the mediator of baptism, makes the ways straight for the Holy Spirit who is to come next.

This is as clear a statement as could possibly be expected that,

34

despite anything that may just have been said, the moment of baptism itself is not the actual moment when the Holy Spirit is given to the candidates; and it is followed in chapter 8 by an equally clear statement that the Holy Spirit descends on them at the hand-laying. These two statements taken together are of decisive importance for fixing the moment when Tertullian believed the Spirit to be given to the initiates. To treat them otherwise is to explain them away.

In that case, however, what becomes of the words in chapter 5 which at least seem to imply that man recovers the Spirit of God at his baptism? Seeing a real contradiction here, Lampe (p. 161) asserted that there was confusion in Tertullian's mind. But there ought to be an answer to the question which does not accuse Tertullian of flatly contradicting in one sentence what he had just said in the previous sentence. Two answers are possible. Either the spirit of God which man recovers at baptism is not to be equated with the Holy Spirit, in which case in chapter 6 Tertullian was warning his readers against a possible misunderstanding about the nature of the gift conferred at baptism. Or, if the Spirit of God is in fact the Holy Spirit, then we may suppose with Mason (pp. 63f) that in chapter 5 Tertullian did not strictly confine himself to the blessings conferred at baptism itself. The unity of the rite of initiation was such that it was easy to pass in thought from the blessings associated with one part of the rite to those conveyed in another. In chapter 6, then, Tertullian hastened to correct the false impression which he felt he might have created, by adding that we do not actually receive the Holy Spirit in the water, but by implication later.

It seems clear, however, that, while he believed that baptism itself by the operation of the Holy Spirit conveyed remission of sins and eternal salvation, Tertullian attributed the actual giving of the Spirit to the ensuing hand-laying. Lampe (pp. 161f) condemned such a distinction between the regenerating activity of the Holy Spirit and his personal indwelling as an unwarrantable and unintelligible differentiation between those modes of the Spirit's activity. But in trying to appreciate Tertullian's line of thought Western liturgiologists of the twentieth century labour under one heavy disadvantage, namely, that they have lived in and inherited a situation where those who receive the laying on of the hand have usually been baptized many years previously; in consequence, they find it well nigh impossible to divest their minds of the notion that baptism in water and the laying on of the hand are two separate and independent rites. It may be freely granted that the blessings which Tertullian ascribed to baptism and to hand-laying respectively are from the theological point of view in the last resort indivisible. But in his day both acts formed part of a rite which was a single whole, in which baptism in water, unction, consignation and imposition of the hand followed one another without any appreciable interval of time between them. The real question which needs to be asked is not how Tertullian could differentiate between regeneration by the Spirit at baptism and the giving of the Spirit at the hand-laying, but how the Western church could allow the hand-laying to become detached from baptism and assume the appearance of an independent rite. As Ratcliff has well said, 'in the early and patristic periods, the relation between confirmation and baptism is one of essential unity rather than of mere liturgical association'.[19]

The discussion evoked by the use of the word 'seal' in the second century literature makes it necessary to consider Tertullian's use of this term. In *de Spectaculis* 4 he referred to 'our seal' in the context of the baptismal profession of faith and renunciation of Satan, and to the 'seal of faith', again in the context of the renunciation. Similarly in *de Baptismo* 6 he wrote of the cancelling of sins granted 'in response to faith signed and sealed in the Father and the Son and the Holy Spirit'; and in chapter 13 of the same work he said that for those who believe in Christ's nativity and passion and resurrection 'the sacrament has been expanded and the seal of baptism added, in some sense a clothing for the faith which was previously unattired.'[20] Yet again, in *de Paenitentia* 6.16 he called the laver the sealing of faith. In all these instances the 'seal' bears the same general sense, that baptism in water consummates and sets the mark of the divine approval upon the faith of the Christian convert. This assists the interpretation of the seal in some of the writings of the second century, for example, the statement of Hermas that the seal is the water. In none of these passages is there any suggestion that the seal confers the Holy Spirit. The nearest that Tertullian came to saying this was in *de Pudicitia* 9: 'So the apostate also will receive again his former robe, the garment of the Holy Spirit, and receive once more his ring, the seal of the laver.' Lampe (pp. 122f) took Tertullian to mean that the ring, which is the seal of baptism, was synonymous with the robe which is the garment of the Holy Spirit; in other words that which man lost at the Fall is recovered by the gift of the Spirit at baptism. But, as Dewar[21] pointed out, since in the parable of the prodigal son the ring and the robe are not identical, there is no reason to suppose that Tertullian equated the two in such a way as to make them both symbols of baptism in water. Secondly, Tertullian was referring not to the Fall but to the act of apostasy. Thirdly, he spoke of the seal of the laver, not the seal of the Spirit, using the term in the same sense as in the passage already noticed. Hence the ring probably contains an allusion to baptism in water and the robe to the hand-laying which followed it.

In support of his claim that Tertullian believed the Holy Spirit to be given in baptism Lampe (p. 159) cited *adv. Marcionem* 1.28, where in discussing the spiritual benefits of baptism Tertullian asked *inter alia* how Marcion's baptism could be the imparting of the Spirit. This question, however, needs to be studied in its context. Tertullian began by asking a number of rhetorical questions about Marcionite baptism, 'If it is the remission of sins . . . if it is the loosing of death . . . if it is the regeneration of a man . . . if it is the imparting of the Holy Spirit.' Now it is true that remission of sins, loosing of death, and regeneration are gifts conferred by baptism itself, even when baptism has become a complex rite, as had Marcion's. So Marcion may well have attributed the gift of the Spirit to the anointing or consignation which formed part of his rite of baptism.

In this connection it has to be borne in mind that Tertullian described a rite which included baptism in water, unction, consignation and laying on of the hand under the title, *On Baptism*, so that it was much easier for him than for us to say that the grace which belonged to the hand-laying was conferred in baptism. While it is true that for Latin Fathers the act of dipping in water was called baptism, the same word could be used also in a wider sense to cover the whole rite of initiation, of which dipping in water was the most prominent feature. Dix went too far when he said that for Tertullian *baptismum* meant not only baptism in water but other things as well,[22] because there are a number of instances, such as *de Bapt.* 3, 4, 12 and *Adv. Jud.* 8, where he used the word 'baptize' specifically in connection with water, although there are other occasions when he used the verb *tinguere* to denote the act of baptism in water. On the other hand Lampe (p. 160) went too far in the opposite direction when he said that normally Tertullian meant no more by baptism than baptism in the strict sense of the word. When Tertullian wrote in *de Bapt.* 7, 'So also in our case the unction flows upon the flesh, but turns to spiritual profit, just as in the baptism itself (*ipsius baptismi*) there is an act that touches the flesh . . .', he showed an awareness of the narrower and broader senses in which the word 'baptism' could be used: 'baptism itself' meant the act of dipping in water, whereas by implication 'baptism' could cover the whole rite of baptism, including the anointing.

Part of Wirgman's main purpose was to prove that Tertullian and all the ancient Fathers believed the Holy Spirit to be given in baptism itself. Confronted with the fact that in *de Baptismo* 8 Tertullian clearly stated that the Holy Spirit was received at the hand-laying, he (p. 112) tried to extricate himself from this difficulty by alleging that here 'Holy Spirit' bore a different meaning. According to his theory baptism in water conveyed '*the* Holy Spirit', while the hand-laying conveyed 'Holy Spirit', that is, certain graces of the Holy Spirit, as opposed to the Holy Spirit himself. If this theory were tenable, it would be possible to argue that where Tertullian said that the Holy Spirit was given in baptism, he was referring to the gift of the Holy Spirit himself, and where he said that the Spirit was given at the hand-laying he was referring to the gift of further graces of the Holy Spirit.

37

So an apparent contradiction would be conveniently removed. But not only is it impossible to prove that the presence or absence of the definite article before 'Spirit' can thus affect the meaning, but also it is hard to see how a Latin writer could express the supposedly different meanings of 'Spirit' in a language which had no definite article.

Without having recourse to Wirgman's precarious theory, Stone adopted a similar standpoint. He interpreted the clear statement in Acts 8.16 that baptism in the name of the Lord Jesus did not in this instance confer the Holy Spirit as meaning that the Samaritans had not yet received the special confirmation gifts of the Holy Spirit, but that at the laying on of the apostles' hands the Holy Spirit came upon them with these same special confirmation gifts. Similarly he interpreted the gift of the Spirit ascribed by Tertullian to the hand-laying as meaning special confirmation gifts of the Holy Spirit.[23] But this cannot be justified out of scripture, because, while in the Acts of the Apostles it is abundantly clear that new converts received the Holy Spirit at their initiation, the author showed no knowledge of a rite in which they received further gifts of the Holy Spirit over and above the gift which they had received once, and once and for all, at their baptism, or baptism with laying on of hands. The gift of the Spirit which St Peter promised that his first converts would receive if they repented and were baptized must be the same gift that the apostles had themselves received a few hours earlier. The gift received by Cornelius and his companions is most clearly equated with the gift outpoured at Pentecost. There is no justification at all for supposing that the gift received by the Samaritans and the disciples at Ephesus was different from this. The spiritual gift conferred was the same in all cases, although there is uncertainty as to the means by which the gift was imparted. St Luke knew of only one giving of the Spirit to Christian converts; what he has not made clear was the normal means, if there was one, by which the gift was mediated.

So also Tertullian knew of only one giving of the Spirit in Christian initiation. When he said that at the hand-laying the Holy Spirit descended upon our cleansed bodies, he must surely have meant that the Holy Spirit himself was received thereby, because this was hardly the language to use in order to describe the infusion of certain impersonal graces of the Spirit. If, as Stone alleged, Tertullian believed that the Holy Spirit was given in baptism itself, then a second ceremony following almost immediately, and having as its purpose the bestowal of further gifts of the same Spirit becomes otiose in the extreme. Stone's doctrinal position here is intelligible when confirmation is normally received seven or more years after baptism, but is inapplicable to the situation which obtained in the third century when the laying on of the hand normally followed baptism in water at once.

In short, then, the evidence as a whole points overwhelmingly to the conclusion that in Tertullian's view baptism by itself by the operation of the Holy Spirit conferred eternal salvation and remission of sins, while the subsequent hand-laying conveyed the gift of the Holy Spirit to the initiates. In this way we are spared the need to charge Tertullian with inconsistency or muddled thought. Moreover this interpretation of his doctrine of initiation accords with the doctrine of the ancient baptismal liturgies.

To say, however, that the convert received the Holy Spirit at the hand-laying after baptism does not carry with it the implication that he had been untouched by the Holy Spirit up to that moment. The baptism which he had just received was not a mere water-baptism but a baptism of water and the Spirit. When he confessed his faith at his baptism, he was moved by the Spirit, because no man can say that Jesus is Lord but by the Holy Spirit. When he first asked for baptism, he was moved by the Spirit. When he was first moved to give his attention to the preaching of the gospel, he was moved by the Spirit, although he did not know it. The apostles were not untouched by the Spirit until the day of Pentecost. It is the Spirit as experienced at Pentecost that 'was not' until Jesus was glorified, and that was conferred upon new believers at the baptismal hand-laying or anointing.

The circumstances which evoked his letters did not require Cyprian to describe the rite of initiation in full, or to give a balanced commentary on all its component parts. Questions about the age at which infants might be admitted to baptism and questions about clinical baptism required him to deal with baptism in water from a particular angle; and the controversy over rebaptism, in which he was personally involved, necessitated a lengthy discussion about the meaning of the hand-laying given to heretics and schismatics when they were received into the catholic church. Hence if we find in Cyprian's correspondence a fair amount about baptism in water and hand-laying, and little about anointing and consignation, it does not follow that in his eyes these two latter ceremonies were insignificant.

In actual fact Cyprian mentions the unction after baptism once only:

It is necessary that he who has been baptized should also be anointed, so that after receiving the chrism, that is, the anointing, he can be God's anointed and have in him the grace of Christ. Moreover it is at the eucharist that the oil with which the baptized are anointed is consecrated on the altar.[24]

Like Tertullian, Cyprian believed this unction to confer membership in Christ, and related it with the Second rather than with the Third Person of the Trinity. In Lampe's (p. 177) opinion Cyprian regarded this anointing as a subsidiary ceremony, demonstrating that the person just baptized had now been incorporated into Christ; that is, it was not itself an efficacious act but merely declared one of the effects of the act of baptism itself. This, however, is less than what Cyprian said, because his words evidently imply that the anointing accomplished something, in that he who was anointed became thereby the anointed of God, having the grace of Christ within him. It is much more likely that to Cyprian the whole rite of initiation was sacramental, and that in it there was no sharp differentiation between acts which were efficacious means of grace and other acts which were bare signs.

Cyprian made three brief references to a sealing at the time of baptism. If heretical baptism, he argued, could procure remission of sins, the Holy Spirit could be received outside the church, in which case it was superfluous to lay the hand on heretics who wished to enter the church 'so that they might obtain the Holy Spirit and be sealed.'[25] Further on in the same letter he said that according to the custom of the Catholic Church baptized persons were presented to the bishops for the laying on of the hand with prayer, so that they might receive the Holy Spirit and be perfected with the Lord's seal. In neither of these cases did Cyprian make it absolutely clear whether or not the seal was another liturgical act. But all doubt on this score is removed in Cyprian's third reference, where he wrote of people who had been reborn and signed with the sign of Christ, and, in order to show the meaning of the sign, quoted Ezek. 9.4.[26] In his *Liber Testimoniorum*, 2.22 he said that through the sign of the cross salvation was secured for all who were marked upon their foreheads. The Lord's seal, therefore, is the sign of the cross imprinted on the foreheads of the baptized, and emphasizing the eschatological aspect of initiation. Whether the sign of the cross was made with oil, as in later times, is a point with which Cyprian did not deal.

With regard to the reception of heretics into the church, Cyprian made it abundantly clear that the hand-laying administered on those occasions had the purpose of conveying the Holy Spirit, as is demonstrated in the following quotations from his letters:

Ep. 72.1: . . . it is not enough to lay the hand on them so that they may receive the Holy Spirit, unless they also receive the church's baptism.

Ep. 73.6: . . . but if somebody could have been baptized outside the church with a distorted faith and receive the remission of his sins, with that same faith he could also have received the Holy Spirit, and it is not necessary that when he comes to us a hand should be laid upon him so that he may receive the Holy Spirit and be sealed.

Ep. 69.11: So let those who support heretics and schismatics answer us whether they have or have not the Holy Spirit. If they have, why, when they come to us, is the hand laid upon those baptized among them so that they may receive the spirit . . . ?

Ep. 74.5: Or if they attribute the effect of baptism to the majesty of the name, so that those who are baptized in the name of Jesus Christ anywhere and anyhow are adjudged to have been renewed and sanctified, why is not the hand also laid upon him who has been baptized there in the name of the same Christ so that the Holy Spirit may be received?

Ep. 74.7: Furthermore a person is not born again through the imposition of the hand when he receives the Holy Spirit, but in baptism so that having first been born he may receive the Spirit.

Ep. 73.9: And therefore those who had received the lawful baptism of the church had not to be baptized again, but only that which was lacking was done by Peter and John, that when prayer had been made for them and the hand laid upon them the Holy Spirit might be invoked and poured upon them. This even now is our practice, that those who are baptized in the church are presented to the prelates of the church and through our prayer and the laying on of our hand receive the Holy Spirit and are perfected with the Lord's seal.

In these quotations from Cyprian's correspondence the number of times that he associated hand-laying with the gift of the Holy Spirit is highly impressive. If he had done this once only, it might have been possible to accuse him of expressing himself loosely or carelessly. But six times he said quite plainly that the hand-laying in initiation was for the imparting of the Spirit. This must be allowed to establish the moment when he believed the Holy Spirit was given.

In the course of his argument, however, Cyprian not only made abundantly clear his views about the grace conveyed by the hand-laying, but also showed what he held to be the grace conveyed by baptism itself. In the passages quoted above it is twice said that baptism confers remission of sins: it renews: it creates a temple for God: it is a spiritual birth. Thus whatever the significance Cyprian ascribed to the hand-laying, he was very far from treating baptism itself as an event of minor importance on a par with the baptism of John.

Furthermore Cyprian evidently believed that the Holy Spirit was present and active at baptism itself. 'The water', he wrote in *Ep*. 70.1, 'must first be cleansed and sanctified by a bishop so that it can in baptism wash away all the sins of the man who is baptized.' The effect of consecration was briefly touched upon by Cyprian when he said in *Ep*. 74.5 that water alone cannot cleanse unless it also has the Holy Spirit. Thus Cyprian was at one with his *magister*, Tertullian, in holding that the Holy Spirit, given to the water at its consecration, was the agent through whom the blessings of baptism were conferred.

41

Indeed when Cyprian wrote about the work of the Holy Spirit in baptism itself, he expressed himself in terms which have seemed to a number of scholars to imply that he believed the Holy Spirit to be given at the very moment of baptism, and consequently to contradict what he said about the effect of the hand-laying. Thus he wrote of the possibility of evil spirits remaining in the body of a man, 'in whom, baptized and sanctified, the Holy Spirit begins to dwell.'[27] If we did not know what Cyprian has said about the hand-laying, we would have to treat this as a clear statement that the Spirit is given in baptism itself. But since baptism in water was normally followed at once by the imposition of the hand, we cannot be certain that Cyprian here confined his thought to the grace actually conferred at the washing in water.

Besides, 'baptized' and 'sanctified' are not necessarily synonyms. There are a number of occasions when Cyprian used the verb 'sanctify' in conjunction with another verb, such as 'baptize', 'quicken' or 'purify'. For instance, he commented upon the view that the precedent of circumcision required infants to be 'baptized and sanctified' before the eighth day from birth.[28] He was asked whether those who came from the profane baptism of Novatian ought to be 'baptized and sanctified' with the true baptism of the church.[29] If Novatian was not within the church and did not preside over a church, he could not 'baptize and sanctify' anybody.[30] Novatianists and other schismatics could not 'baptize and sanctify', since their clergy had not the power to baptize.[31] Those who came from the profane water of heretics were to be 'washed and sanctified'.[32] He who was outside the church could not be 'quickened and sanctified'.[33] Those who recognized heretical baptisms implied that the enemy and adversary of Christ had the power to 'wash and purify and sanctify' a man.[34]

The repeated phrase 'baptize and sanctify' suggested to Mason (p. 65n) the possibility that the two words signified two liturgical acts, baptism in water and either unction or consignation. In support of this conjecture appeal can be made to the words of Tertullian, 'the flesh is anointed that the soul may be consecrated.' Nevertheless it can be argued that the words 'baptize and sanctify' are an indication that sometimes Cyprian enjoyed using two words where one might have sufficed, or that 'baptize' refers to the outward act and 'sanctify' to its inward effect. In support of this interpretation can be cited the fact that in *Ep.* 73.12 Cyprian wrote, 'If he has retained remission of sins, he has been sanctified, he has been made a temple of God,' and in *Ep.* 74.5, 'he who having put away his sins in baptism has been sanctified . . .'

Again Cyprian wrote, 'Moreover by baptism the Holy Spirit is received, and so those who have been baptized and received the Holy Spirit come to drink the Lord's chalice.'[35] If by baptism Cyprian here

42

meant the act of baptism in water and nothing more, then this is a flat contradiction of what he said many times elsewhere in unequivocal language, that the Holy Spirit was given through the hand-laying. Nevertheless Stone,[36] Wirgman (pp. 113f), and Lampe (p. 171) have contended that despite the contradiction Cyprian here used 'baptism' in its narrower sense. The latter argued strongly that whenever Cyprian spoke of baptism he meant the act of dipping in water, no more than that; he quoted two phrases used by Cyprian, 'the washing of baptism' in *Ep*. 74.6 and 'the baptism of saving water' in *Ep*. 63.8: and he drew attention to the statement in the same letter that 'whenever water alone is mentioned in the holy scriptures baptism is proclaimed.' Lampe urged that the point of this exegetical theory would be blunted if baptism meant more than baptism in water. On the other hand, water, where mentioned in the Old Testament, can be treated as a type of baptism without necessarily implying that the rite of baptism included dipping in water but nothing further. If it is argued that in New Testament passages where bread is mentioned there is a reference to the eucharist, it would obviously be wrong to suppose that only bread was used and not wine also. So even if there are a number of instances where Cyprian used the word 'baptism' specifically of the dipping in water, the term seems to have been elastic enough to be able to be used on occasion to denote the whole rite of initiation.

Once this possibility is granted, then the words 'by means of baptism the Holy Spirit is received' do not conflict with what Cyprian said many times about the hand-laying, and we are spared from having with Lampe (p. 170) to accuse Cyprian of muddled thought. Again, the words which immediately follow in this context should be noticed: 'after being baptized and after receiving the Holy Spirit, men come to drink the Lord's chalice.' Now there is no doubt that in the African rite of initiation men were baptized in water, then anointed and then received a hand-laying which over and over again is said to confer the Holy Spirit, and finally participated in the eucharist. Hence the words 'baptized' and 'receiving the Holy Spirit' have every appearance of referring to baptism and the subsequent imposition of the hand, in which case 'baptism' in the preceding sentence must mean baptism in the wider sense.

Where in *Ep*. 64.3 the subject of infant baptism came up for discussion, Cyprian observed that the actual grace given to the child was not granted in greater or less measure according to the age of the recipient. 'The Holy Spirit is not bestowed by measure but by God's fatherly love and graciousness, and is the same for all.' From this Wirgman (p. 115) and Lampe (pp. 171f) concluded that Cyprian believed the Holy Spirit to be given in baptism in the narrower sense of the word even to infants. But at this time infants who were baptized normally received also anointing, hand-laying, and communion, so that it cannot be ruled out as impossible that Cyprian was here thinking of infants who had received not only baptism in water but a full initiation, including the hand-laying for the imparting of the Spirit.

In *Ep.* 1.3 Cyprian recounted his experience at his own baptism:

'. . . but when with the help of the life-giving wave the taint of my past life had been wiped away, and into my reconciled and cleansed breast light from above poured in, when after I drank the Spirit from heaven a new birth restored me to a new man, then in a wonderful way doubtful things were seen to be corroborated . . . so that I had to admit that something of God which the Holy Spirit animated had begun.

There is no hint that there was a hand-laying or an anointing or a consignation at Cyprian's own baptism, or that the rite concluded with the eucharist. The explanation seems to be that he was thinking of his spiritual experience on that memorable occasion without relating it to the liturgical acts in the rite.

In *Ep.* 69.13f Cyprian had to allay misgivings about baptism by aspersion:

Have they indeed received the grace of the Lord but in a smaller and lesser measure of the divine gift and of the Holy Spirit, so that they are to be indeed reckoned Christians, but not treated as equal to the others? No, the Holy Spirit is not given by measure but is poured out in his fullness on the believer.

This seems to suggest that the Holy Spirit was given in all his fullness at the moment of baptism itself. But the question is what Cyprian meant in this context by the outpouring of the Spirit. As we have seen, Cyprian, like Tertullian before him, believed that the water for baptism was by consecration imbued with the Holy Spirit. So with regard to clinical baptism the question arose whether a person baptized by affusion, having had his body only partially touched by the saving water, as a consequence received less of the Spirit who indwelt the water. That is, did the Holy Spirit grant him only a partial regeneration and remission of sins? Cyprian replied that the grace received at baptism did not depend upon the amount of water used; the activity of the Holy Spirit remained unimpaired when only the sick person's head was touched by the water. It seems that Cyprian was here thinking of the grace received through the agency of the Spirit in the water rather than of that gift of the Spirit which elsewhere he most clearly linked with the laying on of the bishop's hand.

Lampe (p. 172) asserted that according to Cyprian the essential gift of the Spirit was conferred upon the clinically baptized at their baptism and not at any subsequent hand-laying or anointing. While it is easy enough to place this interpretation upon this particular passage, it is not so easy when all the evidence from Cyprian is taken as a whole. Mason (p. 66) solved the problem by supposing that baptism and hand-laying were so much a unity that, in describing the grace received in clinical baptism, Cyprian included the grace which those baptized would have received through the hand-laying when they recovered. But it is likely that many of those baptized in sudden emergency did not survive. Mason's attempted solution would be more convincing if the African church had been in the habit of administering the whole rite of initiation whenever baptism was required in haste. Augustine tells a story of an infant baptized in great haste: 'he was baptized, he was sanctified, he was anointed, the hand was laid upon him; when all the Sacraments were completed, he was taken.'[37] In this instance the entire rite was performed by presbyters. But we do not know whether this was normal practice in Africa in Cyprian's time; and in Rome it was customary for the sick to be baptized as occasion demanded and for a bishop to supply the missing anointing and hand-laying if and when they recovered.

If this is what happened in Carthage also, and if Lampe is right in maintaining that in the case of clinical baptisms baptism in water without any other ceremonies sufficed to procure the gift of the Holy Spirit, then another difficulty arises, in that it becomes very hard to see why the clinically baptized, if they recovered, were expected to receive the anointing and hand-laying which had so far been omitted, or what grace remained for these ceremonies to convey. This question is illustrated by the famous case of Novatian, who when he was gravely ill was baptized upon his bed of sickness. Pope Cornelius wrote in a letter to Fabius, bishop of Antioch, that, after having been baptized by affusion on the bed where he lay, Novatian, 'when he recovered from the illness, never obtained the other things which a man ought to partake in according to the church's rule, and was never sealed by the bishop. But before having received this, how could he have received the Holy Spirit?'[38] In this instance there was no problem because Cornelius, unlike Lampe, did not believe that Novatian had received the full gift of the Holy Spirit at his baptism. Lampe's view that the Spirit was fully given in clinical baptism makes the gift imparted by the subsequent anointing and hand-laying received by those who recovered an inexplicable duplication of the gift received at baptism.

In expounding the theology of initiation Cyprian used the analogy of building a temple for God. He asked why, if a person born outside the church could become the temple of God, it was not possible for the Holy Spirit to be poured upon the temple:

For he who having got rid of his sins in baptism has been sanctified

45

and spiritually reformed into a new man has been made fit to receive the Holy Spirit, since the apostle says, 'Whoever of you have been baptized in Christ have put on Christ'. If a person baptized among heretics is able to put on Christ, much more is he able to receive the Holy Spirit whom Christ sent. Otherwise he who was sent will be greater than him who sent him, if you say that one baptized outside the church has indeed begun by putting on Christ but cannot receive the Holy Spirit, as if either Christ can be put on without the Spirit or the Spirit can be separated from Christ.[39]

From this Wirgman (pp. 120f) took Cyprian to mean that putting on Christ in holy baptism involved a union with that indwelling Spirit who could not be separated from Christ the incarnate Lord. Hence he found support here for his main argument that the putting on of Christ and the reception of the Holy Spirit were so essentially one that they could only be imparted simultaneously, and therefore were imparted by the one sacramental act of baptism in water. Similarly Lampe (p. 172) concluded that Cyprian refused to distinguish between baptismal remission of sins and the gift of the Holy Spirit.

Now it is true that, when a temple is prepared for God, it is not expected that it will remain unoccupied. But it does not follow that Cyprian believed that at the moment of baptism the temple was prepared and also the divine tenant took up his residence in it. For Cyprian actually said that he who had put away his sins in baptism was made fit to receive the Spirit. This agrees exactly with the statement of Tertullian that in the water we are made clean by the action of the angel, and made ready for the Holy Spirit; and Tertullian made it clear that the Holy Spirit came into the temple made ready for him at the subsequent hand-laying. If it is unthinkable that the temple should remain empty and untenanted, the right conclusion to draw is not that the Holy Spirit must therefore be given at the very moment of baptism when the temple is prepared, but that the hand-laying must follow the baptism immediately.

Similarly when Cyprian argued that Christ could not be put on without the Spirit, nor the Spirit separated from Christ, the consequence is not necessarily that the Spirit must be supposed to be given at the actual moment of baptism when Christ is put on, but rather that the hand-laying which conveys the Spirit must not be separated from baptism. Cyprian's doctrine requires baptism and hand-laying to be seen as an organic unity. If Cyprian was right about the meaning of the hand-laying, then it was an integral part of baptism; if he was wrong, then it is redundant.

Evidently Cyprian did not expect the temple to remain cleansed but unoccupied. Any suggestion that a soul could be emptied of sin in baptism and remain empty for any length of time is open to the most damaging criticism, as Augustine[40] observed: 'Then after the remission of sins unless the Holy Spirit dwells in the house made clean, does not the unclean spirit return with seven others, and the last state of that man is worse than the first?'

The close connection between baptism and hand-laying was again stressed by Cyprian when he referred to the creation of Adam and his reception of the breath of life:

> Moreover a man is not reborn through the laying on of the hand, when he receives the Holy Spirit, but in baptism, so that he is born first and then receives the Spirit, as happened in the case of the first man Adam. God created him first, and then breathed into his nostrils the breath of life. For the Spirit cannot be received without the prior existence of the man to receive him.[41]

Here in very clear terms Cyprian asserted that spiritual rebirth took place at the moment of baptism, while the ensuing hand-laying conferred the gift of the Spirit. To argue that, because God breathed into Adam the breath of life as soon as he had made him, therefore the gift of the Spirit belongs so closely to the regeneration of baptism that it must of necessity be conferred by the same act is to miss the point and overlook what Cyprian said about the hand-laying. Again, what Cyprian's analogy demands is not that we should suppose that the gift of the Spirit cannot but be given simultaneously with the gift of regeneration at the moment of baptism itself, but that the hand-laying, which Cyprian said plainly enough conferred the Holy Spirit, should follow the actual baptism as soon as possible, as was the normal practice of the Church of Carthage at that time.

In conclusion, then, Cyprian's doctrine of initiation, virtually identical with that of Tertullian, requires a liturgical practice where baptism, anointing, consignation, and hand-laying with prayer are seen to be an organic whole. There is no ground for disagreement as to the spiritual blessings conferred by the whole rite; the difficulty arises when the attempt, unavoidable in the circumstances of today in the West, is made to distribute the blessings among the particular moments in the rite. While there is no doubt that the gifts of renewal, regeneration, and remission of sins belong to the moment of baptism itself, there is room for argument to which moment Cyprian assigned the giving of the Spirit. But when all the evidence is taken into account, it seems clear that the hand-laying was the moment with which Cyprian, like Tertullian before him, linked the imparting of the Spirit, although he was very far from holding that there was no operation of the Spirit in baptism itself. Where Cyprian seems to have associated the gift of the Spirit with the actual moment of baptism, we have argued that it is possible to interpret those particular passages in such a way as not to contradict the numerous clear statements that the Holy Spirit was given at the hand-laying.

It is not the easiest of tasks to interpret Cyprian's doctrine of initiation in a consistent manner: and doubtless there are those who will deny that the attempt here made to do so has been successful. Yet what is the alternative? First, we could say with Stone that baptism confers the Holy Spirit and the hand-laying confers special 'confirmation' gifts of the same spirit. This may be a tenable position to adopt when confirmation has become detached from baptism to the extent that it has done in the West. But in Cyprian's day the situation was very different. If a man receives the full gift of the Holy Spirit at the moment of baptism, it does not make sense to have another rite a few minutes later to bestow further gifts of the same Spirit. The African Fathers, as also the New Testament, show knowledge of a moment when new converts received the Spirit: the real question is not whether the Spirit was received more than once in initiation but whether that one moment was baptism itself or hand-laying.

Or we could follow Lampe in holding that Tertullian and Cyprian contradicted themselves, being far from clear in their thought on the subject. Now the literary remains of these two Fathers are extensive enough for the most sympathetic critic not to expect complete consistency throughout on all points. But here it is not a case of a writer contradicting in a later work what he has written in an earlier work, or of changing his mind after mature reflection: rather is it a case, if Lampe is right, of a writer contradicting himself in the same tract or the same letter. The kind of muddled thought which Lampe claimed to have found in these writers is such as to invite the retort that he has not fairly represented their mind.

The fewest difficulties are encountered if we adopt the position that in the African church of Tertullian and Cyprian regeneration and remission of sins were held to be conveyed by the agency of the Spirit in baptism itself, while the gift of the Spirit belonged to the hand-laying which followed at once.

Finally in the writings of Tertullian and Cyprian we can see clearly for the first time the ceremonies out of which has sprung the rite now known as confirmation. As yet they are not known by this name because they were integral parts of baptism. They were related to the imparting of the baptismal gift of the Holy Spirit, the emphasis being on a precious gift which God conferred. They had nothing to do with the personal confession of faith or renewal of baptismal promises, because the personal confession of the faith was one of the necessary preliminaries of baptism, and its was pointless to renew baptismal promises a few minutes after having made them.

About a hundred years after Cyprian, Optatus of Milevis published his *de Schismate Donatistarum*, in which there is one passage of special interest here, because in 4.7 he drew an analogy between the baptism of a Christian convert and the baptism of our Lord:

> He descended into the water, not because there was that in God which needed to be cleansed, but the water had to come before the oil that was to follow, for the initiation and ordering and fulfilling of the mysteries of baptism: when he had been washed and was held in the hands of John, the sequence of the mystery was observed, and the Father fulfilled what the Son had asked and what the Holy Spirit had announced. The heaven was opened while God the Father anointed him: the spiritual oil immediately descended in the form of a dove, and rested upon his head, and covered him with oil, from which he began to be called Christ, since he was anointed by God the Father; lest the laying on of the hand should seem to have been missing in his case, the voice of God was heard from the cloud saying, This is my Son in whom I am well pleased: hear him.

There is the same sequence of events — baptism, anointing and imposition of the hand — as we have seen in Tertullian and Cyprian. But whereas the latter had much more explicitly linked the gift of the Spirit with the hand-laying, Optatus here at any rate seems to associate the gift with the unction after baptism. Mason (p. 80f), however, cited 7.4 from the same work, where Optatus, in a passage which echoes words of Tertullian's *de Baptismo*, said of the oil that it prepared a throne for the Holy Spirit, 'so that being invited he might there, after removing all roughness, vouchsafe willingly to take up his abode.' It may be, therefore, that Optatus did not tie the giving of the Holy Spirit exclusively to either the anointing or to the hand-laying, although it is clear that he did not connect it with baptism itself.

Although there are in the voluminous writings of Augustine of Hippo many references to an anointing and a hand-laying after baptism, it is open to dispute how far he linked the gift of the Spirit with these acts rather than with baptism itself.

The unction of which he showed knowledge undoubtedly came after and not before the actual baptism. The analogy of baking bread, where the grain is mixed with water before it is baked, requires baptism in water to precede the anointing with chrism which represents the fire of the Spirit.[42] 'There is no bread without fire first. What then does the fire signify? This is the chrism. For the oil is our fire, the sacrament of the Holy Spirit.'[43]

The hand-laying after baptism had the purpose which Tertullian and Cyprian attributed to it:

> For none of his disciples gave the Holy Spirit. They would pray that he would come to those upon whom they would lay the hand, they

themselves used not to give him. This custom the church preserves through its prelates.[44]

Again Augustine wrote: 'For who now expects that those on whom the hand is laid that they may receive the Holy Spirit should suddenly begin to speak with tongues?'[45]

There are, however, a few places where Augustine has been thought to ascribe the gift of the Holy Spirit to baptism itself. The brief sentence, 'It is God who gives the Holy Spirit when even he baptizes,'[46] has been thought by Stone,[47] Wirgman (p. 212), and Lampe (p. 204) to prove this. But it is here a question of what Augustine meant by 'baptize'. In this context he was not dealing specifically with baptism in the narrower sense of the word, but rather was concerned to refute the argument of the Donatists that all sacraments depended for their validity upon the worthiness of the officiant. To this end he declared that prayers said over the water of baptism, or over the oil, or over the eucharist, or over those who receive the imposition of the hand, are heard by God even when uttered by murderers, that is, by clergy who hate their brethren.[48] Coming after this, the word 'baptize' may well bear its wider meaning here.

Similarly when in *Ep.* 187.26 Augustine wrote, 'We say therefore that the Holy Spirit dwells in baptized infants although they know it not', it is once more a question of the meaning of the word 'baptize'. For many centuries it has been safe in the West to assume that an infant, though baptized, has not been confirmed. But in this context such an assumption is totally unwarranted. For when infants were presented for initiation at the traditional seasons, a bishop would be present to lay his hand upon them, as may be inferred from Augustine's own words: 'Or when we laid a hand upon those infants, did each of you wonder whether they would speak with tongues?'[49] It is a fact that in those days infants were admitted to all the sacraments: 'They are infants, but they receive his sacraments. They are infants, but they are communicants at his table, that they may have life in themselves.'[50]

Now it is true that in Augustine's time baptism might be administered on any day in the year;[51] but when this happened it was because haste was required in case an ailing catechumen or newly born infant should die unbaptized. We of today would naturally assume that in these situations a bishop could not be present. But if the number of bishops who attended the Council of Carthage in 256 is any criterion, African dioceses were small enough and African bishops plentiful enough to make it possible to secure the presence of a bishop at least at some of the baptisms which had to be administered in haste. Furthermore we have no certain knowledge that the African church did not in these circumstances, when no bishop was available, delegate the whole rite of initiation to presbyters. Indeed, as we have seen,[52] Augustine has related a story in which this is precisely what happened. Hence when he said that the Holy Spirit dwelt in baptized infants, there is no proof that he had in mind infants who had not received anointing and hand-laying as well as baptism.

So also some words in *de Trin.* 15.46, 'He was pleased to prefigure his body the church, in which the baptized especially received the Holy Spirit', although cited by Wirgman (p. 211) as evidence for the gift of the Spirit in baptism itself, may be taken to refer to baptism in its wider sense, especially as the subject of anointing is prominent in the context. Unless we allow that in these passages Augustine meant by baptism the whole rite of initiation, we make him contradict here what he said elsewhere about the unction and hand-laying as the means by which the Holy Spirit was given.

In one well known passage Augustine treated hand-laying in an almost disparaging manner, denying it any sacramental significance: 'But the laying on of the hand is not, like baptism, incapable of being repeated. For what else is it but praying over a person?'[53] Here, however, Augustine was thinking not of the hand-laying which was the normal accompaniment of baptism in water but of the rite of reconciliation received by heretics and schismatics who, having been outside catholic peace and unity, lacked that charity which is the principal fruit of the Spirit.

Lambot has called attention to a lacuna in the standard editions of the tract, *adv. Fulgentium Donatistam*, usually placed among Augustine's genuine works, although it may be by another author.[54] In the missing passage is found some information concerning the unction in the African rite of initiation. After a reference to Elisha and the widow's cruse of oil, and after the words, 'but you say, If we do not give the Holy Spirit, do you repeat the anointing with chrism',[55] comes the invitation,

> The Spirit can be taken away, circumcision cannot be taken away. He who gave to Christ, when John baptized him, himself gives to the Christian, when the bishop prays, 'Come, receive the Holy Spirit without whom you can be neither sons nor alive'. For whoever are led by the Spirit of God, these are the sons of God.

If these few words are not from Augustine's own pen, yet they are at least from Africa, and show the meaning attached to the chrismation at baptism in the early fifth century.

We shall deal later with the question whether Augustine knew the confirmation prayer of the West, in which the Holy Spirit with his sevenfold gifts is invoked upon the initiates.[56]

3 The West

Although in his *La Liturgie d'Hippolyte* Hanssens has argued at great length for an Alexandrian origin of the *Apostolic Tradition*, the most widely held view is still that this work is by Hippolytus and reflects Roman practice in the early third century.[1] The rite of initiation, which is described in full, may, however, to a certain extent be an ideal liturgy in the sense that it represents what Hippolytus thought that the Roman church ought to do rather than what it actually did. Moreover the church's rites had not yet assumed the fixed form which they were to have at a later date.

When the candidate emerged from the baptismal waters, he was anointed by a presbyter with the oil of thanksgiving with these words, 'I anoint you with holy oil in the name of Jesus Christ'.[2] This unction was probably an unction of the whole body, because it took place as soon as the candidate came up from the water and before he dressed himself. Although the accompanying formula does not clearly express the meaning of this ceremony, a clue is provided by the fact that it was performed with the oil of thanksgiving, which has been consecrated by the bishop at the start of the proceedings. There is an evident reference to Ps. 45.8 (quoted in Heb. 1.9), where God is said to have anointed the Messiah with the oil of gladness above his fellows. Hence this presbyteral unction symbolized the union of the baptized with Christ and incorporation into his Messianic body. It relates to the Second rather than to the Third Person of the Trinity.

There follows the final part of the rite, administered by the bishop:

The bishop laying his hand upon them shall say the invocation: Lord God, who hast made them worthy to obtain the remission of sins by the bath of regeneration, make them worthy to be filled with the Holy Spirit and send upon them thy grace, so that they may serve thee according to thy will . . . Then, pouring some of the oil of thanksgiving in his hand and putting it on the head (of each candidate), he shall say: I anoint thee with holy oil in God the Father almighty and in Christ Jesus and in the Holy Spirit. And after having signed him on the forehead, he shall give him the kiss and shall say: The Lord be with thee. And he who has been signed shall say: And with thy spirit. He (the bishop) shall thus do for each one.[3]

Here is incontrovertible evidence of hand-laying with prayer, anointing, and consignation after baptism. The meaning of these episcopal acts is to be found in the accompanying prayer. Unfortunately here we have to pass into disputed territory, because the original Greek text of the *Apostolic Tradition* no longer survives, so that we are left dependent upon a number of later versions in different languages, and the text of the prayer is not identical in all of them. Following the version in the Latin Verona MS, Easton translated the prayer thus: 'O Lord God, who hast made them worthy to obtain remission of sins through the laver of regeneration of the Holy Spirit, send into them thy grace, that they may serve thee according to thy will . . .'[4] But the Ethiopic and Bohairic versions, the *Testament of our Lord*, and the *Canons of Hippolytus* contain this prayer in a longer form, the few extra words being of cardinal importance in determining the meaning of the hand-laying and unction. Preferring their testimony to that of the Verona MS, Dix translated thus: 'O Lord God, who didst count these thy servants worthy of deserving the forgiveness of sins by the laver of regeneration, make them worthy to be filled with thy Holy Spirit and send upon them thy grace, that they may serve thee according to thy will.'[5] Thus in this longer version the words 'make them worthy to be filled with thy Holy Spirit' make this prayer a petition that the Holy Spirit may be given to the baptized at this point, whereas the shorter version only mentions the Holy Spirit in a reference to the baptism which has just taken place. The problem is to decide whether the extra words of the longer version are a later interpolation, or whether a line has dropped out of the shorter Latin version, perhaps through the error of a copyist.

Dealing at some length with this question, Lampe (pp. 139ff) criticized Dix for regarding as corrupt the shorter Latin text which reads thus:

> . . . qui dignos fecisti eos remissionem mere-
> ri peccatorum per lavacrum regenera-
> tionis spiritus sancti; inmitte in eos grati-
> am. . . .

If the longer version favoured by Dix is genuine, then some words have been omitted, presumably accidentally, from the third line of the Latin text. Assuming for argument's sake that this was so, Lampe suggested that the Latin text might have run thus:

> ... qui dignos eos remissionem mere-
> ri peccatorum per lavacrum regenera-
> tionis dignos fac eos reple-
> tionis spiritus sancti; inmitte in eos tuam grati-
> am. ...

Two consecutive lines beginning with '-tionis' would then provide a reason for a copyist accidentally to miss a line. But since the third line of this reconstructed text is noticeably too short, Lampe rejected the theory that a line has dropped out of the Verona text, and preferred the shorter version as representing more accurately what Hippolytus originally wrote. This, however, leaves unanswered the question, Whence did the longer version obtain the words 'make them worthy to be filled with thy Holy Spirit'?

Now W. G. Wilson has shown that it is possible to insert into the text of the Latin version the words, 'dignos fac eos repletionis', without producing lines of too unequal length. Of more than one possible reconstruction of the text he preferred this one:

> Dne Deus qui dignos fecisti
> eos remissionem mereri
> peccatorum per lavacrum
> regenerationis dignos fac
> eos repletionis spus sci in-
> mitte in eos tuam gratiam ...

The presence of the word 'repletionis' under the word 're-generationis' with its identical ending might well have caused a scribe to omit a line.[6] Botte also preferred the longer text, believing that either the Latin translator had jumped a line, or that he had before him a Greek text in which a line had been omitted.[7] Moreover, Lampe himself in the preface (p. xvii) to his second edition of *The Seal of the Spirit* appears to accept the longer version of this prayer.

In considering possible reconstructions of the Latin text we are necessarily in the realm of speculation. But if nothing less than the discovery of Hippolytus' original text could ever finally settle this problem to the satisfaction of all, there are nevertheless other factors which tell in favour of the longer version of the prayer.

First, Crehan has advanced reasons for believing that the longer text in the Ethiopic version is more likely than the shorter version to reflect what Hippolytus originally wrote.[8] Secondly, the reference to Tit. 3.5 in the first clause of the prayer is incomplete in the shorter version of the Verona MS, because, whereas there is an exact counterpart of the scriptural phrase 'washing of regeneration', there is no such counterpart of the ensuing scriptural phrase 'renewing of the Holy Spirit'. Something seems to have been omitted.

Thirdly, the longer form of the prayer indicates that the purpose of the hand-laying and anointing was to bestow the Holy Spirit upon the baptized. Now this agrees well with what Hippolytus wrote elsewhere on this subject. For instance, in a *Fragment on Susanna* he likened the oil in Susanna 17 to the power of the Holy Spirit, with which after the washing believers are anointed as with unguent; and in *de Christo et Antichristo* 59 he said that it was the Spirit from heaven through whom those who believe in God are sealed.

Fourthly, the rubric which precedes the prayer in question, 'the bishop placing his hand upon them shall say the invocation', is not without significance in that it makes good sense to invoke the Holy Spirit upon the baptized, but not such good sense to invoke impersonal grace upon them; and it will be recalled that at the hand-laying in Tertullian's rite there was an invocation which was addressed to the Holy Spirit himself, and the Holy Spirit himself descended on the bodies cleansed by baptism.

The *Apostolic Tradition*, then, supplies evidence of a hand-laying with prayer and an unction and consignation after baptism, the purpose of which was to convey the gift of the Holy Spirit and so equip the initiates with grace for service. Now if these ceremonies could be incorporated in a work which purported to record a tradition received from the apostles, they can hardly have been newly introduced into the Roman Church at the time when the *Apostolic Tradition* was published, about the year 217. If Justin Martyr's failure to mention them is thought decisive, then they cannot have formed part of the Roman rite of initiation before about the year 170; but if Justin's silence is thought not to be decisive, it is at least arguable, even if it cannot be proved, that they originated in the apostolic age itself.

In his commentary on St Matthew's Gospel, 2.6, Hilary said that the sequence of events in our Lord's baptism was

> in order that we, by those things which were fully completed in the case of Christ, might understand, that after the washing of water, and from the gates of heaven, the Holy Spirit flies down upon us also, and we are covered with the unction of the heavenly glory, and are by the divine voice adopting us made sons of God; for the truth, by things thus actually done, has prefigured a type of the sacrament which for us was to follow the same sequence.

Evidently Hilary, writing *c.* 360, knew an initiatory rite in which baptism in water was followed by an unction which symbolized the gift of the Holy Spirit. That he knew also of a hand-laying after baptism appears in his comment in the same work, 19.3, on our Lord's blessing of the little children, 'who, the Lord says, were not to be forbidden, because of such is the kingdom of heaven. For the bestowal and gift of the Holy Spirit was to be vouchsafed to the Gentiles, without the work of the Law, by means of the laying on of the hand and prayer.'

It is possible, as we shall see later,[9] that Hilary knew the so-called confirmation prayer of the West, in which the Holy Spirit of sevenfold grace was invoked upon the initiates.

Hence Hilary attests an unction and a hand-laying after baptism, their purpose being to convey the gift of the Holy Spirit. Yet for him they were as much part of the rite of baptism as our Lord's reception of the Spirit was part of his baptism.

The Council of Elvira, held about the year 305, sheds some light on initiation in the Spanish church. Canons 11 and 37 reveal a desire that those who are dangerously ill should be baptized; and canon 38 shows that on such an occasion there would be no bishop present. This same canon lays down that a catechumen taken ill at sea or far from a church may be baptized by a faithful layman, but on condition that, if he recovers, he be taken to the bishop to be perfected by the imposition of his hand. Canon 77 shows that a deacon might be in charge of a congregation, and might find it necessary to baptize in the absence of bishop or presbyter, and persons so baptized are to be perfected by the blessing of the bishop; if they die in the meantime, their failure to receive the episcopal blessing will not prejudice their chance of salvation. Clearly the intention is that the baptized person shall receive the laying on of the bishop's hand as soon as possible; no doubt a catechumen taken ill at sea would have received both baptism and the hand-laying if there had been a bishop on board. In normal circumstances this is what always happened. Since the hand-laying is regarded as the perfecting or completion of baptism, it must belong doctrinally very closely with baptism, although nothing is said here about the grace which it confers.

About fifty years later Pacian, bishop of Barcelona, asked whether only the apostles were allowed 'to baptize and to give the Holy Spirit and to cleanse the sins of the Gentiles.'[10] Here at first sight it would seem that Pacian considered the giving of the Spirit and the cleansing from sin as the effects of baptism in water. But later on in the same letter he wrote of the 'power of the laver and of the chrism', showing that the rite of baptism included chrismation. Commenting on John 1.12, he revealed the significance of the chrism:

these things cannot be otherwise fulfilled except by the sacrament of the laver and of the chrism and of the bishop. For by the laver sins are purged; by the chrism the Holy Spirit is poured upon us; and both these we gain by the hand and mouth of the bishop; and thus the whole man is born again and made new in Christ.[11]

Evidently Pacian believed that it was the purpose of the anointing after baptism to impart the Holy Spirit; but he saw a close connection between the anointing and the baptism. A further point to be noticed is his insistence that the bishop is the proper minister of initiation.

Ambrose has provided two fairly full accounts of the Milanese rite of initiation as it was in the late fourth century. After the actual baptism came an unction by the *sacerdos*, or bishop, who prayed, 'God the Father almighty, who has regenerated you by water and the Holy Spirit, and has forgiven you your sins, himself anoint you to eternal life.'[12] After quoting and commenting on Ps. 133.2, Ambrose explained the purpose of this ceremony: 'that you may become a chosen generation, priestly and precious; for we are all anointed with spiritual grace to the kingdom of God and the priesthood.'[13] As in the African rite, the purpose of this anointing was to confer membership in the priestly body of Christ rather than to confer the gift of the Holy Spirit.

The anointing was followed by the ceremony of the feet-washing, with which we are not here concerned. Next came 'the spiritual seal, which you have heard mentioned in the lesson today. For after the font it remains for the perfecting to take place, when, at the invocation of the priest the Holy Spirit is conferred . . .'[14] While the minister who performed this sealing was again the *sacerdos*, or bishop, it is not stated whether chrism was used. Srawley was almost certainly right in suggesting that the seal consisted in an act of consignation,[15] because in *de Sacr.* 6.2.7 Ambrose referred back to the sealing thus: 'Because you were signed with the image of the cross itself unto his passion, you received a seal unto his likeness, that you might rise unto his image, and live after his example, who was crucified to sin and lives to God.' Furthermore, since in *de Sacr.* 6.2.6f—'It is God who anointed you, and the Lord signed you . . . therefore God anointed you, the Lord signed you'—anointing and singing are twice mentioned together, it becomes virtually certain that the signing was in fact performed with chrism.

Now one point is abundantly clear, that the spiritual seal constituted the moment in the Milanese rite when the Holy Spirit was given to the initiates. This is plainly stated three times: in *de Sacr.* 3.2.8, cited above; in *de Sacr.* 6.2.6, 'the Lord signed you and put the Holy Spirit in your heart. You have therefore received the Holy Spirit in your heart;' and in *de Myst.* 7.42, 'God the Father has sealed you, Christ the Lord has confirmed you, and has given the earnest of the Spirit in your heart . . .'

The seal is treated by Ambrose as the perfecting of baptism, the washing in water being completed or consummated by the gift of the Spirit. Here Ambrose was using a term which was often employed both in the East and the West in connection with the post-baptismal

57

anointing by the bishop.[16] The spiritual seal was the final part of a complex rite which was yet an organic whole.

We have seen how in the West the actual baptism was followed by an episcopal sealing with chrism, and sometimes also by a hand-laying. The accompanying prayer is of cardinal importance because it reveals the purpose of these symbolical acts. Yet, if we accept the prayer at this point in the *Apostolic Tradition*, we have to wait till the *Gelasian Sacramentary* for the full text of this prayer. At the consignation of the forehead the bishop prays:

> Almighty God, Father of our Lord Jesus Christ, who hast made thy servants to be regenerated of water and the Holy Spirit, and hast given them remission of all their sins, do thou, Lord, send upon them thy Holy Spirit, the Paraclete, and give them the spirit of wisdom and understanding, the spirit of counsel and might, the spirit of knowledge and godliness, and fill them with the spirit of the fear of God . . .[17]

The first point to be considered is the antiquity of this prayer. The chief manuscript of this sacramentary emanated from Gaul not earlier than the eighth century, although, if Chavasse[18] is right, its rite of initiation reflects Roman usage as far back as the sixth century. But there is more to be said.

The prayer invokes the Holy Spirit upon the initiates, and ends by enumerating the seven gifts of the Holy Spirit in Is. 11.2. Now it is highly significant that Augustine wrote with reference to this text of Isaiah: 'The Spirit of wisdom and understanding, of counsel and strength, of knowledge and godliness, the Spirit of the fear of God, this is the sevenfold Spirit who is invoked upon the baptized.'[19] And again: 'The Spirit himself is invoked upon the baptized that God would give them, according to the prophet, the Spirit of wisdom and understanding . . .'[20] This would strongly suggest that the Gelasian prayer was in use in Africa at least as far back as the early fifth century.

In commenting on the spiritual seal, Ambrose said that at the invocation of the bishop 'the Holy Spirit is bestowed, the spirit of wisdom and understanding, the spirit of counsel and strength, the spirit of knowledge and godliness, the spirit of holy fear, as it were seven virtues of the Spirit.'[21] Ambrose repeated this in *de Myst.* 7.42. This would seem to show that the Gelasian prayer, perhaps not in identical words, was used in Milan in the late fourth century. Moreover since in *de Sacr.* 3.1.5 Ambrose said that except in the matter of the feet-washing the Church of Milan followed the type and form of the Roman Church in all things, there is a strong probability that the Gelasian prayer was used in Rome also in the late fourth century.

Indeed the prayer may have been known to pope Siricius, who in

385 ordered that Arians were to be received into the communion of the catholic church by the invocation of the sevenfold Spirit and the imposition of the bishop's hand.[22] Since the rite by which heretics were received into the church was very similar to the latter part of the rite of initiation, it looks as if a knowledge of the Gelasian prayer led him to refer in this context to the Spirit as seven-fold. Similarly when in 416, Innocent I wrote in his well-known letter to Decentius of Gubbio of the right of bishops alone 'to seal and give the Spirit the Paraclete,'[23] these last four words, coming in this context, sound like an echo of the same prayer.

The seven loaves in our Lord's miracle led Hilary to think of the seven gifts of the Spirit in Is. 11; and, referring to the salvation of the Gentiles, he added that 'they are called to the gift of the sevenfold Spirit.'[24] Here, too, it is just possible that there is an allusion to the bishop's prayer at the chrismation.

Ratcliff[25] argued that a prayer in which the sevenfold Spirit was invoked upon initiates was known to Justin Martyr in the mid second century. Even if he is right, the evidence of Hippolytus does not support him, because the prayer in the *Apostolic Tradition*[26] is noticeably different from the Gelasian prayer, in that the opening relative clause quotes Tit. 3.5 and not John 3.5, and the sevenfold gifts of Is. 11.2 are not mentioned at all.

It seems, then, that this prayer was almost certainly in use in the late fourth century; but whether it is older still is a matter for speculation.

More important than the antiquity of this prayer is its doctrine. It begins with a relative clause, 'who hast made thy servants to be regenerated of water and the Holy Spirit, and hast given them remission of all their sins.' That is a succinct summary of the gifts conferred at the actual baptism which has just taken place a few minutes previously. Moreover, the prayer presupposes that the baptism will have taken place only a little while before the episcopal chrismation, because, when, as is now the case in the West, there is an interval of years between baptism and confirmation, the candidates for chrismation will have had time to commit many actual sins which will not have been remitted at their baptism.

The prayer continues: 'do thou, Lord, send upon them thy Holy Spirit, the Paraclete, and give them the spirit of wisdom and understanding ...' This is the gift to be conveyed through the episcopal sealing with chrism. Innocent I claimed that this latter part of the rite could only be administered by a bishop, since bishops alone had the power to impart the Holy Spirit, a prerogative which, he said, could be justified from tradition and from Acts 8.17, where it was apostles who laid their hands on those baptized by Philip the deacon. The gift of the Spirit conferred at the chrismation by the bishop is the same gift of the Spirit that was conferred at Samaria by St Peter and St

John by the imposition of their hands with prayer, and also the same gift of the Spirit which the apostles themselves had received at Pentecost.

If it was this gift of the Spirit that the candidates received at the chrismation after baptism, it nevertheless does not follow that they had in no sense received the Holy Spirit before this. The Holy Spirit had been invoked upon the water in which they had been baptized; and it was through him that they received regeneration and remission of sins. Many today would say that persons who had received this much had indeed received the Holy Spirit. But while this may in a sense be true, it is not what is meant when it is said that the candidates receive the Holy Spirit at the chrismation. The prayer shows clearly that the sealing with chrism is a sacramental act in which there is an objective giving of the Holy Spirit; it is not treated as a bare sign merely calling attention to a grace that has already been given and received. If we say that the Holy Spirit is given in baptism itself, we have to avoid making the gift of the Spirit at the chrismation a mere duplication of this. If the gift of the Spirit in the chrismation is the same gift as that initially outpoured at Pentecost, we have to consider whether we do justice to it if we treat it as an enlargement of a gift already bestowed at baptism. Faustus of Riez asserted that the gift conferred in confirmation was an addition of a new kind.[27]

Finally, if it is held that the regenerating and sin-remitting activity of the Holy Spirit at baptism is theologically inseparable from the giving of the Spirit at the chrismation, it has to be remembered that the acts which symbolized and conferred these gifts were two moments in a rite which was far more of a unity than we readily appreciate today.

4 *Egypt*

A contemporary of Tertullian but a man of very different outlook, Clement of Alexandria made a number of allusions to the subject of initiation, but never in terms which reveal clearly the content of the rite.

After saying that our Lord was perfected by the laver alone and sanctified by the descent of the Spirit, he added:

> the same takes place also in connection with ourselves, whose pattern the Lord is made. Being baptized we are enlightened; being enlightened, we are adopted as sons; being adopted, we are perfected; being perfected, we are rendered immortal . . . But this work bears various names, gift of grace, and enlightenment, and perfection, and laver; laver, by means of which we are cleansed from the filth of sins; gift of grace, whereby the penalties due to our sins are remitted; enlightenment, through which that holy light which is our salvation is set before our eyes, that is, our sight is quickened to see God; by perfection we understand the lack of nothing: for what is wanting to one who knows God?[1]

The style of this passage makes it impossible to determine the nature of the rite which underlies Clement's comments. That it included baptism in water is evident: whether it included any further ceremonies is a matter for conjecture. Mason (p. 261) contended that the phrase 'laver alone' gave a hint that there was a whole sequence of baptismal rites. Such an interpretation does not follow easily when this passage is considered by itself, as his critics were not slow to point out. Wirgman (p. 129), for instance, thought it very evident that Clement was here referring to baptism *per se*, while Lampe (p. 156) saw no reason for supposing that the gift of the Spirit, separated from the baptismal blessings listed by Clement, was to be associated with another moment in the rite of initiation, and R. P. C. Hanson was convinced that Clement was not expounding the successive stages in that rite but four different aspects of one and the same event.[2]

Where Clement used the term 'seal', it is not always evident to what it referred, or even whether it always bore the same meaning. For example, one topic with which Clement dealt was the matter of sin 'after the seal and redemption'.[3] Hanson called attention to the fact that the seal is mentioned before the redemption.[4] If the seal here stands for 'confirmation', then these words, at first sight at any rate, do not support the case that from the earliest times baptism in water was followed by confirmation in the form of hand-laying or anointing, although they could be cited in support of Dix's theory that originally confirmation preceded baptism.[5] However this could be a simple case of *hysteron proteron*. Nor is it clear whether the seal here refers to another act distinct from baptism itself, or denotes the inward redemption wrought by the outward act of baptism.

There is a similar ambiguity in *Protrepticus* 12, where Clement wrote: 'I become holy while I am being initiated: the Lord is the interpreter of holy things and seals the initiate as he enlightens him, and commends him that has believed to the Father to be guarded for ever and ever.' If in speaking of the seal as a protective Clement was influenced by Ezek. 9.4, then the seal could be a mark placed upon the faithful at their initiation.

In an attack on the doctrine of Basilides, Clement complained that it left no reason either for baptism or for the blessed seal.[6] If, which is doubtful, there is any significance in the order of the words, then it is to be noted that in this instance Clement mentioned the seal after baptism. But unless he is to be convicted of tautology, the seal here must surely, as Wirgman (p. 130) and Mason (p. 257) alleged, refer to something distinct from baptism, although Lampe (p. 153) rejected any exegesis which saw an allusion to confirmation.

In *Prophet. Eclog.* 12, where Clement wrote of the need to empty the soul of evil and fill it with good, the seal followed in order that 'that which is holy may be kept for God.' This could be a reference to the protecting power of the sign of the cross; but even if this is not so, Hanson can hardly be right in saying that it indubitably meant water baptism.[7]

Clement also told the story of a young robber said to have been entrusted by St John to the care of a presbyter who took him home, 'nourished him, kept him in, fostered him, at last enlightened him. And after this he withdrew from further care and guardianship of him, as having set upon him the perfect safeguard, the seal of the Lord.'[8] Lampe (pp. 115, 153), Hanson,[9] and Leeming[10] considered that the seal was certainly to be identified with the baptism at which the youth had been enlightened. This view rests on the assumption that baptism in water and enlightenment are entirely synonymous. While this assumption could in this instance be right, another interpretation is not necessarily ruled out, because the verb 'having set upon him' (*epistesas*) suggests a mark placed upon the person of the young man at his baptism. So there could be here another allusion to the protective powers of the sign of the cross.

Commenting on the tribute money handed to our Lord, Clement said that the believer 'has through Christ the name of God written on him and the Spirit as an image. Even brute beasts through this branding show whose is the flock, and the branding-mark establishes a claim to them. Thus the soul of the believer, who has received the seal of truth, bears the marks of Christ upon it.'[11] Lampe (pp. 153f) understood the seal here to be the character imprinted on the believer's soul at baptism, the mark of Christ's ownership. But this does not sufficiently account for Clement's analogy of the mark put upon the coin and his reference to the branding of animals. Clement's words probably imply that a mark was placed upon the baptized, while the phrase 'the stigmata of Christ' suggests that the mark was the sign of the cross.

So too when in *Strom.* 5.11 Clement wrote that the three days would be the mystery of the seal, through which God is believed in truth, the reference may be not only to the baptismal confession of faith in the Trinity, but also to the Paschal *triduum*, because Clement has just quoted Gen. 22.3f, where on the third day Abraham saw afar off the place where he was to sacrifice Isaac. Since, therefore, the thought of sacrifice was present in Clement's mind, good sense would be obtained if the seal were understood as the emblem of our Lord's sacrifice. Thus in this instance the seal may well have stood for a consignation during the rite of baptism.

Since, however, the passages so far considered do not indicate whether the sign of the cross was made with chrism, we pass now to some other passages where Clement may have shown a knowledge of anointing at baptism. The expression in *Protrep.* 12, 'the unguent of faith' must surely be understood in a metaphorical sense. But in *Strom.* 7.7 Clement said that the true Gnostic refers to God 'the solemn enjoyment of food, or drink, or unction, and offers the firstfruits to the Giver of all, giving him thanks both by the gift and by the anointing.' Since food and drink and firstfruits are material objects, the unction must in this context surely be an unction with material oil. Possibly, as Mitchell (p. 52) suggested, the reference is to an actual anointing at baptism, when a man became a true Gnostic.

Again, Clement found a mystical meaning in the anointing of our Lord's feet: 'These feet of the Lord which were anointed are the apostles, it being a prophecy of the sweet savour of the chrism, after becoming partakers of the Holy Spirit.'[12] Here, although it can be understood metaphorically, the expression 'sweet savour of the chrism' could also refer to a physical anointing which imparts the Holy Spirit. The possibility of a physical anointing arises also in *Strom.* 4.18, where the Christian is said to exhibit the mark, the shining mark, of righteousness: 'I speak of the chrism of well-pleasing, the quality of disposition which is produced upon the soul when it is made glad according to the coming upon it of the Holy Spirit.' Although the chrism of well-pleasing is a metaphorical expression, it could refer to the spiritual effects of a physical anointing at baptism.

Without saying for what purpose it was to be used, Clement dealt in *Excerpt. Theodot.* 83 with the consecration of oil by the followers of Theodotus: 'The bread and the oil are sanctified by the power of the name, and, contrary to appearance, are no longer the same things as they were when they were taken, but have been changed by power into spiritual power.' This does not prove that the Catholic Church was already using holy oil in its rites and ceremonies, still less that it was using it in its rite of baptism, except insofar as there was a similarity between the rites of the Church and those of the heretical sects.

So far we have been on uncertain ground. But it becomes firmer when we consider a statement by Origen that according to the form handed down to the churches we have all been baptized in the visible waters and in the visible chrism.[13] For a chrism which is visible like the water of baptism cannot possibly be interpreted in a purely figurative sense. Furthermore, since this twofold baptism in water and in chrism was in accordance with the form handed down to the churches, it cannot have been a recent innovation, but must go back at least to the time of Clement, if not further back still.

On the subject of hand-laying there are only two passages in Clement's works which are at all relevant. In *Paed.* 3.11 he condemned the feminine practice of wearing false hair on the ground that a presbyter would then lay his hand not on the woman so adorned but on the other person's hair, and consequently on a different head. But since, as Lampe (p. 157) pointed out, hand-laying was used in solemn blessings, this affords no proof that it was now to be found among the ceremonies of baptism.

More important, Clement has supplied clear evidence that the Valentinians included hand-laying in their rite of initiation:

Wherefore also in the laying on of the hands they say at the end, Into the angelic redemption, that is, the redemption which the angels possess, in order that the man who has obtained the redemption may be held to have been baptized in the same name in which his angel also has been previously baptized.'[14]

Now if, as is quite possible, the Valentinians had inherited this practice of hand-laying at baptism from their founder, then here is evidence of a baptismal hand-laying, albeit in a heretical sect, as far back as the mid-second century, Valentinus having died about the year 160. Furthermore, it is arguable that the Church would not have adopted a liturgical practice peculiar to a heretical sect, and that the

Valentinians included this hand-laying in their rite of initiation because it was already customary in the church from which they seceded . . . Moreover, if Epiphanius is to be trusted when he said that Valentinus was an Egyptian who grew up in Alexandria,[15] then Hanssens[16] may well have been right in suggesting that the Valentinian rite of initiation with its hand-laying was inspired by the practice of the church of Alexandria. Indeed Clement's phrase 'in the laying on of hands' rather suggests that this act was well known, common both to the Church and to the Valentinians, except that, as Mason (p. 270) thought, the latter attached a novel meaning to it.

Of the gift of the Holy Spirit in Christian initiation Clement said very little, and nothing which reveals clearly the context in which the gift was imparted. Yet it is significant that in two of the passages quoted above oil is treated as a symbol of the Holy Spirit. In this connection there is a passage in *Paed.* 1.12 which is relevant: 'I believe that he (i.e. the Word) both formed man out of the dust, and begat him again with water, and increased him with the Spirit, and tutored him with the spoken word, unto adoption and salvation . . .' While Wirgman (p. 130) saw in the words 'increased him with the Spirit' a reference to confirmation, and Mason (p. 265) a reference to a second and different movement of divine grace, Lampe (p. 156) rejected the notion of an increase of the Spirit being given later in time than the regeneration of baptism. As between these two points of view, it seems that there is no more reason for treating the clause 'increased him with the Spirit' as identical with the preceding clause 'begat him again with water', than there is for treating this latter clause as identical with the clause before it, 'formed man out of the dust.'

Further evidence of the gift of the Spirit is found in *Strom.* 5.13, 'But we affirm that the Holy Spirit is breathed in a new way upon him who has believed.' The occasion when this happened is presumably the great occasion when the believer confessed his faith at his initiation. Yet Clement never once described this occasion.

Thus on balance it seems probable that the Alexandrian rite of initiation in Clement's time included an unction with which the gift of the Holy Spirit was associated. The evidence for a hand-laying at baptism is more problematical. But if Clement's evidence for any post-baptismal ceremonies is inconclusive, this is due chiefly to the fact that his main concern was to demonstrate that the Christians were the enlightened ones in possession of the true gnosis, for which reason he treated the subject of initiation, insofar as he treated it at all, from the intellectual and not from the liturgical angle.

In several places Origen appears to assign the giving of the Spirit to the moment of baptism itself. For instance in *Hom. 6.5 in Ezek.* he exhorted catechumens to come to the laver and be washed unto Salvation, and not be washed after the fashion of some who have been washed but not unto salvation—of him who receives the water and does not receive the Spirit. He who is washed unto salvation receives both the water and the Holy Spirit. Because Simon was not washed unto salvation, he received the water, but did not receive the Holy Spirit, thinking that the gift of the Spirit could be purchased with money.

There is a very similar passage in *in Num.* 3.1, where Origen wrote:

Nor are all who have been washed with the water washed then and there with the Holy Spirit also, just as, on the other hand, not all who are numbered among the catechumens are strangers to the Holy Spirit and destitute of him.

In another appeal to catechumens occur these words: 'But you too, who desire to receive holy baptism, and be vouchsafed the grace of the Spirit must first . . . control your barbarous and wild manners so that having received gentleness and humility you can also receive the grace of the Holy Spirit.'[17] Or again we read in *in Jesu Nave Hom.* 5.2: 'Faith is one and baptism is one, and the Spirit is one in whom all are made to drink in baptism.'

All four quotations seem to corroborate the view taken by Lampe and Hanson that Origen believed the Holy Spirit to be given in baptism itself. There are four other passages which point in the same direction. Origen said that whether through baptism or through the grace of the Spirit the word of wisdom or some other gift might be conferred.[18] It is impossible to be baptized again in water and the Spirit for the remission of sins.[19] Christians have been baptized in Christ, in water and the Spirit.[20]

The washing of the new birth was not found with John, but with Jesus by means of his disciples—known as the washing of regeneration—being combined with renewal of the Spirit who even now moves upon the water, since he is from God, but who does not come to be in all after the water.[21]

The inference is that the Holy Spirit in fact comes to be in some and ideally would come to be in all after the water. If Hanson's translation 'along with the water' is preferred, the inference is all the stronger that Origen believed the Holy Spirit to come into a man while he was in the font.[22]

So far the evidence points to only one conclusion, that, as far as Origen was aware, baptism in water without any ancillary ceremonies sufficed to procure the gift of the Holy Spirit. But the situation is more complex because there are other passages which supply proof that Origen knew also of an unction which accompanied baptism. The surest piece of evidence occurs in a passage where Origen was once again stressing the need for those who would receive the grace of baptism to approach with the proper disposition:

> And although according to the form traditionally delivered to the churches we have all been baptized in the visible waters and in the visible chrism, yet only he who has died to sin and is truly baptized in Christ's death, and is buried with him into death, is truly baptized in the Holy Ghost and the water which is from above.[23]

The chrism here cannot be understood figuratively because it is said to be as visible as the water in the font. There is another clear allusion to a physical unction in *in Lev. Hom.* 6.5: '. . . if the word of the law has washed you and made you clean, and the unction of chrism and the grace of baptism have continued in you undefiled.' The significance of this baptismal unction is revealed in Origen's comments on Ezek. 16.9: '*And I washed thee in water*. With the washing and grace of the Holy Spirit and with the sanctifying word. *And I anointed thee with oil*. The chrism is the indwelling of the Holy Spirit in knowledge of the truth.'[24] That the chrism is a symbol of the Holy Spirit is shown even more clearly in the following excerpt: 'The gift of the grace of the Spirit is signified by the image of oil, so that he who is converted from sin can not only obtain purification but also be filled with the Holy Spirit.'[25]

If, however, the anointing at baptism symbolizes the gift of the Holy Spirit, this would seem at first sight to contradict those passages where Origen apparently associated the gift of the Spirit with baptism itself. The contradiction, however, can be resolved. Whatever Origen believed about the chrismation, he quite clearly believed the Holy Spirit to be present at the font. In this connection it is important to notice what he said about the change which came over the baptismal water at its consecration: 'The water is no longer mere water: for it is sanctified by a kind of mystical invocation.'[26] This reads like a reference to the consecration of the font by an invocation of God upon it, such as we have found in Tertullian. Now whereas Tertullian had stated that the effect of consecration was to cause a kind of real presence of the Holy Spirit in the water, Origen said only that the water ceased to be mere water; nevertheless it is probable that he too believed that the Holy Spirit became in some sense conjoined with the water of the font. So for Origen there was no Christian baptism from which the Holy Spirit was absent, the rebirth and remission of sins being conferred in baptism by the agency of the Holy Spirit.

Now it will be recalled that, despite what he said about the activity of the Holy Spirit at the moment of baptism, Tertullian could still say that the Spirit came upon the initiates at the hand-laying after baptism; and it is at least arguable that this affords a clue to the right understanding of Origen's doctrine about baptism and anointing. For instance, when he said that faithful subjects of baptism received both water and the Spirit, he may have meant chiefly that for them the water was not mere water but water indwelt by the Holy Spirit, so that for them the act of baptism was a spiritual as well as a physical washing, whereas unworthy subjects such as Simon Magus received a bodily washing only, their lack of true faith preventing them from receiving the spiritual grace offered at baptism. If that is so, just as Tertullian was not precluded from assigning the gift of the Holy Spirit to the hand-laying after baptism, so Origen may be supposed to have assigned that gift to the unction after baptism.

Indeed there is one passage in Origen's works which suggests that this is how he saw the relationship between baptism in water and the ensuing unction with chrism:

It should be known that the washing by means of the water, symbolical as it is of the cleansing of the soul, as she washes off every stain that comes from wickedness, is . . . to him who yields himself to the divine power of the invocation of the adorable Trinity, the beginning and source of spiritual gifts. For there is a diversity of spiritual gifts. The statement is supported by the account recorded in the Acts of the Apostles, how the Holy Spirit in those days so evidently took up his abode in those who were being baptized, his way being made ready in advance (in the case of genuine receivers) by the water, that even Simon the sorcerer in astonishment desired to receive this grace from Peter . . .[27]

The notion that baptism in water prepared the way for the Spirit who came in a subsequent ceremony in the rite of baptism was, as we have seen, expressed also by Tertullian.

It was, however, unnecessary for Origen to define exactly the moment when the giving of the Holy Spirit took place. Once he expressed a reluctance to go into detail about matters of this kind:

But if and when you have come to the mystical font of baptism, and in the presence of the priestly and Levitical order have been initiated in those venerable and magnificent sacraments which they know who have the right to know, then indeed by the ministrations of priests after crossing the Jordan you will enter the land of promise . . .[28]

Origen's reluctance fully to divulge the Church's mysteries may well explain why some of his other references to initiation are so inexplicit as to permit of more than one interpretation.[29] Again, his mention of venerable and magnificent sacraments, or mysteries, in the plural, prove that the Egyptian rite of initiation at this time consisted in more than a simple act of dipping in water, so that Hanson[30] was probably wrong in seeing here no room between baptism and the eucharist for a ceremony which conferred the Spirit.

Lampe's claim (p. 167) that Origen regarded the anointing as a ceremony which denoted the inward unction of the Spirit conferred in baptism, and consequently as a symbolic but not an efficacious ceremony, while not impossible, is, as Mitchell (p. 52) said, not certainly demanded by the evidence. Rather, it would seem, Origen regarded the whole rite of baptism and chrismation as sacramental, as both symbolic and efficacious. Two extreme positions seem to be untenable. The first is to suppose that Origen so connected the gift of the Spirit with the anointing as to reduce baptism itself to a mere water-baptism from which the Spirit was absent; and the second is so to associate the imparting of the Spirit with baptism itself that the ensuing anointing becomes deprived of any sacramental significance. If this leaves the situation somewhat obscure or confusing, this is partly because Origen never had to face a situation in which baptism and confirmation had been put asunder, and therefore did not have carefully to distribute the various graces conferred by the whole rite of initiation among its component parts. What, however, is not obscure is that all that Origen wrote on the subject of Christian initiation is a witness to the organic unity of the rite, and is a forewarning of the theological riddles which arise if and when the rite becomes divided into two apparently independent sacraments.

Whether Origen knew of a hand-laying after baptism depends on the view taken of two comments which he made in *de Principiis* on the hand-laying in Acts 8. In 1.3.2 he wrote that 'in the Acts of the Apostles through the imposition of apostolic hands the Holy Spirit used to be given in baptism.' It is noticeable that Origen, like Tertullian, could use the word 'baptism' to include laying on of hands as well as dipping in water. This is one more small piece of evidence to illustrate the unity of the initiatory rite at this time. In 1.3.7, a little further on, he wrote: 'So finally through the imposition of the hands of the apostles after baptism the grace and revelation of the Holy Spirit used to be conferred.' Here Origen used the word 'baptism' in its narrower sense to denote only the act which took place at the font. Hence it is unnecessary to suppose with Wirgman (p. 133) that in the second passage he was contradicting or correcting what he said in the first.

Mason (p. 275) argued that Origen had no intention of suggesting that the practice of his own time differed from that of the apostles, and on the contrary was justifying the practice of his own time by showing that it was based upon apostolic precedent. Whether, however, the context justifies this conclusion is doubtful. Indeed an excursus at this point into contemporary liturgical practice would have been something of a digression. Wirgman (pp. 131f) maintained that in the former passage Origen implied that the confirmation gift of 'Holy Spirit' was conferred in the hand-laying, and in the latter passage that '*the* Holy Spirit' was given in baptism—an exegesis which depends on an untenable theory that the meaning of Holy Spirit is affected in this way by the presence or absence of the definite article before it.

To conclude, while it is certain that Origen knew of an anointing which at least in some measure related to the giving of the Holy Spirit, there is no positive proof that he knew of a hand-laying at baptism. The situation, however, would be greatly changed if Hanssens were allowed to have proved his case that the *Apostolic Tradition* of Hippolytus with its hand-laying and two unctions after baptism emanated from Alexandria.[31] But his thesis has found little support, and has been severely criticized by Botte,[32] Davies,[33] and H. Chadwick.[34]

Coquin has shown that the editor of the *Canons of Hippolytus* was probably a presbyter of Alexandria, who had been present at the Council of Nicaea, and was a theologian and teacher of some distinction.[35] Thus these Canons are a revision of the *Apostolic Tradition*, made in order to suit the circumstances of the church of Alexandria about the year 340.

The section with which we are specially concerned begins with the presbyteral unction after baptism, which, being similar to that in the *Apostolic Tradition*, is not related with the giving of the Holy Spirit. Then

> the bishop lays his hand on all the baptized and prays thus: We bless thee, Lord God almighty, that thou hast made these persons worthy to be born again, to be filled with thy Holy Spirit, and to be each a member in the body of the church, not being separated from it by alien deeds: but as thou hast given them forgiveness of their sins, grant them also the firstfruits of thy kingdom . . . Then the bishop signs their foreheads with the oil of unction and gives them the kiss of peace . . . After that they pray with all the faithful and they rejoice with them with joy. Then the deacon begins the liturgy and the bishop performs the eucharist of the body and blood of the Lord.[36]

Here is incontrovertible evidence of some further ceremonies after the actual baptism, namely, hand-laying, signing of the forehead with chrism and the kiss of peace, all administered by the bishop. But some uncertainty surrounds the moment when the Holy Spirit is believed to be given to the initiates. The bishop's prayer at the hand-laying supplies the only data on which a judgment may be formed. Now in that prayer the words 'thou hast made these persons worthy to be born again' are obviously retrospective, referring to the actual baptism which has just taken place. On grammatical grounds the immediately following words 'to be filled with thy Holy Spirit' could equally refer back to the baptism. Nevertheless they could be prospective, looking forward to the hand-laying and chrismation which are about to take place. But the subsequent petition 'grant them also the firstfruits of thy kingdom' decides the issue. This petition is answered in the hand-laying and consignation with chrism; and since it has an allusion to Rom. 8.23, it is a petition that the initiates may now receive the Holy Spirit. So if an unnecessary duplication is to be avoided, the words 'to be filled with thy Holy Spirit' must look forward to the episcopal chrismation.

Some of the prayers found in the *Sacramentary of Sarapion* were used during initiation. In the prayer for the Sanctification of Waters we read:

> 'Look down now from heaven and behold these waters and fill them with Holy Spirit. Let thine ineffable Word come to be in them and transform their energy and cause them to be productive by being filled with thy grace . . .'[37]

Baptism was preceded by an unction not related to the giving of the Holy Spirit, and followed by a chrismation which included a consignation

> 'in order that they who have been baptized, and who are being anointed with it with the sign of the impress of the saving cross of the Only-Begotten, by which cross Satan and every opposing power was routed and triumphed over, they also, as being regenerated and renewed through the washing of regeneration, may become partakers of the gift of the Holy Spirit . . .'

The value of this document depends on the view taken of its authorship. If, as has commonly been supposed, the author was Sarapion, bishop of Thmuis, then we have here prayers used in an Egyptian church by a friend of Athanasius. But Botte[38] has detected in this work an intrusion of Arian doctrine such as could not have emanated from an ally of Athanasius. For it is the Logos and not the Holy Spirit who is invoked upon the baptismal waters, as also upon the eucharistic elements; and similarly it is to the activity of the Logos that the benefits conveyed by baptism and chrismation are attributed. This reads like a deliberate attempt by an Arian, who as such denied the personality and divinity of the Third Person of the Trinity, to play down the role of the Holy Spirit in initiation.

Nevertheless, whatever its doctrine, this rite is Western and not Syrian in pattern, because it associates the giving of the Holy Spirit with the post-baptismal anointing. But it can no longer with confidence be attributed to Sarapion, and in Botte's opinion could be dated as late as *c.* 450.

It is evidently to the chrismation after baptism that Macarius, one of the Egyptian ascetics of the fourth century, referred when he wrote:

'as in the days of the prophets unction in the widest sense was held to be specially precious, since men were anointed to be kings and prophets, so now, spiritual men, being anointed with the heavenly unction, become Christians according to grace, so that they are kings and prophets of Heavenly mysteries'[39]

A little further on in the same homily this unction is said to confer the Holy Spirit:

'. . . how much more do all that are anointed according to the mind and the inner man with the hallowing and joyful-making oil of gladness, heavenly and spiritual, receive the seal of that kingdom of the incorruptible and everlasting power, the earnest of the Spirit, the Holy Spirit the Comforter?[40]

Macarius, however, did not distinguish sharply between the gift of the Spirit in the unction and the operation of the Spirit in baptism itself, because he could say that the foolish virgins in the parable were 'not born from above of the Spirit, not having received the oil of gladness.'[41]

The value of the writings of Athanasius for our present purpose are in inverse proportion to their value for the study of Christology and the doctrine of the Trinity, because they contain few references to initiation, and no explicit reference to the rite as such. But in the light of other evidence from Egyptian sources Athanasius must surely have known an anointing with chrism after baptism. Hence it would be wrong to interpret in a figurative sense his brief statement that 'the Spirit is called chrism and is a seal.'[42]

Athanasius was well aware that 'participating in the Spirit, we have the Son and having the Son we have the Spirit crying in our hearts, Abba, Father.'[43] But if through baptism itself we have the Son, it is not impossible to say that through chrismation we participate in the Spirit, provided that baptism and chrismation are not separated in time. The correct conclusion to draw from these words is not that, if we have the Son in baptism itself, therefore we must have the Spirit in baptism also, but that chrismation is inseparable from baptism.

Hence if baptism included chrismation, Athanasius need not have been tying the gift of the Spirit to the moment of baptism itself when he said that Origen and Theognostus defined the blasphemy against the Holy Spirit as a return to sin by those 'who have been granted in baptism the gift of the Holy Spirit,'[44] or when he wrote that the Holy Spirit is with those only who partake of him in the gift of baptism,'[45] or when in a comment on Gal. 3.2 he asked, 'What had they received but the Holy Spirit who is given to those who believe and are reborn through the washing of regeneration?'[46]

Didymus, the blind head of the catechetical school at Alexandria, appointed to his office by Athanasius, made some clear references to chrismation at baptism. For instance, he mentioned the ointment 'with which we are sanctified and anointed by the priest.'[47] 'With created oil that has been consecrated,' he said, 'the creature is anointed in baptism.'[48] Evidently the unction is regarded as a part of the baptismal ritual. In the very next sentence Didymus related this unction with the Holy Spirit: 'The Saviour as God anointed himself with his uncreated and all holy Spirit above his fellows, that is, above us.' Hence when in a passage a little further back Didymus wrote of the 'saving seal and the divine chrism, the firstfruits . . .', the seal and the chrism must refer to the gift of the Spirit imparted by the outward act of consignation with chrism.

In *de Trin.* 2.14, where he shows a knowledge of Tertullian's *de Baptismo*, Didymus, like Tertullian, used the story of the healing in the pool of Bethesda as a type of baptism:

> the angel also which troubled the water was a forerunner of the Holy Spirit; and, like him, John was both called the angel of the Lord, and was forerunner of the Master and baptized in the waters. And the unction with which Aaron was anointed by Moses and not Aaron only but also all who were anointed from the priestly horn, and were surnamed from the unction anointed ones, bore a type of the consecrated unction received by us. For although this takes place in a bodily manner, the benefit none the less is a benefit to the soul. Only let the faith of the thrice-blessed Trinity come into our hearts, and the spiritual word into our mouths, and the seal of Christ upon our foreheads, only let baptism receive us, and the unction confirm us, and at once the Trinity, which by nature is a giver of good things, is found to be propitious; at once the Trinity comes to us.

Whereas it was the hand-laying with which Tertullian associated the descent of the Spirit, Didymus has concentrated his comments upon the unction, presumably because at this time the Egyptian church no longer practised hand-laying at baptism. Clearly the Egyptian rite of initiation included a sealing of the forehead with chrism, which was the outward sign of the giving of the Holy Spirit.

In the next chapter Didymus wrote of 'the Holy Spirit and his saving sign, sealed with which we are refashioned into the original likeness. A sheep unsealed falls an easy prey to wolves, lacking the defence which comes from the seal.' Here Didymus dwelt upon the protective properties commonly attributed to the sign of the cross.

Equally clear evidence of chrismation after baptism is found in the writings of Cyril of Alexandria. 'For we are copiously anointed with ointment', he wrote, 'during the very time of baptism, making the unction a symbol of the imparting of the Holy Spirit.'[49] So also in *in Joel*. 32 Cyril said:

> We have been given, as it were in rain the living water of holy baptism; and as in wheat the bread of life; and as in wine the blood. And the use of oil, moreover, is foreshown as well, which contributes to the perfecting of those who are in process of being justified in Christ through holy baptism.

Mason's rendering 'in process of being justified' reads more into the present participle than is necessarily there, because Cyril probably meant no more than 'those who are from time to time justified'. Nevertheless the point which he wished to make, that the chrismation was an integral part of baptism, still holds good.

But however closely Cyril connected the giving of the Spirit with the chrismation, he was very far from implying that the Holy Spirit was inactive in baptism itself. For his doctrine of the effect of consecration upon the water of baptism does not differ essentially from that of Tertullian and Origen, although it is stated in a more advanced form:

> By the Spirit the spirit of man is hallowed; by water—hallowed water—his body. For as the water that is poured into caldrons by converse with the energies of the fire, absorbs its power, so through the operation of the Spirit the material water is transelemented to a kind of divine inexpressible power, so as thereupon to hallow any in whom it comes to be.[50]

Seeing, therefore, that consecration effects a real presence of the Holy Spirit in the water, the Spirit himself is the author of all the blessings conferred at the moment of baptism itself.

Hence Cyril could speak of the Holy Spirit as the agent in baptismal regeneration, and identify the Spirit with the water of life.[51] But this renewing and regenerating activity of the Spirit is not entirely identical with the gift of the Spirit effected by the chrismation. If it be argued that renewal and regeneration by the Spirit are inseparable from the gift of the Spirit symbolized by the chrism, the answer is that baptism and chrismation are inseparable.

When in a context where he was speaking of the water of baptism Cyril said that Christ 'removes all defilement from us, so that we become a holy temple of God and sharers in his divine nature through partaking in the Holy Spirit',[52] he had the whole rite of initiation in mind, and in the last clause passed in thought from the water of baptism to the ensuing chrismation.

There are five other places where Cyril mentions the giving of the Spirit in connection with baptism, but not in such explicit terms that he must be supposed to have assigned the gift strictly to baptism itself:

(i) *Thesaur. Assert. 11:* In the days of John and from that time forward the giving of the Spirit and the regeneration unto God through holy baptism is violently seized through faith.

(ii) *in Joan.* 5: . . . the baptized has been born of God . . . and has become a partaker of the divine nature, having the Holy Spirit dwelling within him . . .

(iii) ibid. 12: But the circumcision in the Spirit could not take place in us, if the Holy Spirit had not been made to dwell in us by means of faith on the one hand and holy baptism on the other . . . for he does not dwell in those who are not yet baptized.

(iv) *in Is.* 3.3: . . . a sure water is given, namely that of the holy baptism which makes those to whom it is vouchsafed sure and steadfast. For the grace of the Holy Spirit is given to those who have been cleansed through holy baptism.

(v) *in Luc.* 5.21: For believing in Father, Son and Holy Spirit, and making this appointed confession before many witnesses we are cleansed from every defilement caused by sin. We are rich by our sharing in the Holy Spirit, and we are perfected by becoming partakers in the divine nature, and we enjoy the grace of adoption to sonship.

In all the above passages Cyril was dealing with the blessings conferred in the whole rite of initiation. Since the rite was an organic whole, it was easy to think of the grace of baptism and the grace of chrismation together without carefully distinguishing between them. But Cyril's theology presupposes a unified rite, and is not applicable to the disintegrated rite which now obtains in the West.

In *de Adorat.* 11 Cyril made some comments upon the scriptural use of laying on of hands:

And Aaron lifted up his hands and blessed the people. See again, I pray you, imposition of hands upon the people used for the first time by Aaron. For the true Aaron blesses all alike, priests and people, the small with the great, as it is written, all but laying his hands upon them. And this laying on of hands may serve as a clear prefiguration of the injection of the all holy Spirit into us.

It cannot, however, be confidently inferred from this that in Cyril's time hand-laying was included among the meaningful ceremonies of baptism.

The evidence from fourth-century Egypt is quite clear. Baptism included a sealing with chrism which conferred the Holy Spirit upon the initiates, although justice has to be done to the vital role played by the Holy Spirit in baptism itself. The evidence from Origen points, perhaps not quite so clearly, in the same direction, but that of Clement is of such a character that it is difficult to draw any firm conclusions from it either way.

5 *Jerusalem*

If we accept that Cyril is the author of the *Mystagogic Catecheses* usually ascribed to him, then we have a fairly full account of the rite of initiation used in Jerusalem about the year 348. Those who take a different view of the authorship attribute them to his successor, John, and give them a date about fifty years later.

In the rite of Jerusalem there was a pre-baptismal unction performed with exorcized oil. Cyril's comments in *Cat. Myst.* 2.3 suggest that it should be understood as an exorcism:

> Just as the breath of the saints and the invocation of God's name burn like a fierce flame and drive out devils, likewise the exorcized oil, through invocation of God and through prayer, is invested with such power as not merely to cleanse all traces of sin with its fire, but also to pursue all the invisible powers of the wicked one out of our persons.

But just before this Cyril had said:

> Next, after removing your garments you were rubbed with exorcized oil from the hair of your head to your toes, and so you became sharers in Jesus Christ, who is the cultivated olive tree . . . The exorcized oil, then, symbolized your partaking of Christ's richness.

So, because this unction had not only the negative purpose of expelling the evil spirit but also the positive purpose of grafting into Christ, it cannot be interpreted solely in terms of exorcism. One point, however, is abundantly clear, that this anointing was not connected with the giving of the Holy Spirit.

Cat. Myst. 3 is devoted to a post-baptismal anointing of forehead, ears, nostrils, and breast. In section 3 Cyril explains the effect of consecration upon the chrism, and shows that the purpose of this unction was to impart the Holy Spirit:

> But be sure not to regard the chrism merely as ointment. Just as the bread of the eucharist after the invocation of the Holy Spirit is no

longer just bread, but the body of Christ, so the holy chrism after the invocation is no longer ordinary ointment but Christ's grace, which through the presence of the Holy Spirit instils his divinity into us. It is applied to your forehead and organs of sense with a symbolic meaning; the body is anointed with visible ointment, and the soul is sanctified by the holy, hidden Spirit.

In the beginning of this lecture Cyril drew an analogy between this anointing and our Lord's reception of the Spirit at his baptism:

Christ bathed in the river Jordan, and having invested the waters with the divine presence of his body, he emerged from them, and the Holy Spirit visited him in substantial form, like coming to rest on like. In the same way, when you emerged from the pool of sacred waters you were anointed in a manner corresponding with Christ's anointing. That anointing is the Holy Spirit, of whom the blessed Isaiah spoke.

(The reference is to Is. 61.1 and Luke 4.18.) In Cyril's view, therefore, baptism and chrismation were as much a unity as were our Lord's baptism and the descent of the Holy Spirit upon him. As our Lord was anointed figuratively with the Holy Spirit at his baptism, so the Christian's chrismation was a visible and effective sign of his anointing with the Spirit at his baptism.

In sections 1 and 5 of this lecture Cyril treats chrismation as part of the Christian's christening:

You have become anointed ones by receiving the sign of the Holy Spirit . . . Now that you are reckoned worthy of this holy chrism, you are called Christians, and this title you substantiate by your new birth. For before being thought worthy of this grace you did not strictly merit such an address. You were still advancing along the path towards being Christians.

To a Greek-speaking Christian the intimate connection between chrism, Christ, and Christian was far more obvious than to a Latin- or English-speaking Christian, who can talk about christening without any thought of anointing in his mind, and who can call people Christians without any awareness that he is calling them anointed ones, members of the Anointed One, so called because he was anointed with the Holy Spirit.

Cyril saw the rite of initiation as a drama, a dramatic representation of the scene at the Jordan. When baptism and chrismation are seen in this way as a drama, the time factor ceases to have the importance that it has for some modern minds—that is to say, the fact that baptism in water and anointing with chrism, while conveying graces which are theologically inseparable, were not administered simultaneously is irrelevant.[1] It is still possible to claim that the baptismal gift of the Holy Spirit is conferred by chrismation after baptism in water without implying any disintegration of doctrine, provided, of course, that there is no interval of time in between the two acts. Consequently Cyril did not have to differentiate carefully between the activity of the Holy Spirit in baptism and in chrismation respectively. If the main purpose of the unction after baptism was to signify and effect the gift of the Holy Spirit, this in no way implies that the Holy Spirit was absent from the font, or was in no sense given there.

Indeed Cyril had much to say about the operation of the Holy Spirit in baptism itself. In *Cat.* 3.3 he described the significance of the blessing of the font:

Do not regard the laver as mere water, but regard the spiritual grace given with the water. For as the things which are offered on altars, being mere things by nature, become defiled by the invocation of idols, so on the other hand mere water after receiving the invocation of the Holy Spirit and of Christ and of the Father acquires the power of sanctifying.

Here Cyril's doctrine closely resembles that of Tertullian. Because as a result of the consecration there is a real presence of the Holy Spirit in the water, Cyril can say:

The water cleanses the body, but the Spirit seals the soul, in order that, with our heart sprinkled with the Spirit and our body washed with clean water, we may draw near to God. You who are going to descend into the water, do not regard the bare element of water, but by the power of the Holy Spirit receive salvation; for without both you cannot be perfected.[2]

So also Cyril said of Simon Magus that he 'came once to the laver, he was baptized but not enlightened; he dipped his body in the water, he did not enlighten his heart with the Spirit; his body went down and came up, but his soul was not buried together with Christ, nor raised together with him.'[3] That is, he who comes to baptism without the proper disposition receives a physical washing only, as if the Spirit were not in the water. In *Cat.* 17.36 Cyril expressed the same thought: 'If you pretend, men now baptize you but the Spirit will not baptize you. But if you draw near in faith, men minister as far as can be seen, but the Holy Spirit gives what is not seen.' Or again in *Cat.* 17.14, commenting on Pentecost, Cyril said: 'For as he who is immersed in the waters and baptized in them is surrounded on all sides by the waters, so also they were baptized by the Spirit entirely. But the water surrounds externally and the spirit baptizes the soul internally and completely.' Thus Cyril taught that baptism conveys cleansing from sin, sanctification, and eternal salvation, and that all these gifts are bestowed by the Holy Spirit by means of the water. Furthermore in *Cat. Myst.* 2.6 Cyril said that baptism conveyed the gift of the Holy Spirit:

> No one should think, then, that his baptism is merely for the remission of sins and for adoption in the way that John's baptism brought only remission of sins. We know well that not merely does it cleanse sins and bestow on us the gift of the Holy Spirit—it is also the sign of Christ's suffering.

Our problem here is how to interpret this statement that baptism conveys the gift of the Spirit, since elsewhere, as we have seen, he very clearly associates the gift of the Spirit with the chrismation after baptism. It seems unreasonable to accuse an author of Cyril's ability either of inconsistency or of contradicting himself or of not knowing his own mind. Possibly, as Lampe (p. 197) suggested, he felt able to refer to the grace imparted by the agency of the Spirit at the font as 'the gift of the Holy Spirit', without meaning by these words in this context all that they meant when used of the chrismation. Or it may be that he included here, where he was comparing Christian with Johannine baptism, the gift of the Holy Spirit among the gifts conferred in Christian baptism because he could not overlook the fact that this was the notable gift which John's baptism did not convey, although he knew that in fact the Spirit was given in the chrismation which, however, was part of the rite of baptism. Since baptism and chrismation were an organic whole, it was easy to pass in thought from the grace which was received in baptism itself to the grace which, strictly speaking, belonged to the chrismation. Indeed Cyril could say that he was going to explain why 'each of the holy sacraments of baptism was performed,' meaning by that the various ceremonies that together constituted the one rite of baptism.[4] In the same place, too, he talked of proceeding from baptism to the holy altar of God. He could express himself in this way because the chrismation which intervened between the actual baptism and the eucharist was part of baptism.

But although it is not completely clear how Cyril related the gift of the Holy Spirit in baptism with the gift of the Spirit in chrismation, there can be no doubt that, when the evidence is taken as a whole, Cyril believed the chrismation to be the moment in particular when the Holy Spirit was communicated to the initiates. For when he wanted to summarize the gifts conferred at the different moments in the rite, he said that after Easter he would explain how 'you were cleansed from your sins by the Lord in the washing of water in the word, and how in the manner of priests you became partakers in the name of Christ and how the seal of the fellowship of the Holy Spirit was given to you and about the mysteries at the altar of the new covenant.'[5]

Thus, briefly, baptism is the remission of sins and a washing of water in the word, while the ensuing chrismation confers the title of 'Christ' and is the seal of the Spirit.

In this last passage Cyril uses the word 'seal' in connection with the chrismation. This raises two questions, first, whether the seal included or denoted an act of consignation, and secondly, how far Cyril used this term in connection with chrismation rather than baptism.

With regard to the first question Cyril said that Christians frequently made the sign of the cross upon themselves. In exhorting his hearers not to be ashamed to confess Christ crucified, he urged them to make the sign of the cross as a seal on their foreheads 'when eating bread, or drinking from cups, when coming in or going out, before sleep, when going to bed or getting up, when travelling or resting.'[6] 'It is the sign of the faithful and a terror to demons.'[7] Hence it becomes reasonably certain that consignation took place during initiation since Cyril said: 'You receive weapons terrible to the demons. And if you do not throw away your weapons but have the seal upon your soul, the demon does not come near you, because he is frightened; indeed in the Spirit of God demons are cast out.'[8] Thus Cyril was thinking not only of the prophylactic properties of the cross but also of the power of the Holy Spirit imparted to Christians at their initiation.

Just before this Cyril had said that the Holy Spirit 'is present ready to seal your soul and gives you a kind of heavenly and divine seal at which demons tremble, as it has been written, in whom also having believed you were sealed with the Holy Spirit of promise.' All this points to the conclusion that the seal was the sign of the cross imprinted upon the initiates when they were anointed with the chrism, the sign of the Holy Spirit.

But when in *Cat.* 5.6 Cyril said that like Abraham after coming to faith we receive a spiritual seal, being circumcised in the Holy Spirit by the washing,[9] the seal clearly refers to baptism itself. To Cyril, it seems, the seal was a term wide enough to be used both of baptism or chrismation.

There is no evidence that the rite of Jerusalem included a hand-laying after baptism. On this subject Cyril said that our Lord's disciples not only possessed the Holy Spirit themselves but also through the laying on of their hands communicated him to believers.[10] This, however, is a reference to Acts 8.17 and 19.6, and does not necessarily throw any light on the practice of the fourth century. But in *Cat.* 16.26 Cyril again referred to the laying on of hands in scripture:

Under Moses the Spirit was given through imposition of hands, and Peter through imposition of hands gives the Spirit. To you who are being baptized is the grace about to come. But I do not say how, because I do not anticipate the time.

81

Here Cyril shows no awareness that the practice of his own church was in any way incongruous with this scriptural precedent. It may be that Cyril was more concerned with the fact that Christians at their initiation still received the same gift of the Spirit that in Acts was conferred through hand-laying with prayer than with the actual means by which they now received that gift.

The post-baptismal chrismation which Cyril described was, as we have seen, an anointing of the forehead, ears, and nostrils, but not apparently of the eyes, and also of the breast. There is a similarity between this procedure and that found in the later Byzantine rite, where after the baptism there is an anointing with holy oil, the sign of the cross being made on forehead, eyes, nostrils, mouth and both ears. The formula used at this point is 'The seal of the gift of the Holy Spirit'.[11] In view of this we may ask whether Cyril has not in fact alluded to a similar formula used at the same point in his rite when he said that 'to you is given the seal of the partaking of the Hôly Spirit.'[12]

The rite of Jerusalem, then, included a post-baptismal chrismation for the imparting of the Holy Spirit, a feature not found in the contemporary Syrian church. If the Syrian rite without any post-baptismal ceremony for conferring the Holy Spirit is the more primitive, whence did the church of Jerusalem derive its anointing after baptism? Ratcliff asked whether it was introduced in imitation of Western practice, or through the influence of the *Apostolic Tradition*, although he felt that no certain answer could be given.[13] Mitchell (p. 44) saw some similarities between the rites of Hippolytus and Cyril. Both used exorcized oil for the unction before baptism. Again in the two rites the method of baptizing is the same, consisting in a threefold series of question, answer, and dipping, whereas in Eastern rites the officiant pronounced a Trinitarian formula over the candidates. There are, however, also notable differences between the two rites. There was a hand-laying after baptism in Hippolytus' rite but not, it seems, in Cyril's. The prayer which Hippolytus gives at the hand-laying has no parallel in Cyril's rite. The chrismation in Hippolytus was of the forehead only; Cyril's post-baptismal chrismation is Eastern, not Western. While, of course, it is true that many pilgrimages were made to Jerusalem, so that the church in Jerusalem would be well informed about liturgical developments in other parts of the church, it still seems unlikely that the post-baptismal chrismation was inserted into the rite of Jerusalem in imitation of Roman practice. So little is known of the rite used in Jerusalem before Cyril's time that we are not in a position to say that Cyril's chrismation after baptism had not been in use for some considerable time before he delivered his catecheses, unless we suppose that the Syrian rite without any unction after baptism is primitive and original, and that all other Eastern rites are as a consequence later developments of this archetype.

6 Syria

So far the matter in dispute has been whether in the early church Christian converts received the Holy Spirit through baptism itself or through a further ceremony or ceremonies after baptism though closely allied with it. There is, however, clear evidence that in the third and following four centuries there were in use in Syria initiatory rites which had an anointing before baptism but neither anointing nor hand-laying between the baptism and the ensuing eucharist. This prompted Raes to ask 'Où se trouve la Confirmation dans le rite Syro-Oriental?'[1] and Thompson to say that the pre-baptismal unction in the Syrian rites was really the unction of confirmation,[2] and Green to declare that the Antiochene rite did not have confirmation in an unusual place but lacked it altogether.[3] Much of the evidence which has to be studied before these questions can be answered has been set out by Connolly,[4] Maclean,[5] and Duncan.[6]

The *Acts of Judas Thomas* have been thought to furnish evidence of the Syrian order with its one anointing before baptism. This work contains brief accounts of five initiations, each the result of the missionary work of Judas Thomas.

Gundaphorus and his brother besought Judas Thomas 'that they also might now receive the seal of the Lord . . . But the apostle said to them: I also rejoice and pray you to receive this seal, and to share with me in this eucharist and feast of blessing of the Lord, and be made perfect in it . . . And he commanded them to bring oil, that through the oil they might receive the seal.'[7] Initiation, therefore, consists in a sealing with oil and communion. After he had poured the oil on their heads and chrismed them, the apostle uttered a long invocation which concluded with the words, 'Come Holy Spirit, and purify their reins and their heart and give them the added seal in the name of the Father and Son and Holy Spirit.' Finally the apostle broke bread and made them partake in the eucharist of Christ. There is no mention of baptism in water or of wine at the eucharist.

In the Syriac version of these *Acts* there is a baptism as well as an anointing before the eucharist; but Bornkamm has shown that it is a later interpolation due to Catholic influence.[8]

The initiation of a woman out of whom a devil had been cast is very briefly described:

> But the woman besought him, saying: Apostle of the Most High, give me the seal, that the enemy may not return to me again. Then he made her come near to him, and laying his hands upon her sealed her in the name of the Father and of the Son and of the Holy Spirit. And many others also were sealed with her. And the apostle commanded his servant (deacon) to set a table before them; and spreading a linen cloth upon it set on the bread of blessing . . .[9]

As in the previous case there is no mention of baptism or of wine at the eucharist; and again the Syriac version differs by substituting baptism for sealing, due to the desire of a redactor to bring this rite more into line with the usage of the Catholic Church.

Both the Greek and the Syriac versions of these *Acts* include in Mygdonia's initiation an anointing and baptism in water:

> And Mygdonia said: Give me the seal of Jesus Christ, and I will receive a gift from thy hands before thou depart from life . . . Mygdonia stood before the apostle with her head bare; and he taking the oil poured it on her head, saying: Holy oil given to us for sanctification, hidden mystery in which the Cross was shown to us . . . Let thy power come; let it be established upon thy servant Mygdonia; and heal her through this unction. And when the oil had been poured out he bade the nurse unclothe her and gird a linen cloth about her. Now there was a spring of water, and going to it the apostle baptized Mygdonia in the name of the Father and of the Son and of the Holy Spirit. And when she was baptized and clothed, he broke bread and took a cup of water, and made her partake in the body of Christ and the cup of the Son of God, and said: Thou hast received thy seal, and obtained for thyself eternal life.[10]

Then the nurse, Marcia, asked for the seal: and 'giving it to her the apostle said: The zeal of the Lord be about thee, as about the others.'

Mygdonia received the seal when the oil was poured upon her. The words 'hidden mystery in which the cross was shown to us' may signify that when Mygdonia was anointed the sign of the cross was made upon her with the oil. Again we have to ask whether the baptism given to Mygdonia is not a later insertion into the original text due to Catholic influence. It could be that when Mygdonia was undressed, it was not in order to be baptized but in order that her whole body might be anointed, and that where the extant text says that she was baptized in the name of the Trinity the original said that she was sealed, that is, anointed, in the name of the Trinity. Furthermore even in the extant texts it does not appear that Marcia was baptized; rather she asked for and received the seal, which we have found reason to believe meant the anointing.

Siphor requested Judas Thomas that

we may receive the seal from thee, that we may become servants to the true God . . . And he began to speak about baptism: This baptism is forgiveness of sins. It brings to new birth a light that is shed around . . . Glory be to thee, renewal through which are renewed the baptized who take hold of thee with affection. And when he had said this he poured oil upon their heads and said: Glory be to thee, the lover of compassion. Glory be to thee, name of Christ. Glory be to thee the power established in Christ. And he commanded a basin to be brought, and baptized them in the name of the Father, the Son and the Holy Spirit. And when they were baptized and clothed, he set bread upon the table and blessed it and said, Bread of Life, those who eat of which remain incorruptible . . .[11]

Now it is to be noticed that this passage begins with a request for the seal, which in the previous cases means the anointing. Then, instead of immediately performing the anointing, the apostle expatiates on the grace conferred by baptism in water; yet when he has finished this, he does not baptize the candidates but anoints them. The sequence is not logical. But it becomes logical if the apostle's words about baptism and the baptism itself are omitted. This gives ground for believing that these are later interpolations inserted by a redactor who believed that baptism in water was indispensable to initiation.

Finally, the initiation of Vazan also opens with a request for the seal. The apostle prayed:

Be thou their guide in a land of error . . . make them thy holy temples, and let thy Holy Spirit dwell in them. When the apostle had thus prayed for them, he said to Mygdonia: Unclothe thy sisters. And she unclothed them, girded them with girdles, and brought them. But Vazan had come forward before, and they came after him. And Judas took oil in a silver cup, and spoke thus over it . . . And when the apostle had said this, he poured it first on Vazan's head, then on the heads of the women, saying, In thy name, Jesus Christ, let it be to these souls for remission of sins, and for the turning back of the adversary, and for salvation of their souls. And he commanded Mygdonia to anoint them (the women), but he himself anointed Vazan. And when he had anointed them he led them down to the water in the name of the Father and of the Son and of the Holy Spirit. But when they had come up from the water he took bread and a cup and blessed and said . . .[12]

The unction was twofold, first of the head and then of the whole body. The apostle could without impropriety anoint the heads of candidates of either sex; but it had to be left to Mygdonia to anoint the bodies of the women. This is in accordance with the practice found in the third-century *Didascalia*, a work emanating from the orthodox Syrian Church. While much is said about the unction, little by comparison is said about the baptism. Again we may ask whether the baptism was inserted into the narrative as a result of Catholic influence.

When the evidence is taken as a whole, it seems certain that the author of the original Syriac *Acts of Judas Thomas* knew an initiatory rite which consisted in an unction of the head and of the whole body—this action constituting the seal—and the eucharist in which the elements used were bread and water, seeing that wine is never mentioned. The baptisms briefly described are probably interpolations added at a later date when a Syrian and a Greek editor worked over the original Syriac material. But even if the case that they are interpolations is rejected, nevertheless baptism in water is treated as comparatively unimportant, because, whereas the unction and the prayer which accompanied it are recorded at length, nothing is said about baptism, save in one instance, beyond a bare statement that it was administered in water in the name of the Trinity. If, however, we are dealing with interpolations, then the interpolators, believing that baptism was essential to initiation, inserted it after the unction and not before it. This, as we shall see, agrees with the known practice of the orthodox Syrian Church, where at this time initiation consisted in unction followed by baptism in water without any post-baptismal ceremonies.

The importance of the *Acts of Thomas* for our recent purpose lies in the fact that they have been cited as evidence that the Syrian Church had only one unction in its initiatory rite, and that before baptism, and secondly that this pre-baptismal unction was the Syrian equivalent of confirmation. Maclean included these *Acts* among the authorities which supplied evidence that this pre-baptismal unction took the place of confirmation.[13] The prayer of invocation said over the oil seemed to Ratcliff[14] to indicate that the Spirit of holiness was conveyed to the individual before he descended into the water, so that the liturgical anointing was not a confirmation or completion but an inception, the giving of the Spirit being the beginning of initiation.

Against this Whitaker has urged that the epiclesis over the oil proved that the unction was for the purpose of healing and for the expulsion of Satan, and consequently was not to be regarded as confirmation but as an exorcism.[15] Whitaker cited with approval the opinion of Woolley[16] that these prayers over the chrism were forms for the blessing of oil to be used in a pre-baptismal exorcism. The petition, 'Come, Holy Spirit, and purify their reins and their heart,' seemed to

Whitaker to show that the purpose for which the Spirit came was purification, something quite different from what is commonly meant by confirmation.

But in the *Acts of Thomas* the unnamed woman asked for the seal 'that that enemy may not return to me again.' If the purpose of exorcism is to cast out the evil spirit, then that woman had already been exorcized, and the purpose of the sealing with oil was to deny the evil spirit a chance to re-enter. If, as was probably the case, the chrism was applied crosswise, then we have here an instance of the commonly held belief that the sign of the cross imprinted on the foreheads of the baptized was an effective deterrent to the evil spirits.

Again, the thoughts expressed in the prayers said over the oil range over too wide a field for the unction to be interpreted solely as an exorcism. The power invoked upon the oil is said to be not only a physician in a land of wickedness but also a guide in a land of error. The words 'make them thy holy temple and let thy Holy Spirit dwell in them' suggest that one of the purposes of the unction was to effect the indwelling of the Spirit; and the notion of making a temple and inviting the Holy Spirit to take up his residence in it was applied by ancient writers not to the preceding exorcism but to initiation itself, as can be seen in Tertullian's *de Baptismo*, 4f and in Cyprian's letters, 64.5 and 69.12, and also in the *Gelasian Sacramentary*, 44.[17]

Furthermore when Siphor said that he and his wife and daughter intended to live henceforth in holiness and purity, he obviously expected the seal which he requested to give them the power to do this, and to enable them to become servants of the true God. Similarly Vazan expected the seal to enable him to be a keeper of God's commandments. Here we have passed from the realm of exorcism, because the subject now is not the expulsion of Satan but initiation into God's people and the power to live accordingly.

There remains the question how far the ritual in the *Acts of Thomas* may be taken to reflect the practice of the third-century Syrian Church. Now the first point to be made is that it is impossible to read the invocations over the oil without feeling that they breathe the atmosphere of Gnosticism. If, as has been argued above, in the original Syriac text of these *Acts* initiation consisted in sealing with chrism and participation in a eucharistic meal, without any baptism in water, then the *Acts of Thomas* cannot have emanated from an orthodox milieu. This conclusion is reinforced by the fact that in the five references to the eucharist there is no mention of wine, in four cases bread alone being mentioned, and in the fifth a cup of water. This objection to the use of wine is evidence that these *Acts* come from a Gnostic sect with Encratite tendencies, which can be seen throughout the work, as, for example, in the several instances where wives after their initiation refused to cohabit with their husbands because Judas

Thomas had won them over to a belief in a purely spiritual marriage.

Secondly, if the references to baptism are in fact interpolations, we do not know exactly when they were inserted into the text; but we can no longer be sure that this happened during the third century. Consequently the *Acts of Thomas* are quite useless when we are trying to determine whether the Syrian order of sealing with oil before baptism without any anointing after baptism is primitive, or the original pattern of Christian initiation. But they do furnish evidence of an initiatory rite, however heretical, in which there was no sacramental act corresponding with the post-baptismal ceremonies attested by Cyril of Jerusalem, Tertullian and Hippolytus.

In the *Acts of Xanthippe and Polyxena*, written about the middle of the third century, Xanthippe's slave, replying to the question, What cure is there to heal such sickness?, said, 'The invocation of a new name, and the unction of oil, and the laver of water.' When Xanthippe asked to be sealed, St Paul baptized her in the name of the Trinity. 'Then he took bread and gave thanks and gave it to her, saying: Let this be to thee for the remission of sins and the renewal of thy soul.'[18] Here oil, water, and eucharist are all mentioned, and the oil is mentioned before baptism. In the next chapter Probus is baptized and made to partake of the eucharist of Christ without apparently having been anointed at all.

The *Acts of John the Son of Zebedee*, probably written in the late fourth century, recorded two baptisms. The first is the baptism by St John of the procurator of Ephesus: 'the holy man drew nigh, and took oil in his hand, and made him a cross on his forehead, and anointed his whole body, and brought him nigh to the cistern, and said to him: Descend, my brother . . .'[19] Previously the apostle had made the sign of the cross on the oil, but the words he said do not indicate what was the purpose of this unction.

The second baptism was that of some priests of Artemis. On this occasion the apostle invoked the Holy Spirit upon the oil and the water:

> Lord God Almighty, let thy Spirit of holiness come, and rest and dwell upon the oil and upon the water; and let them be bathed and purified from uncleanness; and let them receive the Spirit of holiness through baptism; and henceforth let them call thee Our Father who art in heaven.[20]

At the actual baptism

> John drew near, and washed them clean of the soot (which they wore in token of grief), and anointed them with oil, and baptized them in the name of the Father and the Son and the Spirit of

holiness, for the forgiveness of debts and the pardon of sins. And St John said to the procurator: Command that they go and fetch fine white bread and wine.

Seeing that the Holy Spirit was invoked upon both, it is possible that the oil and the water were regarded as symbolic of the gift of the Spirit. But however this may be, initiation is seen to consist first in an anointing of the head and of the whole body, secondly of baptism in water and thirdly of the eucharist. This accords with the known practice of the Syrian Church which lacked any hand-laying or further unction between the baptism and the eucharist.

In the life of Rabbula, bishop of Edessa from 411 to 435, it is stated that on his conversion he went to Palestine in order to be baptized in the Jordan.

> He persuaded the priests, and repeated before them the faith. And they anointed him, and baptized him . . . But when he had been communicated with the holy mysteries of the body and blood of our Lord, and had been fully initiated in the whole divine mystery, he returned to his own city.[21]

As Siman observed,[22] this account of baptism is probably the baptismal rite of Edessa as the author knew it.

Similarly a Syriac story of the baptism of Constantine recounts how the emperor was anointed with oil, baptized in water and communicated.[23]

Although the baptisms in the *Acts of Xanthippe and Polyxena* and in the *Acts of John the Son of Zebedee* are fictitious, they reflect the baptismal practice known to their authors; and their evidence agrees well with that just quoted. We are presented with an initiatory rite which consisted in a twofold anointing and baptism in the name of the Trinity, followed without any intervening ceremonies by the eucharist.

We pass now from apocryphal Acts which contain much legendary material and are not devoid of heresy to the *Didascalia Apostolorum*, another Syrian work of the late third century, whose orthodoxy nobody has impugned.

The anonymous author of this pseudo-apostolic set of instructions addressed his readers as persons 'who have received the power and fellowship of his Holy Spirit.'[24] He said that to call a layman a fool meant calling a fool one in whom dwelt the Holy Spirit of God. It was even worse to speak evil of the bishop

> through whom the Lord gave you the Holy Spirit, . . . and through whom you were sealed, and through whom you became the sons of light, and through whom the Lord in baptism, by the imposition of

hand of the bishop, bore witness to each one of you and uttered his holy voice, saying: 'Thou art my son: I this day have begotten thee.'[25]

Evidently, therefore, the writer regarded Christians as persons who had received the Holy Spirit through the ministration of a bishop at their sealing and baptism. The bishop, then, was the proper minister of baptism, who presided over the whole rite, even if he did not administer it all in person. What is not clear from these passages is the meaning of the seal, the significance of the hand-laying at baptism, and whether there was an anointing.

This last point is cleared up in 3.12 where the duties of deaconesses are described:

> In the first place, when women go down into the water, those who go down into the water ought to be anointed by a deaconess with the oil of anointing; and where there is no woman at hand, and especially no deaconess, he who baptizes must of necessity anoint her who is being baptized. But where there is a woman, and especially a deaconess, it is not fitting that women should be seen by men: but with the imposition of hand do thou anoint the head only. As of old the priests and kings were anointed in Israel, do thou in like manner, with the imposition of the hand, anoint the head of those who receive baptism, whether of men or of women; and afterwards— whether thou thyself baptize, or thou command the deacons or presbyters to baptize—let a woman deacon, as we have already said, anoint the women. But let a man pronounce over them the invocation of the divine names in the water, let the deaconess receive her, and teach and instruct her how the seal of baptism ought to be (kept) unbroken in purity and holiness.

Here the author seems to equate the seal with baptism, but without making it clear in what sense baptism was a seal.

The next point that arises is whether the unction here mentioned preceded or followed the actual baptism. Ysebaert argued that the sentence beginning 'in the first place' refers to an anointing before baptism, while the later sentence which comes after the allusion to the unction of priests and kings, and begins 'and afterwards' refers to a second unction after baptism.[26] This, however, is not the most natural interpretation of the words. It is much more likely that Connolly was right in saying that 'and afterwards' meant after the bishop had anointed the head, not after the baptism itself.[27] In support of this Connolly cited *Apostolic Constitutions* 3.16, where the editor had the *Didascalia* for his main source: 'and first in the baptism of women, the deacon shall anoint only their foreheads with the holy oil, and after this the deaconess shall anoint them: for there is no necessity that the women shall be seen by men.'[28] Again, the instructions to the deaconess immediately after the baptism do not suggest that another unction then occurred. Hence it seems reasonably certain that the Didascaliast knew only one unction in initiation, and that before baptism.

A further important point is the significance of this pre-baptismal unction. Ratcliff maintained that its purpose was to convey the Holy Spirit, that is to say, that it could be understood as confirmation, on the ground that the readers, having seen it compared with the unction of priests and kings in the Old Testament, would naturally recall to mind those biblical passages where the spiritual effect of this anointing was described.[29] The passages which Ratcliff cited are Lev. 8.12, 1 Sam. 10.1–6, 16.13, 1 Kings 1.39. Of these the third is the most interesting: 'Then Samuel took the horn of oil, and anointed him in the midst of his brethren: and the Spirit of the Lord came upon David from that day forward.' Now although it is perfectly possible that the Didascaliast interpreted the unction in the light of these passages of scripture, and therefore regarded it as the vehicle of the Holy Spirit, he did not actually say as much. Hence one cannot absolutely rule out Whitaker's argument (p. xvii) that the reason why the analogy was drawn between the baptismal unction and that of kings and priests was simply the fact that both were unctions of the head, the spiritual effects not entering into the matter at all.

In this connection Whitaker cited a prayer from the *Statutes of the Apostles*:

> God, . . . stretch out thine hand invisible upon the fruit of this olive with which thou anointedst the priests and the prophets; and thou hast given power to it with thine own hand, that for those who shall be anointed therewith it may be for healing and safety and benefit in all diseases and sicknesses, and for the extermination of every Satanic adversary; make an unction by thine own grace, really for them for whom it is given, the Holy Spirit, through the name and through the power of our Lord Jesus Christ.[30]

As Whitaker pointed out, although the Holy Spirit is invoked in this prayer, he is invoked for purposes of exorcism rather than of confirmation. From this Whitaker inferred that the prayer in the *Didascalia*, where the pre-baptismal unction is compared with that of kings and priests in the Old Testament, need not be understood, *pace* Ratcliff, as symbolizing the gift of the Spirit in confirmation, but could well be an exorcism. On the other hand Ephraem Syrus[31] also made the comparison between the pre-baptismal unction and the unction of priests and kings, but did not regard it as an exorcism; rather it was the means by which the Holy Spirit imprinted the seal upon his sheep. If, therefore, Ephraem associated the unction before baptism with initiation proper and not with a preparatory exorcism, Whitaker's argument loses much of its force, and it becomes correspondingly easier to suppose that the Didascaliast interpreted this unction in similar terms.

There is, however, a further factor to be taken into account. For at the baptism of a man his head and whole body could be anointed by a male minister without impropriety, while in the case of a woman modesty forbade a man to do more than anoint her head. Hence the need of a deaconess to anoint the woman's body. But despite the difficulty of preserving decency a bishop was required to anoint her head. He could delegate the anointing of her body to a deaconess; he could delegate the actual baptizing to a presbyter or deacon, and the recital of the baptismal formula to a man.[32] But he alone could anoint the head of a female candidate, although it would have been more convenient to delegate this task also. Evidently the role of the bishop and the gift conveyed by his anointing of the head were of vital importance. As for the reason, it will be recalled that it was the bishop through whom the Lord gave the Spirit, through whom Christians were sealed, by the imposition of whose hand the Lord in baptism bore witness to the initiate's adoption to sonship. It is probable, therefore, that at least part of the unction before baptism had to be reserved to the bishop because he was the minister in particular who under the sign of oil conferred the Holy Spirit.

In the passage just quoted mention is made of an episcopal hand-laying at baptism. Again in 3.12 at the initiation of women the bishop was ordered with the imposition of his hand to anoint the head only, and in the case of those who receive baptism, whether men or women, with the imposition of the hand to anoint their heads. Yet it is uncertain what meaning the author attributed to this episcopal act. If it had no meaning, it is odd that he took the trouble to mention it three times in this way. There is no ground for supposing that he had in mind the hand-laying in Acts 8.17 and 19.6. Probably he was thinking of the hand-laying which formed part of the act of baptizing when the officiant placed his hand on the candidate's head in order to dip it in the water.

In his instructions about the reception of penitents the Didascaliast associates the giving of the Holy Spirit with hand-laying and also with baptism:

> And as thou baptizest a heathen and then receivest him, so also lay thy hand upon this man (i.e. a baptized person who is a penitent), whilst all pray for him, and then bring him in and let him communicate with the church. For the imposition of hand shall be to him in the place of baptism; for whether by the imposition of hand, or by baptism, they receive the communication of the Holy Spirit.[33]

The man who sins after baptism has made himself a stranger to the church which admitted him into its fellowship and to the Spirit who indwells the church. When such a person repents, the episcopal hand-laying effects his restoration to the fellowship and in a kind of second baptism gives him once more the Holy Spirit. Hence penance is regarded as a sacrament which restores the gift of the Spirit.

But quite apart from what it says about the fruits of penance, this passage says clearly that by baptism the Holy Spirit is received. The penitent recovers the Holy Spirit through the laying on of the bishop's hand: the convert receives the Holy Spirit through baptism. Now there are other places where the writer clearly connects the giving of the Holy Spirit with baptism itself. For instance, he commented on Matt. 12.43–5 thus:

> A believer is filled with the Holy Spirit, and an unbeliever with an alien spirit. He therefore who has withdrawn and separated himself from the unclean spirit by baptism, is filled with the Holy Spirit; and if he do good works, the Holy Spirit continues with him, and he remains fulfilled; and the unclean spirit finds no place with him, for he who is filled with the Holy Spirit does not receive him.[34]

In the withdrawal from the evil spirit there is a reference to the renunciation of Satan, and the filling with the Holy Spirit is accomplished by baptism. In the same chapter we read: 'For through baptism they receive the Holy Spirit, who is ever with those that work righteousness.'

But although the writer believed that the Holy Spirit was given in baptism itself, this does not mean that he denied any giving of the Holy Spirit in the preceding unction. Whereas Western rites of initiation tended to associate the giving of the Spirit with one particular moment in the rite, Syrian Christians regarded the whole rite as a sacramental means of imparting the Spirit. We shall see later that anointing, baptism, and eucharist were all related to the giving of the Spirit.

Ephraem Syrus, a great Syrian doctor, poet, and biblical commentator of the fourth century, wrote two hymns for the Epiphany which yield information about the Syrian rite of baptism. The order and content of the rite are revealed in Ephraem's comment on the cleansing of the leper: 'When the leper of old was cleansed, the priest used to seal him with oil, and to lead him to the waterspring. The type has passed and the truth is come. Lo, with chrism have ye been sealed, in baptism ye are perfected, in the flock ye are intermixed, from the body ye are nourished.'[35] This is a reference in chronological order to anointing, baptism, and eucharist. In similar strain he wrote in Hymn 8.22 of Christians being anointed with fire by oil, clothed in water, fed by bread and inebriated by wine. Here again oil is mentioned before water. When he invited the candidates to enter the font he said, 'Descend, my sealed brethren, put on the Lord ...'[36] The seal received before the descent into the font was in the first passage quoted identified with the anointing with chrism. Again, in one of his hymns on virginity Ephraem wrote, 'April recreates those who are fasting, anoints, baptizes and whitens them.'[37] The mention of April indicates that Easter was the normal season for initiation.

There are a number of other places where Ephraem connected the seal with the chrism. For instance, in the third Hymn on the Epiphany, section 1, we read: 'Christ and chrism are conjoined; the secret with the visible is mingled. The chrism anoints visibly, Christ seals secretly the lambs newborn and spiritual ... From the people he separated the People by the former seal of circumcision; but by the seal of anointing the peoples he separates from the People.' That the seal consisted in the sign of the cross may be inferred from 3.12: 'The sheep of Christ leaped for joy to receive the seal of life, that ensign of kings which has ever put sin to flight. The wicked by thy sign is routed, iniquities by thy sign are scattered. Come, ye sheep, receive your seal which puts to flight them that devour you.'

Expounding the meaning of the anointing, Ephraem said that, as Jacob poured oil on a stone, so this unction was a sign of bodies being consecrated by oil that they might become temples for God.[38] Further on Ephraem returned to the idea of the soul of the Christian being made a dwelling place for the Holy Spirit: 'Your anointing which ye have is greater, for your minds are censers, in your temples the Spirit exults, a chamber for ever shall ye be unto him.'[39] The anointing of David elicited from Ephraem this comment:

As for the anointing of David, my brethren, the Spirit came down and made sweet savour in the heart of the man wherein he delighted; the savour of his heart was a the savour of his action. The Spirit dwelt in him and made song in him. Your anointing which ye have is greater, for Father and Son and Holy Ghost have moved and come down to dwell in you.[40]

In 7.6 Ephraem wrote:

The oil is the agent of the Holy Spirit and his minister, and followed him as his disciple. Through oil the Spirit signed priests and kings. The Holy Spirit through oil imprinted the seal upon his sheep, as a ring which impresses its seal in wax. Even so the Spirit impresses the hidden seal upon the bodies through oil when they are anointed in baptism and signed in baptism.

The last words here quoted are highly significant because they show how closely the unction and the actual baptism were united in

94

Ephraem's thought, anointing and sealing both being parts of baptism.

Now clearly as he said that the Holy Spirit was given in the unction before baptism, this did not preclude Ephraem from saying that the Holy Spirit was also given in the water of baptism. For example, referring to the passage of the Red Sea, he said: 'The People passed through and believed not: the Gentiles were baptized in this and believed and received the Holy Spirit.'[41] Or again in 5.1 he invited his hearers to descend and 'put on from the waters of baptism the Holy Spirit.' On our Lord's baptism Ephraem commented thus:

> The Spirit came down from on high, and hallowed the waters by his brooding. In the baptism of John he passed by the rest and abode on One; but now he has descended and abode on all that are born of the water. Out of all that John baptized on One it was that the Spirit dwelt: but now he has flown and come down, that he may dwell on the many, and as each after each comes up, he loves him and abides on him.[42]

Siman cited another passage to the same effect:

> And the Son comes to John to receive from him baptism, to mix with the visible water the invisible Spirit, so that the spirits may receive the gift of the Spirit while the body received the moisture of the water.[43]

Thus Ephraem has associated the giving of the Holy Spirit with baptism as clearly as he has associated it with the preceding unction. The whole rite, unction and baptism, not just one moment in it, effected the giving of the Spirit. Furthermore, Ephraem taught that those who had been anointed and baptized received the Holy Spirit yet again in the eucharist which concluded the rite of initiation. For instance, Siman quoted from a Hymn on Faith: 'Fire and Spirit are in our baptism; in the bread and the chalice also are fire and Spirit', and from a sermon on Holy Week, 'Henceforth you will eat a Passover pure without blemish, a bread leavened and perfect which the Holy Spirit has kneaded and caused to be cooked; I have for you to drink a wine mingled with fire and Spirit, the body and blood of God who becomes a victim for all men.'[44] In a sermon on Maundy Thursday Ephraem said: 'He called the bread his living body, he filled it with himself and the Holy Spirit . . . He who eats it with faith, he eats fire and Spirit . . . Take, eat of it all of you; and through him eat the Holy Spirit.'[45]

Siman showed that this notion of receiving the Holy Spirit in holy communion was not peculiar to Ephraem, because in the *Testament of our Lord Jesus Christ* 2.10 the author wrote: '. . . he who gives the communion will say, The body of Jesus Christ, the Holy Spirit, for the healing of soul and body.'[46] We shall find similar thoughts expressed by Chrysostom and Theodore of Mopsuestia.[47]

Thus in Syrian thought the Holy Spirit was present and active and communicated himself throughout the whole rite of initiation from the pre-baptismal unction to the final eucharist.

The *Demonstrations* of Aphraates, 'the Persian Sage', were written, the first ten in 336/7, and the last twelve seven years later.[48] Their references to baptism indicate a rite of the Syrian pattern with no unction after baptism. Thus Aphraates twice wrote of baptism and the eucharist in terms which imply that there was no further ceremony between them: in *Dem. 4 de Oratione*: 'But if they had been washed in the water of baptism and had received the body and blood of Christ, blood would have been expiated with blood and body purified with body,' and in *Dem. 12*, '. . . then he proceeds to baptism, the consummation of the true circumcision, he is joined to the people of God, he participates in the body and the blood.'

Aphraates has not explained clearly what meaning he attached to the seal, when he wrote of the giving of the seal with baptism according to its proper observance.[49] In the light of known Syrian practice it was probably a signing of the forehead with oil before baptism. It is such an anointing to which Aphraates seems to have been alluding when he called our Lord the splendid olive tree, wherein is the sign of the sacrament of life, whereby Christians and priests and kings and prophets are perfected.[50] There is further evidence that Aphraates knew of an unction received by believers, although the occasion is not mentioned: 'And Jacob called that place Bethel, and Jacob erected there as a memorial a pillar of stone upon the top of which he poured oil. And Jacob our father prefigured another mystery by pouring oil on those stones: for the people who have believed in Christ, behold it is they who are anointed . . .'[51] Since some very similar words of Ephraem refer to the pre-baptismal anointing, Aphraates' words very probably also refer to this.

It is difficult to come to any firm conclusion how far Aphraates linked this unction with the gift of the Holy Spirit. But in commenting on the blessing of the font he wrote: 'For from baptism we have received the Spirit of Christ: and at the same hour in which the priests invoke the Spirit, the heaven opens and he descends, and rests upon the waters, and those who are baptized put him on. For from all who are born of the body the Spirit is absent, until they come to the regeneration of water; then they receive the Holy Spirit.'[52] This is as clear a statement as could be expected that according to Aphraates the Spirit was given in baptism itself. Yet in view of what we have discovered already, this does not necessarily mean that he believed that there was no giving of the Spirit in the preceding unction.

The *Liturgical Homilies* of Narsai, an eminent Christian teacher who lectured in Edessa from 437 to 457 when he moved to Nisibis, contain much information about initiation, although the author's unusual style raises some problems of interpretation. Homily 22, which should precede Homily 21, deals with the renunciation of Satan, the confession of the faith and the function of sponsors, whereupon it passes immediately to the unction, the consecration of the oil, the sealing with it and the blessings conferred thereby. The priest makes the candidate for baptism

> to stand as a sheep in the door of the sheepfold; and he signs his body and lets him mix with the flock. The sign of the oil he holds in his hand, before the beholders: and with manifest things he proclaims the power of things hidden. And as by a symbol he shews to the eyes of the bodily senses the secret power that is hidden in the visible sign.[53]

That the power latent in the visible sign of oil was the Holy Spirit becomes apparent in the following words:

> O thou dust-born, that signest the flock with the sign of the Lord, and sealest upon it his hidden name by the outward mark. Ah, dust-born, that holds the Spirit on the tip of his tongue, and cuts away the iniquity of the soul and body with the word of his mouth . . . Ah, pauper, son of paupers, that is grown rich on a sudden, and has begun to distribute the wealth of the Spirit which his fathers had not.[54]

The candidate was signed with the oil in the name of the Father, Son and Holy Spirit: 'the iron of the oil the priest holds on the tip of his fingers; and he signs the body and the senses of the soul with its sharp (edge) . . . The three names he recites in order, one after the other; and in triple wise he completes and performs the mystery of our redemption.'[55] The oil was first consecrated by an invocation of the Trinity upon it: 'the three names he casts upon the oil, and consecrates it, that it may be sanctifying the uncleanness of men by its holiness. With the name hidden in it he signs the visible body; and the sharp power of the name enters even unto the soul.'[56] The signing was made upon the forehead: 'on their forehead they receive the spiritual stamp, that it may be bright before angels and men.' And then, as in the *Didascalia*, the whole body was anointed: 'the three names he recites, together with (the rubbing of) the oil upon the whole man; that hostile demons and vexing passions may not harm him.'

Towards the end of the homily the unction is described again, this time in less cryptic language:

> he calls the king's servants by their names and marks their faces with the brand of the oil . . . The name of the Divinity he mixes in his

hands with the oil; and he signs and says 'Father' and 'Son' and 'Holy Spirit.' The priest does not say, 'I sign', but 'is signed'; for the stamp that he sets is not his, but his Lord's. He is (but) the mediator who has been chosen by a favour to minister; and because it is not his it drives out iniquity and gives the Spirit . . . This power the oil of anointing imparts: not the oil but the Spirit that gives it power. The Spirit gives power to the unction of the feeble oil, and it waxes firm by the operation that is administered in it.

Evidently, then, the anointing of the forehead with the sign of the cross and the anointing of the whole body were held to confer the gift of the Holy Spirit.

There is, however, one passage in this homily which refers to the water of baptism, and has been interpreted in more than one way. After dealing with the consecration of the oil Narsai wrote: 'With the external sign he touches the hidden diseases that are within; and then he lays on the drug of the Spirit with the symbol of water'. Clearly the *rushma*, or signing of the forehead with oil, preceded the act of baptizing. What is not so clear is the precise meaning of the laying on of the drug of the Spirit when it is here associated with the symbol of water. Maclean thought that the laying on of the drug of the Spirit referred to the gift of the Spirit in the pre-baptismal unction which is the subject of this lecture[57]; while Whitaker[58] considered that these words clearly connected the gift of the Spirit with the baptismal washing. It would seem that the 'external sign' is a reference to the unction, and that in the second half of this sentence Narsai allowed himself to pass in thought from the subject under discussion to the baptism which followed the unction.

In Homily 21 Narsai once more used the expression 'drug of the Spirit': 'The drug of the Spirit he casts into the water, as into a furnace; and he purifies the image of men from uncleanness. By the heat of the Spirit he purges the rust of body and soul.'[59] Here quite certainly the reference is to the blessing of the font, which effects the presence of the Spirit in the water. Consequently the benefits conferred in baptism are due to the activity of the Holy Spirit in and through the water. 'The defilement of men he cleanses with water: yet not by water, but by the power of the name of the Divinity which there lights down. The power of the Divinity dwells in the visible waters, and by the force of his power they dissolve the might of the evil one and of death.'[60]

Narsai, then, in common with other Syrian authorities believed that there was a giving of the Holy Spirit in baptism and also in the unction which preceded it. Furthermore he seems, like Ephraem, to have believed that the Holy Spirit was also received in holy communion. Communicants 'suck the Spirit after the birth of baptism.'[61] 'The power of the Spirit comes down unto a mortal man, and dwells in the bread and consecrates it by the might of his power . . . A corporeal being takes hold with his hands of the Spirit in the bread.'[62] Hence the act of communion involves a feeding upon the Holy Spirit.

In support of his case that Narsai knew of only one giving of the Spirit, and that in baptism itself, Whitaker has argued that the pre-baptismal unction, having the property of turning away the power of evil and of promoting healing, should be regarded as an exorcism.[63] Now it is perfectly true that Narsai treated the unction as a medicine to heal sickness: 'The office of a physician, too, he (i.e. the priest) exercises towards the members; . . . To body and soul he applies the remedies of his art; and the open and hidden (disease) he heals by the divine power. Divinely he mixes the drug that is given into his hands; and all diseases he heals by its power without fail.'[64] But because unction is treated as a remedy for spiritual sickness, it does not necessarily have to be regarded as an exorcism. For instance, writing of the blessing of the font, Tertullian said that the waters in some sense acquired healing power by an angel's intervention;[65] yet obviously he believed the healing to be conveyed by baptism, not by exorcism. Moreover, some of the blessings which Narsai ascribed to the unction cannot be interpreted in terms of exorcism:

> An armour is the oil with which the earth-born are anointed, that they may not be captured by the (evil) spirits in the hidden warfare. It is the great brand of the King of kings with which they are stamped, that they may serve (as soldiers) in the spiritual contest . . . As athletes they descend (and) stand in the arena, and they close in battle with the cowardly suggestions that are in them. This power the oil of anointing imparts . . . By its firmness it makes firm the body and the faculties of the soul, and they go forth confidently to wage war against the evil one.[66]

The act which conveys grace such as this cannot be regarded as an exorcism.

The evidence so far considered has come mostly from East Syria. The author of the *Acts of Judas Thomas* may have lived in Edessa. Narsai lived first in Edessa and then in Nisibis. Aphraates lived in Persia. According to Connolly the place of origin of the *Didascalia* was roughly speaking between Antioch and Edessa, although lower Syria or even Palestine could not certainly be ruled out. But this Syrian order of initiation with the one and only unction coming before baptism was also known in West Syria, and in particular in the church of Antioch.

The *Apostolic Constitutions*, a West Syrian work generally dated *c.* 375, include in the third book the regulations concerning baptism in the *Didascalia*, interspersed with other material. The need for a deaconess to assist at the initiation of woman is stated in words taken from the *Didascalia*: but new material is added in the directions for the pre-baptismal unction:

> but in the laying on of hands the bishop shall anoint her head only as the priests and kings were formerly anointed, a royal priesthood, and an holy nation . . . Thou therefore, O bishop, according to that type, shalt anoint the head of those that are being baptized, whether men or women, with the holy oil, for a type of the spiritual baptism.[67]

There are two indications here that the unction was held to impart the Holy Spirit. First, it is said to make people Christians after Christ the anointed one, who was so called because he was anointed with the Spirit. Secondly, it is called a type of spiritual baptism. All doubt on this score is removed in the next section: 'the water is instead of the burial, and the oil instead of the Holy Spirit; the seal instead of the cross; the chrism is the confirmation of the confession.' The chrism here mentioned was applied to the candidates by the bishop after the baptism. Here, therefore, we see evidence of a belief that the Syrian rite of initiation should be brought into closer conformity with the rite of Jerusalem and with Western practice by having two unctions, one before and one after baptism. But the gift of the Holy Spirit is still assigned to the pre-baptismal unction in accordance with early Syrian usage, and not to the second anointing, as in the rite of Jerusalem.

In 7.22 the editor of the *Apostolic Constitutions*, using the baptismal instructions in the *Didache* as his main source, added to them other material so as to produce a rite which had an unction before baptism and another one after it, the *Didache* itself having had no unction at all:

> But thou shalt first anoint the person with holy oil, and afterward baptize him with water, and finally shalt seal him with chrism; that the anointing with oil may be a participation of the Holy Spirit, and the water a symbol of death, and the chrism a seal of the covenant.

Here again, while there is a resemblance with the rite of Jerusalem in that there is a sealing with chrism after baptism, nevertheless the gift of the Spirit is still ascribed to the unction before baptism.

Further on in the same book there is yet another, and fuller, account of baptism. Before the actual baptism there was an anointing with oil 'blessed by the priest for the remission of sins, and the first preparation for baptism.'[68] In the consecration of this oil the priest 'calls upon the unbegotten God . . . that he would sanctify the oil in the name of the Lord Jesus, and impart to it spiritual grace and efficacious strength, the remission of sins, and the first preparation for the confession of baptism, that so the candidate, when he is anointed, may be freed from all ungodliness and may become worthy of initiation . . .' Contrary to what is found in 3.16 and 7.22, there is no suggestion here that this anointing is intended to confer the gift of the Holy Spirit.

After the actual baptism came an anointing with chrism, the significance of which can be gauged from the accompanying prayer: 'O Lord God . . . do thou grant at this time that this chrism may be efficacious upon him that is baptized, that so the sweet odour of thy Christ may continue upon him firm and fixed; and that now he has died with him, he may arise and live with him.'[69] While this rite too resembles that in Cyril's *Catecheses* in including an unction with chrism after baptism, it remains silent about any gift of the Spirit. Indeed the rite described in 7.39–45 does not reveal any awareness that one of the purposes of Christian initiation was to confer the Holy Spirit.

In conclusion, the *Apostolic Constitutions* show knowledge of an anointing before baptism and of a second anointing after baptism; but it is with the first and not the second anointing that the gift of the Holy Spirit is conjoined: and there is no explicit statement that the Holy Spirit is given in baptism itself.

Whitaker (p. xxi) has called attention to a passage in 7.22, where after the explanation of the meaning of the anointing, the baptism and the sealing with chrism the following instruction is given: 'But if there be neither oil nor chrism, the water is sufficient both for the anointing, and for the seal, and for the confession of him that is dead, or indeed is dying together with Christ.' From this Whitaker concluded that, so long as the baptism in water was duly performed, the candidate received the whole effect and benefit of Christian initiation, including the gift of the Spirit. If, he said, some parts of the baptismal complex lapsed, the Syrian Church had a clear answer: 'The water is sufficient.'

But it is doubtful whether this regulation, found in only one of the editor's three baptismal rites, fairly represents the mind of the Syrian Church in this matter. In any case the regulation only applied in emergencies where there was no oil or chrism available. In all normal circumstances both would have been available and used. At one stage in the second world war the present writer experienced difficulty in obtaining communion wine. The very Protestant lady in the off-licence regretted that she could not help him in his difficulty. When he told her that in that case he would have to adopt the Roman Catholic practice of giving communion in one kind only, she soon produced for him from behind the scenes a bottle of port. If she had not done so, he would have had to say to his congregation, 'The bread is sufficient.'

The value of the evidence in the *Apostolic Constitutions* would be far greater if we knew who the editor was and where he lived, and how far he was describing rites which had been in use in some particular church. Although this book obviously emanated from Syria, Botte considered that it did not in every point represent pure Syrian tradition.[70] The chief interest of the book lies in the fact that it shows a rite of initiation in a state of transition from the earlier stage where the giving of the Holy Spirit was ascribed to the one and only unction before baptism to the later stage when the gift of the Spirit will be transferred to the chrismation immediately after baptism.

7 Syria—Chrysostom, Theodore, Theodoret

The case that John Chrysostom knew an initiatory rite of the Syrian pattern rests chiefly upon the information found in some recently published instructions on baptism, which he probably delivered in the years 388 and 390 while he was still in Antioch. As a result we are now in possession of two parallel accounts of the rite which he knew, the first in the series of instructions discovered in 1909 by A. Papadopoulos-Kerameus, which we shall refer to as PK, and the second in the series found by A. Wenger in 1955 in the monastery of Stavronikita on Mount Athos, to which we shall refer as S. This latter was published in Paris in 1957 under the title *Huit Catéchèses Baptismales Inédites*. An English translation has been provided by P. W. Harkins in his *St John Chrysostom, Baptismal Instructions*. The date of these instructions has been discussed at length by Wenger (pp. 48–65), Harkins (pp. 14–18), and by T. M. Finn in *The Liturgy of Baptism in the Baptismal Instructions of St John Chrysostom*.

In the PK series the renunciation of Satan and declaration of adherence to Christ are seen to have been followed immediately by a consignation of the forehead with chrism:

> After these words, after the renunciation of the devil and the covenant with Christ, inasmuch as you have henceforth become his very own and have nothing in common with that evil one, he straightway bids you to be marked and places on your forehead the sign of the cross. In this way does God hold in check all the frenzy of the Evil One; for the devil will not dare to look upon such a sight. Just as if he had beheld the rays of the sun and had leaped away, so will his eyes be blinded by the sight of your face and he will depart; for through the chrism the cross is stamped upon you. The chrism is a mixture of olive oil and unguent; the unguent is for the bride, the oil is for the athlete.[1]

Much the same is said in S:

> After that contract of renunciation and attachment, after you have confessed his sovereignty and by the words you spoke have attached

yourself to Christ, in the next place, as if you were a combatant chosen for the spiritual arena, the priest anoints you on the forehead with the oil of the spirit and signs you (with the sign of the cross), saying: 'So-and-so is anointed in the name of the Father and of the Son and of the Holy Spirit' . . . the priest anoints you on the forehead and puts on you the sign of the cross, in order that the enemy may turn away his eyes. For he does not dare to look you in the face when he sees the lightning flash which leaps forth from it and blinds his eyes. Henceforth from that day there is strife and counter-strife with him, and on this account the priest leads you into the spiritual arena as athletes of Christ by virtue of this anointing.[2]

Clearly, then, this unction consisted in a signing of the forehead with chrism, the officiant reciting a Trinitarian formula in the passive voice.

As we have found in other Syrian documents, this signing of the forehead was followed by an anointing of the whole body. For in PK we read: 'After he anoints all your limbs with this ointment, you will be secure and able to hold the serpent in check,' and in S, 'Next after this, in the full darkness of the night, he strips off your robe and, as if he were going to lead you into heaven itself by the ritual, he causes your whole body to be anointed with that olive oil of the spirit, so that all your limbs may be fortified and unconquered by the darts which the adversary aims at you.'

This unction undoubtedly came before and not after the actual baptism, because in the PK series Chrysostom said, 'After the anointing, then, it remains to go into the bath of sacred waters,' and in S, 'After this anointing, the priest makes you go down into the sacred waters.'[3]

As for the significance of this pre-baptismal anointing, Finn and Whitaker (p. xviii) have claimed that it had much in common with exorcism. That exorcism was included among the preliminaries of baptism is not in doubt, because in S we read:

You must understand why, after this daily instruction, we send you along to hear the words of the exorcists. For this rite does not take place without aim or purpose; you are going to receive the king of heaven to dwell within you. This is why, after we have admonished you, those appointed to this task take you and, as if they were preparing a house for a royal visit, they cleanse your minds by those awesome words, putting to flight every device of the wicked one and making your hearts worthy of the royal presence. For even if the demon be fierce and cruel, he must withdraw from your hearts with all speed after this awesome formula and the invocation of the common Master of all things.[4]

But there are three reasons for believing that this exorcism was something quite distinct from the pre-baptismal anointing. In the first place this exorcism preceded, whereas the unction came after, the renunciation of Satan and the declaration of adherence to Christ. Secondly, the exorcism was performed by exorcists, persons appointed to this task,[5] who, according to the evidence of *Apostolic Constitutions* 8.26, may have been laymen, whereas the unction was administered by a priest (*hiereus*), who in the case of the sealing of the forehead was probably the bishop and in the anointing of the whole body was a priest, assisted presumably by a deaconess in the case of female candidates. Thirdly, the purpose of exorcism is to expel the evil one. As Chrysostom says, the exorcists put to flight every device of the wicked one, and make him withdraw from the hearts of the candidates. But the demon having been expelled does not meekly accept defeat; again, as Chrysostom says, the enemy is furious when he sees his former subjects renouncing him and defecting to the other side; henceforth there is continual strife between the Christian convert and the demon who tries his hardest to regain what he has lost. The purpose of the unction is not to effect the initial expulsion of Satan, which is accomplished in the exorcism, but to equip the convert with the spiritual resources with which to resist Satan successfully in the future. This is the natural sequel to exorcism, but it is not itself exorcism.

To illustrate the theme of lifelong combat between the Christian and his adversary, the devil, Chrysostom turns to the thought of the athlete in the arena:

> So also for you, these thirty days (of preparation for baptism) are like the practice and bodily exercise in some wrestling school. Let us learn during this time of training the grips he uses, the source of his wickedness, and how he can easily hurt us.[6]
>
> How true it is that Christ does not stand aloof but is entirely on our side you may see from this: he anointed us with the oil of gladness, but he bound the devil with fetters that cannot be broken to keep him shackled hand and foot for the combat.[7]

Some of Chrysostom's thoughts about the meaning of the unction arise from the fact that the oil was applied to the forehead in the sign of the cross. Now the sign of the cross made on a Christian was a token of divine ownership and a pledge that God could be trusted to protect his own property. It was also the sign of our Lord's conquest of death and sin, and his victory over the powers of darkness. For this reason Christians used to sign themselves with the cross on a great variety of occasions, a custom which had come into being long before the time of Chrysostom. Tertullian, for instance, had said that Christians habitually signed themselves at every going out or coming in and on numerous other occasions.[8] Chrysostom said that, if on entering a synagogue a Christian signed himself, he would be protected from the evil power that dwelt therein;[9] the signing of a Christian at his initiation provided him with safety.[10] Whether used at baptism or on other occasions, the cross was a great good, a saving weapon, an invincible shield matched against the devil.[11]

Now Chrysostom's views about the protective properties of the cross were by no means peculiar to him. But when reference is made to this topic by other early writers, it is often not in the context of exorcism. For example, in a comment on the ceremonies of baptism Tertullian said that the flesh is signed so that the soul may be fortified.[12] But this consignation took place not at the pre-baptismal exorcism but after baptism. Cyril of Jerusalem described the mystical chrism as the whole armour of the Holy Spirit, enabling the Christian to stand against the power of the enemy and to vanquish it: it was a spiritual preservative of the body and safeguard of the soul.[13] But the chrismation to which Cyril refers was not an exorcism but the concluding ceremony of baptism, which conferred the seal of the Holy Spirit. For these reasons the attempt to interpret Chrysostom's pre-baptismal anointing solely in terms of exorcism must be rejected.

Whether this unction can be regarded as confirmation depends on the question whether Chrysostom believed it to convey the gift of the Holy Spirit. Now although he never actually says as much, there are reasons for believing that he did not entirely dissociate the giving of the Spirit from this unction. First, Chrysostom called the oil used 'the olive oil of the Spirit.' Secondly, in the PK series he quoted in connection with this unction 2 Cor. 1.21, 'It is God who is warrant for us and for you in Christ, who has anointed us.'[14] Now while it is true that Chrysostom stopped short of quoting it here, the very next verse contains the words, 'who hath also sealed us, and given us the earnest of the Spirit in our hearts.' Moreover in *Hom. 3.5 in 2 Cor.* he shows that he linked anointing and sealing with the gift of the Spirit, because on the same text he wrote, 'What does it mean, anointed and sealed? Giving the Spirit, through whom he did both these things, making us also prophets and priests and kings; for these kinds of persons in former times were anointed.' Again in *Hom. 2.2 in Eph.* he commented, 'The Israelites, too, were sealed but by circumcision, as sheep and irrational creatures; we also are sealed but as sons with the Spirit.'

If, then, there are reasons for believing that in Chrysostom's thought the anointing before baptism was not unrelated to the giving of the Spirit, it still remains true that he nowhere said plainly that the purpose of this anointing was to impart this gift. Furthermore, if there was one specific moment in the rite with which Chrysostom connected the giving of the Spirit, there is reason to hold that that moment was the moment of baptism itself. But further enquiry may show that it is wrong to look for one such moment.

Although Chrysostom does not mention any formal blessing of the font such as is found in all the ancient baptismal liturgies, he believed in a kind of real presence of the Holy Spirit in the water of the font: 'When you come to the sacred initiation, the eyes of the flesh see water; the eyes of faith behold the Spirit.'[15] 'For it is not a man who does what is done, but it is the grace of the Spirit which sanctifies the nature of the water . . .'[16] Hence in common with all the Fathers Chrysostom believed the Holy Spirit to be present at the font and to be the author of the blessings there bestowed.

Now there are a number of passages where Chrysostom says quite clearly that the Holy Spirit is received in baptism. Thus in commenting on the rushing mighty wind and the dove Chrysostom said, '. . . not only for this reason, but in order that you may learn that on you too when you are baptized the Spirit comes.'[17] Again in *de Compunct. ad Demetr.* i.8 he wrote: 'for you too enjoyed divine grace when you were baptized and partook of the Spirit', and in *de Bapt. Christi* 5, 'for (Christian baptism) gets rid of sins and washes the soul clean, and supplies the Spirit', and in *Hom. 24.2 in Joan.*, 'If you are not born from above, if you do not partake of the spirit by the washing of regeneration, you cannot come to a right belief about me.' Comparing Christian baptism with Jewish circumcision, Chrysostom said, 'But our circumcision, I mean the grace of baptism, involves a painless operation, and conveys to us manifold blessings, and fills us with the grace of the Spirit.'[18] Of those who have been baptized Chrysostom said, 'they are . . . not only fellow heirs but also members, not only members but also a temple, not only a temple but also organs of the Spirit.'[19] A little further on Chrysostom again expounded the blessings of baptism:

> Did you see how many are the gifts of baptism? And yet to many it seems only to confer the gift of remission of sins, but we count ten blessings. For this reason we baptize infants also although they have no sins, so that there may be given to them sanctification, justification, adoption to sonship, inheritance, brotherhood, being members of Christ, becoming the dwelling place of the Spirit.

In most of these instances it is possible to argue that the Spirit was thought to be given in the rite of baptism as a whole, and not necessarily at the actual moment of baptism itself. Against this, however, there is very clear evidence that Chrysostom associated the giving of the Spirit with the imposition of the officiant's hand during the act of baptizing.

Our bodily eyes see the priest as, from above, he lays his right hand on the head and touches (him who is being baptized) : our spiritual eyes see the great high priest as he stretches forth his invisible hand to touch his head. For, at that moment, the one who baptizes is not a man but the only begotten Son of God.[20]

Similarly in S we read:

... when you see the bath of water and the hand of the priest touching your head, you may not think that this is merely water, nor that only the hand of the bishop lies on your head. For it is not a man who does what is done, but it is the grace of the Spirit which sanctifies the nature of the water and touches your head together with the hand of the priest.[21]

In this same lecture Chrysostom made it clear that the Holy Spirit was imparted through the prayer and hand-laying of the officiant:

After this anointing the priest makes you go down into the sacred waters . . . It is at this moment that, through the words and the hand of the priest, the Holy Spirit descends upon you . . . When the priest says: So-and-so is baptized in the name of the Father, and of the Son, and of the Holy Spirit, he puts your head down into the water three times and three times he lifts it up again, preparing you by this mystic rite to receive the descent of the Spirit.

Elsewhere Chrysostom asked for prayer for the archbishop 'through whose hands and words you gained these blessings.'[22] Again, in emphasizing that the minister is only the instrument through which God bestows his favours, Chrysostom said, 'Neither angel nor archangel can do anything with regard to what is given from God; but the Father, the Son, and the Holy Spirit, dispense all, while the priest lends his tongue and offers his hand.'[23]

Chrysostom saw the baptism of a Christian as a re-enactment of the scene at Jordan, where John the Baptist had his hand upon our Lord's head as he baptized him:

And what happened in the case of our Master's body also happens in the case of your own. Although John appeared to be holding his body by the head, it was the divine word which led his body down into the streams of Jordan and baptized him. The Master's body was baptized by the Word, and by the voice of his Father from heaven which said: This is my beloved Son, and by the manifestation of the Holy Spirit which descended upon him. This also happens in the case of your body.[24]

Clearly Chrysostom considered that in the act of baptizing the imposition of the officiant's hand symbolized and effected that giving of the Holy Spirit which was imparted to our Lord at his baptism.

Now this hand-laying was an integral part of the act of baptizing, not a separate action such as in Acts 8.17 and 19.6, where the apostles imposed their hands after the actual baptism was over. In his homilies on Acts, Chrysostom did not relate these hand-layings with contemporary practice in Syria. But in *Hom. 9.2 in Heb.*, where he was commenting on Heb. 6.2, he wrote: '*And of laying on of hands*. For thus they received the Spirit. For when Paul laid his hands upon them, he says, the Holy Spirit came.' Since he believed that St Paul wrote the Epistle to the Hebrews, Chrysostom here assumed that the apostle was referring to his own teaching about baptisms and laying on of hands. So, if Chrysostom could suppose that in St Paul's time baptism was normally accompanied by hand-laying for the imparting of the Holy Spirit, without apparently seeing any discrepancy between scriptural practice and that of his own church, it may be that the explanation lies in the meaning which he attached to the hand-laying included in the act of baptizing.

Next we have to consider the important question whether Chrysostom's rite of initiation included an anointing after baptism, such as is found in the rite of Jerusalem. The answer to this question depends on the amount of weight placed upon the account in S about what happened after the baptism:

> As soon as they came forth from those sacred waters, all who are present embrace them, kiss them, rejoice with them, and congratulate them, because those who were heretofore slaves and captives have suddenly become free men and sons and have been invited to the royal table heavy laden with countless favours, where they taste of the Master's body and blood, and become a dwelling place for the Holy Spirit.[25]

These words seem without doubt to imply that immediately after their actual baptism the candidates were welcomed into the congregation, received the kiss of peace and assisted at the eucharist, without the intervention between the baptism and the eucharist of any symbolical action which had a purpose as important as that of imparting the Holy Spirit. Hence, if that is so, Chrysostom's rite conforms to the Syrian pattern in that it includes an unction before baptism but none after it.

Now it can be argued convincingly that if Chrysostom had known of a sacramental act which had the vitally important function of communicating the Holy Spirit to the baptized, and which came between the baptism and the eucharist, then he would surely have mentioned it in his baptismal homilies, and expounded its meaning; his failure to do so can lead to only one conclusion.

But is this case unassailable? Is it possible that Chrysostom's account of initiation is incomplete in the same way that Justin's, as some think, is incomplete? For it is a fact that in the passage quoted Chrysostom has not mentioned all that happened between the actual baptism and the ensuing eucharist. Although he said that straightway after they came up from the waters, the candidates were greeted and led to the holy table, he has not mentioned the fact that they had to dry and dress themselves and be conducted from the privacy of the baptistery into the main body of the church. Perhaps he thought this too obvious to require mention.

But, more important, he refers more than thirty times to the garment assumed by those who have in baptism put on Christ. Now although it is possible to interpret these references to the garment in a metaphorical sense, it seems likely, especially in view of the known practice of other churches at this time, that Chrysostom knew of the custom of vesting the baptized in white robes. Yet he has not mentioned this in his baptismal instructions. One further point is that his use of the word 'straightway' should not be pressed too far, since it need not mean 'immediately' in a quite literal sense.

Wenger thought that silence was not sufficient argument to settle the issue whether Chrysostom knew a second unction after baptism.[26] The fact that a post-baptismal sealing with chrism was known to Cyril of Jerusalem and to Theodore of Mopsuestia suggested to him that a negative conclusion should not be drawn from Chrysostom's silence; and it seemed to him possible that Chrysostom dealt with the post-baptismal ceremonies, such as they were, in the series of exhortations addressed to the newly baptized in Antioch in Easter week. But this is at best only a conjecture. We know that Cyril of Jerusalem and Ambrose delivered their addresses on the actual rite of initiation in Easter week, after the candidates had been fully initiated. Evidently the *disciplina arcani* prevented them from divulging in detail the sacramental practices of the church to catechumens who did not yet belong to the body. But although he was well aware of the *disciplina arcani*, Chrysostom did not feel constrained to keep silent in this way about the administration of baptism or about the Holy Spirit or the seal, because his baptismal instructions were delivered before Easter to persons who were still waiting for their baptism. Moreover such instructions as Chrysostom is known to have given after baptism were concerned not with the sacraments as such but with moral teaching.[27]

Again, Chrysostom's comment on the text, 'We all drank of one Spirit', has been thought to show a belief that the Holy Spirit was given after baptism. The relevant sentence was translated by Mason (p. 365) thus: 'My own opinion is, that he is now speaking of that coming of the Spirit, which takes place in us directly after baptism and before the mysteries.' Wirgman's translation of this passage (p. 172) was almost identical. Now it can be argued that in the interests of their own respective theses Mason and Wirgman mistranslated the words *apo tou baptismatos*, on the ground that they really mean not 'after baptism' but 'as a result of baptism'. Their translation, however, is supported by the translation of these words in the *Nicene and Post-Nicene Fathers*.[28] Indeed there would seem to be an antithesis between *apo tou baptismatos* and *pro to mysterion* which is lost unless *apo* here has a meaning exactly opposite to *pro*. Lampe (pp. 204f), however, has cited other instances of the phrase *apo tou baptismatos* where *apo* does not mean 'after'.

Since there is no other evidence that Chrysostom knew of any post-baptismal ceremony for the conferring of the Holy Spirit, and, since his baptismal instructions point unmistakably to the conclusion that no such ceremony then formed part of the Antiochene rite, the case which Mason and Wirgman advanced on their understanding of the meaning of the preposition *apo* in this context must be rejected. So also Wenger cannot be taken to have proved his point. We are left, therefore, with only one conclusion, that, although Chrysostom undoubtedly believed that the Holy Spirit was given in the rite of initiation, that gift was not received at a hand-laying or anointing after baptism.

There is, however, a further factor to be considered in that once in his lectures Chrysostom said that the Holy Spirit comes to dwell in the initiate when he communicates at the baptismal eucharist: 'For straightway after they come up from the waters they are led to the awesome table of the Master's body and blood, and become a dwellingplace for the Holy Spirit.'[29] Similarly in *Hom. 30.2 in 1 Cor.* Chrysostom said: 'Why did he not say, We feed on the same body and drink the same cup? Because in mentioning the Spirit he expressed both, both the blood and the flesh: for by means of both we drink of the one Spirit.' Siman[30] has shown that the notion that, when the faithful receive the body and blood of Christ, they also receive the Holy Spirit occurs often in Syrian tradition.

In the light of this it would seem that Chrysostom believed the Holy Spirit to be present throughout the whole rite of initiation, and that, when he said that the Spirit was given at the baptism with its hand-laying, he did not intend to imply that the Spirit was not given at other moments in the rite. The Syrian rite, it seems, was so far a unity that it was not necessary for him to ask, as a modern Western Christian has to ask, whether the Holy Spirit was given in baptism or in confirmation, or to try to pinpoint the moment when the Spirit was given.

Yet if, as we must, we accept that Chrysostom's rite of initiation was complete without any post-baptismal anointing, there are still difficulties remaining. For his baptismal homilies are believed to have been delivered in Antioch in 388 and 390, and yet the *Apostolic Constitutions*, which are generally supposed to have been compiled about the same time and in the same part of Syria, include a post-baptismal unction. Now the *Apostolic Constitutions*, if they do not actually antedate Chrysostom's baptismal instructions, are so nearly contemporary with them that it is difficult to say that they show the Syrian rite at a later stage of development after Chrysostom had delivered his lectures. Rather, it would seem, there was some variety of practice in West Syria, and not all churches felt obliged to follow closely the use of Antioch.

Again the baptismal homilies of Theodore of Mopsuestia contain a post-baptismal anointing related to the giving of the Holy Spirit. These, too, may have been delivered while he was still a priest in Antioch,[31] in which case they are almost exactly contemporary with Chrysostom's catecheses. This leads to the conclusion either that for some reason for which no convincing explanation can be offered Chrysostom omitted to mention an unction after baptism, or that the post-baptismal anointing apparently attested by Theodore is a later interpolation. If, however, Theodore's lectures can be given a date after 392, when he became bishop of Mopsuestia in Cilicia about a hundred miles away from Antioch, then there is no need to postulate an interpolation, and all that we have to suppose is that in matters liturgical Mopsuestia was not so far under the influence of Antioch that it felt obliged to follow the Antiochene use. But only if these homilies are to be dated in Theodore's episcopate can we say that they represent the West Syrian rite of initiation at a later stage of development.

Before we leave Chrysostom, however, there is one further point to notice, namely, that he treated the hand-laying in Acts 8.17 and 19.6 in a different way from that which we find in the Western Fathers, who saw these two events as the origin of that post-baptismal ceremony which became known as confirmation. The Samaritans, he said, had received the Spirit of remission of sins at their baptism but not the Spirit of signs.[32] As for the reason why this was so, Chrystostom answered:

> Presumably because Philip had not conferred this gift out of deference to the apostles: presumably because he did not have such a power (for he was one of the Seven): which is the preferable view. . . . Therefore when he baptized he did not give the Spirit to the baptized: for he did not have the authority; for this was the prerogative of the Twelve alone.

Commenting on the disciples at Ephesus, Chrysostom said:

> We have a summary of the blessings conferred by baptism: remission of sins we received and sanctification, partaking in the Spirit, adoption, eternal life. What more do you want? Signs? But they have ceased. You have faith, hope, love, the things which endure. Seek these: these are better than signs.[33]

This point that the Holy Spirit can be received without any visible manifestations was emphasized by Chrysostom in *de Sancto Pentecoste Hom. 1.2*, where, after referring to the raising of the dead and the cleansing of lepers, he asked, 'But now how shall we show that the Holy Spirit is present in us? Fear not: for I show you that now too the Holy Spirit is in us. How and in what way? For if the Holy Spirit is not in us, how could these people who have been enlightened during this holy night have been released from their sins? For it is impossible to be released from one's sins without the activity of the Spirit.' Again in *de Compunct. ad Demetr. 1.8* we read: 'For you too enjoyed divine grace at your baptism and partook in the Spirit, even if not to the extent of performing signs, but sufficiently in order to follow a straight and correct manner of life.'

Whatever may be thought of Chrysostom's views about receiving the Spirit of signs, it is clear that he believed that Philip's Samaritan converts had in a real sense received the Holy Spirit when they were baptized and before St Peter and St John laid their hands upon them. He believed also that the Ethiopian eunuch, who received no hand-laying, also had the Spirit given to him.[34] But since he believed that the hand-laying in Acts 8.17 and 19.6 conveyed a gift which had long been withdrawn, it follows that he did not see a close connection between these two passages of scripture and the rite of baptism as practised in his own time.

The chief interest in Chrysostom's views about the giving of the Spirit of signs is that they anticipate the teaching of Luther and Calvin in the sixteenth century.

At the beginning of the homilies on baptism delivered by Theodore of Mopsuestia there is what purports to be a synopsis of his lectures, whereas it is probably an already existing order of baptism on which he has based his commentary. Theodore's account of initiation can be read in a French translation by Tonneau and Devréesse, and in an English translation by Mingana, which is reproduced in Whitaker's *Documents of the Baptismal Liturgy*, and also in Yarnold's *Awe-Inspiring Rites of Initiation*.

In the synopsis or older work on which Theodore is lecturing the section of chief interest here runs thus:

The bishop, wearing light, shining vestments of linen, signs your forehead with the oil of anointing, saying: N. is signed in the name of the Father and of the Son and of the Holy Spirit. Your sponsor, standing behind you, spreads a linen stole over your head and raises you to your feet. Then you come forward to be baptized. First you strip completely; then you are anointed all over with the oil of anointing in the prescribed manner. The bishop begins the ceremony with the words: N. is anointed in the name of the Father and of the Son and of the Holy Spirit. Then you go down into the water that has been blessed by the bishop. The bishop stands and lays his hand on your head saying: N. is baptized in the name of the Father and of the Son and of the Holy Spirit . . . Then you come up out of the font and put on a dazzling garment of pure white. The bishop comes to you and puts a seal on your forehead saying: N. is sealed in the name of the Father and of the Son and of the Holy Spirit.[35]

It can safely be assumed that the ritual here described had been in use already for some time before Theodore delivered his addresses upon it, because in Sermon 3 he referred to the ceremonies which immediately preceded baptism as performed 'according to an early tradition.'[36] Mingana[37] concluded that this rite, being shorter and more archaic, antedated the rites in the *Apostolic Constitutions*, in which case it must have been in use in the patriarchate of Antioch not long after the middle of the fourth century.

The noteworthy feature of this rite is that besides the unction of the forehead and of the whole body before baptism it also contains a sealing of the forehead after baptism, although it gives no clear indication whether this sealing was also performed with oil. Since no prayers over the oil are included, it is impossible to determine what purpose the two signings served, or to ascertain whether either of them was held to confer the gift of the Holy Spirit.

Theodore's homilies illustrate the meaning which he in the late fourth century attached to the several ceremonies in the rite. The pre-baptismal anointing cannot be interpreted as an exorcism because the exorcisms are shown to have taken place before the renunciation of Satan and before the declaration of allegiance to Christ, both of which preceded the anointing.[38]

When the time for the reception of the sacrament draws nigh and the judgment and fight with the Demon—for the sake of which the words of exorcism have been used—are at an end; and when by God's decision the Tyrant has submitted and yielded to the shouts of the exorcist and been condemned, so that he is in nothing near to you and you are completely free from any disturbances from him . . . you are brought by duly appointed persons to the priest, as it is before him that you have to make your engagements and promises to God.[39]

Clearly after this no further exorcism could be thought necessary.

This anointing of the forehead is called the firstfruits of the sacrament,[40] and is administered by a bishop. It has an initiatory purpose: 'The sign with which you are signed means that you have been stamped as a lamb of Christ and as a soldier of the heavenly king.'[41] This unction does not itself confer the gift of the Holy Spirit, because those who carry the mark of a soldier of Christ then 'receive the remaining part of the sacrament and are invested with the complete armour of the Spirit.'[42] That is to say, it is not itself a means of grace but is a visible pointer to the grace which will be offered later.

Theodore has much to say about the blessing of the font. The water in the font cannot become water of the second birth unless the Holy Spirit comes upon it. 'For this it is necessary that the priest should have beforehand made use of clear words, according to the rite of the priestly service, and asked God that the grace of the Holy Spirit might come on the water and impart to it the power both of conceiving that awe-inspiring child and becoming a womb to the sacramental birth . . .'[43] Consequently 'we who are in a mortal nature rightly receive our renewal through baptism and are refashioned through this same baptism and receive the grace of the Holy Spirit, which hardens us more than any fire can do.'[44] Hence without doubt Theodore believed that there was a giving of the Holy Spirit at the moment of baptism. Holy baptism, he says, 'informs you with the gift of the Holy Spirit the firstfruits of whom you receive when you are baptized.'[45]

This, however, is not the end of the rite. 'After you have received the grace of baptism and worn a white garment that shines, the priest draws nigh unto you and signs you on your forehead and says, So-and-so is signed in the name of the Father and of the Son and of the Holy Spirit.'[46] To explain the meaning of this post-baptismal sealing Theodore immediately refers to our Lord's baptism and reception of the Spirit.

> When Jesus came out of the water he received the grace of the Holy Spirit who descended like a dove and lighted on him, and this is the reason why he is said to have been anointed: 'The Spirit of the Lord is upon me, because of which the Lord hath anointed me', and 'Jesus of Nazareth whom God hath anointed with the Holy Spirit and with power'; texts which show that the Holy Spirit is never separated from him, like the anointment with oil which has a durable effect on the men who are anointed, and is not separated from them. It is right, therefore, that you also should receive the signing on your forehead.

> When the priest (i.e. bishop) signs you he says, So-and-so is signed in the name of the Father and of the Son and of the Holy Spirit, so that it may be an indication and a sign to you that it is in the name of the Father, Son and Holy Spirit that the Holy Spirit descended on you also, and you were anointed and received grace.

Two questions immediately arise. First, if Theodore ascribed the gift of the Holy Spirit to baptism itself, does this sealing also confer the

Holy Spirit? Secondly, how can the presence of a post-baptismal sealing here be reconciled with the absence of such a sealing in Chrysostom's lectures?

With regard to the first question, since there is no specific mention of oil or chrism or *myron*, Botte thought it likely that there was no physical anointing at this point.[47] Similarly Lampe (p. 202n) argued that Theodore's language about anointing was to be taken not literally but as a reference to the inward unction of the Spirit conferred in baptism itself. Against this, however, the reference to our Lord's anointing at his baptism and the statement that the anointment with oil has a durable effect on the men who are anointed would lose their point if the sealing was performed without oil.

At first sight Theodore seems to attribute to this sealing after baptism a gift of the Holy Spirit hardly distinguishable from that which he attributed to baptism. Lampe's assertion that the mention of the Holy Spirit in connection with this sealing is no more than a reference back to the inward and spiritual unction of baptism itself, and Yarnold's[48] that it is an explication of a grace conferred in baptism itself, reduce this act from a sacramental means of grace to a visual demonstration that something has already happened.

But if they are right, it is hard to see why Theodore, after mentioning the baptism and sealing of the candidate's forehead immediately referred to our Lord's baptism and reception of the Holy Spirit, unless there is a parallel between our Lord's baptism and anointing with the Spirit and the Christian's baptism and sealing with the Spirit. It is significant that Theodore said that 'the Holy Spirit descended on you also and you were anointed and received grace immediately after mentioning the signing of the forehead in the name of the Trinity.' At this stage in his lecture Theodore is surely describing the meaning of the signing of the forehead in the threefold name and not referring back to the baptism in the threefold name. It seems, then, that Theodore believed that there was a giving of the Holy Spirit both in the baptism and in the sealing which followed it.

A further factor to bear in mind is that Theodore, like Chrysostom, used language which implies that the Holy Spirit is also received in holy communion. An epiclesis over the people at the eucharist included these words: 'The bishop also prays that the grace of the Holy Spirit may come upon all the assembly.'[49] On this Theodore commented: 'Thus we shall look upon God with a pure heart: we shall not incur punishment by communicating in the Holy Spirit when we are divided in our views . . . By our harmony, peace and good works . . . we shall show that we are waiting to receive the Holy Spirit.'[50] Further on Theodore said: 'He set the bread and the chalice before us, and they are his body and blood, by which we eat the food of immortality while the grace of the Holy Spirit flows down on us, feeding us and so making us immortal and imperishable in hope.'[51] This participation in the Holy Spirit in holy communion is treated as an anticipation of the feeding on the Holy Spirit without sacraments and signs in the age that is to come.

Theodore evidently regarded the rite of initiation as an organic whole in which the Holy Spirit was present and bestowed himself throughout. Indeed it is noteworthy that after describing the post-baptismal sealing, which Western Christians of today would regard as confirmation, Theodore said, 'Such, then, is the second birth which we receive at baptism,' and again, 'When you have undergone the sacramental birth of baptism in this way . . .'[52] Baptism and the seal are so far one that together they constitute the sacramental birth of baptism.

With regard to the second question, why Theodore differs from his contemporary, Chrysostom, in having a post-baptismal sealing, there is a problem difficult to resolve. Theodore must have delivered his homilies after the year 381 because in *Rom.* 9 there is a reference to the Council of Constantinople. It is not so easily proved that they belong to the period when he was a priest in Antioch—a period which ended in 392 when he became bishop of Mopsuestia. Tonneau thought it probable that the lectures were given in Antioch, on the ground that certain points in the ritual of baptism presupposed that there were available resources of clerical personnel such as only a big city could provide.[53] Altaner[54] favoured a date between 388 and 392, while Theodore was still in Antioch. We have, therefore, to reckon with the possibility that Chrysostom and Theodore delivered their baptismal addresses in the same city and almost in the same year. Yet one mentioned a sealing after baptism and the other did not.

Yarnold solved this problem by supposing that Theodore's more complex rite represents a later stage in the evolution of the Antiochene rite than Chrysostom's.[55] If this were so, then on the assumption that Chrysostom delivered his instructions in 388 and 390 and that Theodore went to Mopsuestia in 392, the latter must have given his addresses in 391 or within a few months of that year, and the post-baptismal sealing which he attests must have been introduced into the Antiochene rite that very year. But although all innovations have to have a beginning in time, there is one factor that has to be taken into account, namely, that Theodore professed to be giving instructions about a rite which, at any rate in part, was performed according to ancient tradition, and which must consequently antedate Chrysostom's lectures.

Another possible solution to the problem is to suppose that Chrysostom's account of initiation is incomplete, having omitted all mention of a post-baptismal sealing—and we have already noticed the insuperable difficulties which this would encounter. Or we could suppose that Theodore's inclusion of a sealing after baptism is a later interpolation into his text. Siman favoured this latter possibility on the ground that there is no anointing after baptism in the homilies of Narsai, who made considerable use of Theodore's lectures.[56] Mitchell (pp. 41f) also supported the hypothesis of a later interpolation on the ground that Theodore's post-baptismal sealing reads like a doublet of the pre-baptismal sealing. In support of his view he quoted the opinion of Mgr Gabriel Khouri-Sarkis, who believed that the post-baptismal sealing was introduced into Theodore's text in the sixth century when Theodore's work was translated from Greek into Syriac.

Rejecting this solution as too arbitrary, Yarnold[57] argued that, if a later translator had interpolated the post-baptismal sealing in order to make Theodore's rite conform more closely with the then contemporary usage, he would surely have made it clearer than he has that there was an actual anointing at this sealing, and that it conveyed the Holy Spirit. Brock[58] also thought Mitchell's theory improbable, because all commentators from the area of Antioch later than Theodore are consistent in their attestation of an anointing after baptism. Again, if Mitchell were right, then Theodore's words, 'Then you come up out of the font to receive the completion of the mystery', would be left with nothing to which they could refer.[59] In short, while one of the attempted solutions to this problem may be right, none of them is free from all objection.

Another distinguished member of the Antiochene school, and a renowned biblical exegete, was Theodoret, born about 390, a student under Theodore of Mopsuestia, who became bishop of Cyrus about 420. While his works, therefore, belong to the generation after Chrysostom and Theodore, his doctrine concerning initiation has a close affinity with theirs.

That somewhere in the course of the initiatory rite there was an unction which conferred the gift of the Holy Spirit is made abundantly clear in this passage:

> If you care for a more mystical meaning, remind yourself of the sacred initiation, in which those who are being initiated, after the renunciation of the usurper and the confession of the King, receive as it were a kind of royal seal, the unction of the spiritual ointment, receiving in the ointment as a figure the invisible graces of the most Holy Spirit.[60]

The fact that this anointing is said to come after the renunciation of Satan and the declaration of adherence to Christ, and the further fact that it included a sealing, serve to identify it with the pre-baptismal unction described by Chrysostom and Theodore. More clearly than either of them, Theodoret said that this anointing conferred the gift of the Holy Spirit.

To this unction Theodoret applied St Paul's words in 2 Cor. 1.21f: 'God is the author of these good things. For it is he who gave us a firm faith in Christ: he it is who anointed us, and granted us the seal of the all Holy Spirit, conferring this grace as a kind of firstfruits of good things to come.'[61] Theodoret, therefore, must be included among those Syrian authorities who believed that the pre-baptismal unction and sealing had the purpose of conferring the Holy Spirit.

But although he interpreted this unction in this way, Theodoret did not so restrict the giving of the Spirit to it as to preclude any giving of the Spirit at the moment of baptism itself. Like Chrysostom, Theodoret believed that John the Baptist in baptizing our Lord laid a hand upon his head, and saw some spiritual significance in this action: 'And in fact Christ our Master also . . . came to John's baptism and ordered the servant's hand to be placed upon his head, and showed the most holy Spirit coming on him in the form of a dove.'[62] This needs to be borne in mind when we consider Theodoret's commentary on Heb. 6.2: 'Those who have believed . . . come to baptism, and through the priestly hand receive the grace of the Spirit . . .' It would seem that the mention of the priestly hand refers to the laying on of the officiant's hand in the act of baptizing. In this way Theodoret could treat the hand-laying in Heb. 6.2 as the normal means by which the Holy Spirit was received in apostolic times and yet find nothing incongruous with this in the practice of his own church.

Like other Syrian writers, Theodoret believed that the Holy Spirit was received both in baptism and in the unction which preceded it. The rite of initiation as a whole 'not only grants remission of past sins, but also confers the hope of the good things which have been promised, and makes us sharers in the Lord's death and resurrection, and bestows participation in the gift of the Spirit and shows us to be sons of God.'[63] Although some of the blessings here enumerated are obviously connected with baptism itself, the giving of the Spirit according to the Syrians did not have to be confined strictly to one moment in the rite. In this they differed from the Fathers of the West who, while by no means denying the activity of the Holy Spirit at the font, tended to find one moment in the complex rite of initiation with which specially to link the giving of the Spirit.

Theodoret's references to anointing do not require us to suppose that he knew of a second anointing after baptism.

8 *The Significance of the Syrian Rite*

The significance of the Syrian rite of initiation, conspicuous for its lack of anything corresponding to what the West knows as confirmation, depends very largely on the view taken of its antiquity, whether it shows us the original pattern of Christian initiation.

Traces of an initiatory rite of the Syrian pattern are, it has been alleged, to be found in Christian literature of a very early date. For instance, in the *Testament of Levi*, dated by de Jonge between 190 and 225,[1] there is a Christian interpolation of which the relevant words are: 'From henceforth become a priest of the Lord, thou and thy seed for ever. And the first anointed me with holy oil, and gave to me the rod of judgment, the second washed me with pure water, and fed me with bread and wine, the most holy things, and clad me with a holy and glorious robe . . .'[2] Although the writer is describing the installation of the high priest, it is accepted by de Jonge, Manson,[3] and Siman[4] that here is in fact a description of the contemporary rite of initiation, which is seen to consist in an anointing with holy oil, a washing in water, and the eucharist. While this is the Syrian sequence of events, nothing can be inferred from this about the meaning attached to the unction and the baptism. The value of this piece of evidence would be much greater if we could be sure of the date of the interpolation, which could be much later than the original work.

Secondly, in the *Clementine Recognitions*, a fourth-century work derived mainly from a Syrian romance with a date in the third century,[5] there is found this statement put into the mouth of St Peter: 'But every one of you shall be baptized in ever flowing waters, the name of the Trine beatitude being invoked over him; he being first anointed with oil sanctified by prayer, that so at length, being consecrated by these things he may attain a perception of holy things.'[6] When these last words are translated, as they should be, 'that he may partake of holy things,' a reference to the eucharist becomes apparent. Once more the only unction mentioned at all is an unction with holy oil before baptism. Whether this baptism was mentioned in the original document is uncertain, because it is not found in the parallel *Clementine Homilies*.

Neither of these pieces of evidence takes us further back than the early third century, if as far; and while they provide evidence of the Syrian pattern of initiation, they contribute nothing to our understanding of its doctrine.

Thirdly, Dix[7] cited from the *Epistle of the Apostles*, a work which he believed to have emanated from Asia Minor *c.* 160 or even earlier, this brief sentence, 'Whosoever shall hear you and believe on me, shall receive of you the light of the seal through me and baptism through me.'[8] Here the seal is mentioned before baptism. But, as we have seen, in the second century the seal was a term with more than one meaning; and we cannot be sure that here the author meant a pre-baptismal anointing with chrism which conferred the Holy Spirit.

Dix went further still, claiming that there are signs of the Syrian pattern even in the New Testament itself. Thus in 1 Cor. 10.1f baptism in the cloud and in the sea seemed to him to represent the baptism of the Spirit and baptism in water respectively, the baptism of the Spirit being mentioned first. Now even assuming that his exegesis is correct, Dix's argument turns on the point that St Paul mentioned the cloud before the sea. But this is hardly proof that the Pauline rite of baptism included before the actual baptism a ceremony for the conferring of the Spirit. If it be asked why the apostle mentioned the cloud before the sea, the most probable reason is not that his thinking was influenced by his knowledge of the rite of initiation which he used, but simply that as a matter of historical fact the Israelites passed under the cloud before they entered the Red Sea. To read any more into St Paul's order of words is to stray into the realms of fancy.

Mason[9] argued that there was some connection between 1 John 5.8 and the Syrian order of initiation. In that text are mentioned successively the Spirit, the water, and the blood. From this Manson concluded that, since the water and the blood corresponded with the laver and the chalice, the Spirit probably pointed to a ritual anointing, a physical *chrisma*. Hence in 1 John 5.8 there may be a reference to the gift of the Spirit in an act of anointing, followed by baptism in water and the eucharist, the three events being mentioned, it will be seen, in the Syrian order.

Manson's case, however, though sympathetically received by Daniélou,[10] is as interesting as it is uncertain. Although any claim to have discovered the correct meaning of this notoriously difficult text deserves a generous reception, it rests upon a precarious foundation. If water and blood are material objects, and 'the Spirit' in fact denotes a physical unction, it is hard to see why St John did not write 'the oil and the water and the blood', consistently mentioning the material element in each instance. If Manson's argument is valid, then it is applicable to other texts in the Johannine writings. As Couratin[11] has pointed out, his argument would also prove that in John 3.5, 'born again of water and the Spirit', the anointing, if any, occurred simultaneously with the baptism or after it. Similarly the statement in John 19.34 that blood and water came from our Lord's side would prove that the eucharist preceded baptism.

In this connection Daniélou cited a point made by Kretschmar that in the Acts of the Apostles Cornelius received the Holy Spirit before his baptism, as also did Saul of Tarsus, if the purpose of the hand-laying which he received from Ananias was not only to restore his sight but also to confer the Spirit. Saul's initiation, it may be noticed, took place in Syria. But there is no doubt that the evidence of Acts as a whole points to the conclusion that the Holy Spirit was normally received either at the moment of baptism or at the laying on of hands after baptism.

Another argument in favour of the priority of the Syrian pattern of initiation was based upon the rite by which proselytes were admitted into Judaism. In the Babylonian *Talmud*[12] and in the tractate *Gerim* there are accounts of a rite in which a proselyte was examined, instructed, circumcised, and baptized, after which he offered a sacrifice. While these works belong to the second century A.D., they are commonly supposed to describe a practice which dates back to the pre-Christian era, although this has been denied by Zeitlin[13] and Beasley Murray.[14] Accepting the view that the Jewish proselyte baptism was prior to Christian baptism, Dix considered that the Jewish sequence consisting in the seal of circumcision, baptism, and the offering of sacrifice was imitated by the Church, which at the outset had an initiatory rite consisting in the seal of the Spirit conveyed by an anointing, baptism in water, and communion.[15] Hence, he maintained, the Syrian pattern was the original, although it was soon abandoned in many parts of the church.

There are, however, weaknesses in Dix's case. First of all, although Jewish precedents are likely to have exerted some influence upon the Christian sacraments, and although Gavin[16] has shown the points of similarity between the rite of initiation for proselytes and the rites in the *Didache* and the *Apostolic Tradition*, there still remain, as Lampe (pp. 83–7) has shown, notable differences between the Jewish and the Christian rites; and the similarities between the two are not so close as to prove that the Christian Church must have borrowed the order and structure of its rite from contemporary Judaism.

Secondly, Dix was on uncertain ground when he contended that there was a close parallel between Jewish circumcision and Christian confirmation, on the ground that the term 'seal' was applied to them both. By confirmation Dix meant the seal of the Spirit conveyed to Christian converts at their initiation by an act of anointing with chrism before baptism. But, as we have seen, in early Christian literature the seal did not always have the same meaning, and it did not always signify the giving of the Spirit. Again, even if the Church borrowed from Judaism the practice of anointing, such references as there are in the New Testament to anointing in the context of initiation throw no light whatever on the question whether the anointing, if any, took place before or after baptism. Furthermore the argument that Jews were in the habit of anointing themselves after taking a bath, if it proved anything, would prove that the Church anointed its initiates after their actual baptism.

For these reasons the case that the Syrian type of initiation rite was the original type generally observed in the first age of the church must be regarded as unproven.[17] If it had been the original order everywhere, we should have expected it to have left traces in other parts of the church besides Syria, whereas the extant evidence comes from one area, much of it from countries outside the Roman empire, where the language spoken was Syriac. Yet, since the Syrian pattern was peculiar to one area, Manson[18] took this as evidence that a difference of this magnitude was more likely to be a survival than an innovation. On the other hand Crehan[19] suggested that the Syrian Churches, influenced by the ritual for the cleansing of lepers, deliberately rearranged the order of events in the baptismal liturgy, though, if we agree with him thus far, we may prefer to stop short of condemning this revision as an aberration.

Now whatever the origin of the Syrian rite of initiation with its notable difference from the Western rites, it was eventually revised by the addition of a post-baptismal anointing which brought it into line with the rite of Jerusalem, and which could, though perhaps it should not be, regarded by a Western Christian as the Eastern equivalent of confirmation.

If Cyril is the author of the *Mystagogic Catecheses*, then the rite of Jerusalem included a post-baptismal sealing with chrism, which had the purpose of imparting the Holy Spirit, as far back as the year 348. When the rite of Jerusalem first acquired this ceremony and whence it derived it, are subjects for speculation. Its intention of conferring the Holy Spirit could be attributed to Western influence: but the anointing itself is not Western. Unless we assume that the rite of Jerusalem must originally have been of the Syrian pattern, we are not precluded from believing that Cyril's post-baptismal chrismation was by no means new when he delivered his lectures.

Canon 48 of the council of Laodicea ordered that those being enlightened must after the baptism be anointed with heavenly chrism and become sharers in the kingdom of Christ.[20] It is to be noticed that the chrismation which is now made mandatory is not said to confer the gift of the Holy Spirit. Unfortunately the date of this council is uncertain, Leeming, for instance, dating it between 343 and 381,[21] and Mitchell (p. 54) assigning it to the middle of the fourth century. But it could well be that the influence of this council was responsible for the post-baptismal sealing in the *Apostolic Constitutions*, where also there is no suggestion that it conferred the gift of the Holy Spirit.

About the year 500 there appeared the well known and influential work *On the Ecclesiastical Hierarchy* by Pseudo-Dionysius Areopagiticus, who is generally supposed to have been a Syrian. He described a rite in which baptism and the vesting in white robes were followed by an unction:

> But the perfecting unction of the muron makes the man initiated of good odour, for the holy perfecting of the Divine birth unites those who have been perfected to the supremely Divine Spirit. Now the overshadowing which makes intelligibly of a good savour, and perfect, as being most unutterable, I leave to the mental consciousness of those who are deemed worthy of the sacred and deifying participation of the Holy Spirit within their minds.[22]

Siman[23] quotes three of the *Canons of the Holy Fathers*, issued between 532 and 538, of which *c.* 57 ordered that 'those who have been baptized by priests and have not been sealed with the holy *muron*, should be perfected by the seal of the *muron*, with the prayer that is made over those who are sealed.' Raes[24] has cited evidence of an East Syrian rite of initiation in which baptism was followed by an imposition of hands on each candidate, a sealing with oil and a collective hand-laying. The introduction of these acts is attributed to Icho-yabh III, who was patriarch from 650 to 658, and who, as Connolly[25] observed, had travelled in the West.

Western Christians naturally ask with Raes, 'Where is confirmation to be found in the East Syrian rite?' Raes felt that after the reform of Icho-yabh III the East Syrians could be said to have had a rite of confirmation.[26] Lécuyer thought that the baptismal hand-laying commented upon by Chrysostom was the Syrian form of confirmation.[27] Siman,[28] however, doubted whether Raes' question could properly be asked of the Syrians. If the Western church had one ceremony in its rite of initiation which was specially related to the giving of the Holy Spirit, it is clear that the Syrian church in the third and fourth centuries had no such single ceremony. For while we have the evidence of the *Didascalia*, Ephraem, Aphraates, Narsai, Chrysostom, Theodore, and Theodoret that there was a giving of the Holy Spirit at the moment of baptism, there is also evidence that Ephraem, Narsai, Theodoret, the editor of the *Apostolic Constitutions*, and probably also Chrysostom and the Didascaliast, believed that there was also a giving of the Holy Spirit at the pre-baptismal unction, which is not to be explained in terms of exorcism; and Ephraem,

Narsai, Chrysostom, and Theodore taught that there was also a giving of the Holy Spirit in holy communion. The Holy Spirit was active and bestowed himself on the initiates throughout the rite from the pre-baptismal anointing to the concluding eucharist. It follows from this that the practice of the early Syrian Church cannot rightly be cited in support of the thesis that baptism in water is the complete rite of Christian initiation.

9 *The Emergence of Confirmation*

In the days of Tertullian, Hippolytus, and Ambrose the Church had no rite called confirmation. The sealing with chrism and the hand-laying which came after baptism itself, and which we regard as confirmation, were then integral parts of the rite of baptism. These acts were closely associated with the giving of the Holy Spirit; and it was probably largely for this reason that only a bishop was allowed to administer them. So when initiation took place at Easter in the bishop's church, as was the norm, the bishop would be present in person to perform those parts of the rite which were his special prerogative.

But soon there arose situations which, though abnormal in principle, were of ever more frequent occurrence as the Church expanded, when baptism was required in circumstances which made the presence of a bishop very improbable, if not impossible. One such situation was the initiation of persons who suddenly became dangerously ill, and who, it was thought, must not be allowed to die unbaptized.

With regard to the visitation of the sick, Hippolytus said that it was the duty of deacons and subdeacons to wait upon the bishop and report to him those that were ill, so that he might visit them, because 'the sick man is much comforted that the high priest remembered him.'[1] All that may be legitimately inferred from this statement is that when his subordinates told him of cases of illness the bishop visited them and prayed with them. But supposing his deacons informed him of a catechumen suddenly taken ill or of an infant born to faithful members of his church and not expected to survive, did he merely pray with them, or did he also baptize them? We do not know for certain the answer to that question. But if he baptized them at all, there is no reason to suppose that he did not also lay his hand upon them and anoint them with chrism. However, as the Church grew in numbers and spread outwards from the place where the bishop resided, there would be many more instances when adult catechumens or the infant children of churchpeople were taken seriously ill, and were not within easy reach of a bishop. Hence as soon as it was generally felt that persons in extremis, adult or infant, should not be allowed to die unbaptized, there arose the need to baptize in haste without any chance of securing the presence of a bishop; consequently where and when the rule that only bishops might perform the hand-laying and chrismation was strictly enforced, these ceremonies had to be omitted from the baptism.

But not all those who were baptized in sudden emergency died almost at once. What was supposed to happen in the case of those who recovered is shown in the well known case of Novatian who, when he was thought to be at the point of death, was baptized by aspersion on his bed of sickness, but who on his recovery did not receive the other things which he ought to have received, and was not sealed by a bishop.[2] Evidently if Novatian had followed the correct procedure, he would have received the episcopal anointing missing from his baptism at the earliest opportunity after his restoration to health. An interval of time there had to be between his baptism and his anointing: but the interval was meant to be as short as possible.

In the middle of the third century a contemporary of Cyprian, the unknown Roman author of the tract de Rebaptismate, asked whether or not salvation had been received by the person who had not been baptized by a bishop, and consequently had not received the laying on of his hand, and who had died before he could receive the Holy Spirit.[3] If the person in question had been presented for baptism at the Paschal initiation in the bishop's church, he would obviously have been baptized and also received the Holy Spirit through the imposition of the bishop's hand. We are not told whether this person had been baptized in the absence of a bishop because he had suddenly fallen ill, or because he lived too far away from the bishop's church.

Writing in the second half of the fourth century, when the Church had greatly increased in numbers and many of its members lived in remote rural areas, Jerome said that according to the custom of the churches the bishop hastened to invoke the Spirit and lay his hand upon those baptized by presbyters or deacons far from the bigger cities; 'if only at the invocation of a bishop does the Holy Spirit descend, they are to be mourned who have been baptized by presbyters and deacons in villages and hamlets and in the more distant places, and have fallen asleep before they could be visited by bishops.[4] It seems, therefore, that at this time a bishop with a large diocese would go on tour in order to lay his hand on those whom his presbyters at work in the countryside far from the see city had baptized in his absence. The reason given for this is not that these persons had had to be baptized in haste because of illness, but that they lived far away from the bishop. So even if these persons had been baptized at Easter, the hand-laying would of necessity have been omitted.

The early fourth-century council of Elvira in Spain issued two canons which throw further light on this subject. Canon 38 permitted a faithful layman to baptize a catechumen taken ill at sea or far from a church, with the proviso that if the sick person recovered he must be taken to a bishop to be perfected by the imposition of his hand; and canon 77 required that, if a deacon in charge of a congregation baptized people in the absence of a bishop or a presbyter, the bishop must perfect them with his blessing.[5]

In 385 pope Siricius, without intending to imply that Easter was not the proper season for baptism, expressed the wish that infants and those whose lives are in danger should be baptized with all haste, lest any of them dying unbaptized should be excluded from the kingdom and from life.[6] Not many years later, Innocent I said that there was not a day which did not witness the divine sacrifice and the office of baptism.[7] Even when some allowance is made for exaggeration, it is clear from this that baptisms now took place with great frequency throughout the year; but since the proper seasons for baptism were Easter and Pentecost, these baptisms must have been those of sick persons who could not be reserved without risk for the next solemn initiation at the customary seasons. Clinical baptism was now required so often that an episcopal presence at more than a very few of them is highly unlikely. Since, however, a number of those baptized in emergency may be presumed to have recovered, there must have been many occasions when the bishop's hand-laying and chrismation were administered separately some time after the baptism.

About the year 500 John the Deacon in Rome had to answer a question addressed to him by Senarius, 'whether or not it is any disadvantage to a man, if after having been baptized he should depart this life without the anointing of chrism and the blessing of the pontiff?'[8] While there is nothing in Senarius' question to indicate the age of this person, John's answer indicates that he had in mind the initiation of infants, because in his reply he said that, when an infant had been born and seen the light of this world, it was said that there had been born a perfect man, of the same substance as that of the father who begat him. By this time the population of Rome was almost entirely Christian, and it was accepted that the children of Christian parents must be baptized in infancy. Consequently the supply of adult catechumens had virtually come to an end. Therefore those who were baptized without the anointing of chrism and the bishop's blessing must have been almost entirely the newly born children of the faithful, born with slim hope of survival. When the size of the population of Rome and the infant mortality rate in those days are taken into account, it is evident that neither the pope nor his suffragans would have had the time to attend the many baptisms which now had to be administered with the utmost haste, the bishop's hand-laying and chrismation being received at a later date in the cases of those who recovered from their sickness.

So far, although the bishop's hand-laying and sealing with chrism are frequently separated in time from baptism, they have not acquired the title of confirmation. For the origin of this term we have to go to southern Gaul in the fifth century.

The council of Riez in 439, deciding that the appointment of Armentarius to the see of Embrun was canonically irregular, deposed him without, however, reducing him to the rank of a simple presbyter; he could be placed in charge of a parish so long as it was not in the province of Maritime Alps, of which Embrun was the principal city; and this parish had to be in a village or small town. He was given the status of a *chorepiscopus* or country bishop. Among the episcopal privileges which he was allowed to retain was that of 'confirming neophytes'. But while he could perform this latter function in his rural parish, he was expressly forbidden ever to perform it in the see city or in a large town. Three times, twice in the third canon and once in the fourth, explicit reference was made to the right of confirming neophytes. 'To confirm' is therefore evidently an expression with a meaning already well understood in this part of southern Gaul.[9] Thus by the year 439 the expression 'confirming neophytes' referred to a post-baptismal ceremony normally performed by a bishop, although it could be delegated to a *chorepiscopus*.

At the council of Orange in 441 there assembled bishops from seventeen dioceses, all but one of them in south-eastern Gaul. The second canon issued by this council is as important as it is difficult to interpret.[10] It has been translated by Whitaker (p. 228) thus:

> No minister who has the office of baptizing shall begin without chrism: for it was agreed among us that there shall be one chrismation (in baptism). When anyone for any reason does not receive chrism in baptism, the bishop (*sacerdos*) shall be advised of this at the confirmation. For chrism can only confer its blessing once: and we say this not to any man's prejudice, but that the repetition of chrismation should not be thought necessary.

The first clause of this canon, however, really deals with the matter of the clergy being without chrism, not when they began the office of baptism but when they set out on their pastoral visitations.

The point which exercised the mind of this council was that there should not be more than one act of chrismation in the whole process of initiation. In order to see how this practice of a double chrismation originated it is necessary to consider the pastoral situation envisaged by the canon. The ministers to whom the office of baptizing had been entrusted were presbyters or deacons in charge of rural parishes. When they baptized it was necessarily in the absence of the bishop; and when some time later the bishop completed the baptism with the laying on of his hand, he might anoint with chrism at the same time, thinking, sometimes no doubt mistakenly, that there had been no chrismation at the baptism. The second canon of this council began by forbidding the rural clergy from setting out anywhere without carrying chrism with them. The visitations here alluded to were to chapels in little villages or hamlets without a resident cleric. That this was sometimes the case is shown in canon 21 of the council of Agde, which mentioned an *orarium in agro*.[11] The ruling made in this canon is pointless unless some of the rural clergy had in fact baptized in these remote places without also using chrism. Possibly, as Van Buchem (p. 103) has suggested, they were careless in this matter because they calculated that in any event the bishop would anoint with chrism when later he confirmed those whom they had baptized. On the other hand, if they did in fact also anoint with chrism when they baptized, the bishop, unaware of this, might perform a second chrismation when he confirmed.

The bishops at Orange clearly intended to maintain the Gallican custom of a single chrismation in initiation. Their action had the effect of securing that the one chrismation would always be administered at baptism, and not at the subsequent confirmation, which thereby became a simple act of hand-laying with prayer. Hence baptism, even when administered in the absence of a bishop, was not a simple rite of baptism in water but was always accompanied by an act of chrismation performed by the baptizing presbyter. Although the bishops at Orange were determined that chrismation should not be repeated, they were equally determined that it should not be omitted from baptism. Because their canon was concerned with practice, we are not told whether there was a doctrinal reason for their insistence that the baptism should always be accompanied by chrismation; but their very insistence suggests that this was the case.

Thirteen bishops from southern Gaul attended the third council of Arles, dated between 449 and 461.[12] The question which they had to settle concerned the relationship between the bishop of Fréjus and the abbot of Lérins. With regard to the rights of the former it was laid down that *inter alia* the chrism should be obtained only from him and that neophytes should be confirmed only by him.[13] This latter function, therefore, could not be performed by the abbot of Lérins but was reserved to the episcopate. Moreover since the council claimed to be reiterating decisions made by Leontius, who was bishop of Fréjus from 426 till 433, we have evidence that the episcopal confirmation of neophytes in a rite of hand-laying separate from baptism was known in southern Gaul some ten years before the council of Orange.

So far we have confined our attention to the evidence provided by a number of councils in southern Gaul. With this evidence must be compared that supplied by two authors who belong to this period and to the same region, Salvian and Gennadius, both presbyters of Marseilles.

A few years after the council of Riez, Salvian wrote:

> Perhaps it is asked what are the good things which God allots to Christian men. What, indeed, but all those things which we believe, that is, by which we are Christians? First the Law, then the prophets, thirdly the Gospel, fourthly the apostolic writings, lastly the gift of a new generation, the grace of holy baptism, the anointing of the divine chrism.[14]

In a context such as this Salvian presumably had in mind the norm, that is, initiation as administered in the see city at one of the baptismal seasons. Yet he mentioned neither hand-laying nor the gift of the Holy Spirit.

While there is no hint as to the age of the baptized, Salvian later on in the same work referred to the renunciation of Satan and the confession of the faith in terms which suggest that the candidates were old enough to perform these acts in person.[15] Although it is probable that by this time many infants were admitted to baptism, it would be wrong to conclude that southern Gaul had been so thoroughly converted that there were no longer any adult converts to be baptized. Indeed it is known that Salvian married a woman whose parents at the time of the wedding were both pagans. Hence the persons whom the councils of Riez and Orange show to have been baptized in the country were not necessarily all of them newly born infants. Finally it may be noticed that, as Salvian did not use the word 'confirm', so also he was not dealing with initiation in the countryside.

Gennadius (c. 470) drew a comparison between the catechumen and the martyr:

> The candidate for baptism confesses his faith before the bishop, and answers to his questions: this the martyr does before the persecutor, both confessing his faith and answering the questions. He, after his confession, is either sprinkled with water or plunged in it: the martyr is either sprinkled with blood or bathed in fire. He, by the imposition of the hand of the pontiff, receives the Holy Spirit, the other is made the dwelling place of the Holy Spirit, inasmuch as it is not he that speaks but the Spirit of the Father which speaks in him. The former partakes of the eucharist in commemoration of the Lord's death: the latter dies with Christ himself.[16]

Here is evidence of an undivided rite of initiation consisting in renunciation of Satan, confession of the faith, baptism in water, laying on of the hand, and communion. If the candidates for initiation were infants, the comparison with the martyr would lose its point; and in fact Gennadius assumed that they were old enough to renounce Satan and confess the faith in person. Gennadius, like Salvian, was describing the norm, the rite of initiation as it was celebrated in the see city with the bishop presiding. It is to be noted that, as he was not talking about initiation in the countryside, so he did not use the term 'confirmation'.

Whereas Salvian mentioned after baptism only an unction, Gennadius mentioned only a hand-laying; but Van Buchem (pp. 122f) is probably right in supposing that each writer knew both these ceremonies but saw no need to mention both. Since, however, there were no persecutions or martyrdoms in Gaul in the time of Gennadius, it would seem that in the passage just quoted he had in mind the conditions of a former age. Yet if by his time most of the candidates for initiation were in fact infants, the ceremonies in which the rite consisted probably remained unchanged.

Whereas in this passage Gennadius did not use the word 'confirm', he did use it in chapter 52 of the same work, where he was dealing with the reception of heretics into the church:

> Any who have been baptized among those heretics who baptize in the confession of the Holy Trinity, and then come to us, are to be received indeed as baptized, lest the invocation or confession of the Holy Trinity should be annulled; but they must be taught afresh, and instructed in what sense the mystery of the Holy Trinity is held in the church: and if they agree to believe it, or are willing to confess it, being now purified by integrity of faith, they should be confirmed by the imposition of the hand. But if they are little children, or dull of comprehension, and unable to take in doctrine, those who present them, according to the custom of baptism, answer for them; and so being fortified by the imposition of the hand and chrism, they are admitted to the eucharistic mysteries.

Here there is every reason to believe that Gennadius was referring to contemporary practice. Here, too, although the subject under discussion was the reception of heretics rather than ordinary initiation, it would seem that there was a close resemblance between this form for the reception of heretics and the post-baptismal ceremonies in the initiatory rite normally used in southern Gaul at this time.

Finally, Gennadius' observations apply to initiation in the see city where a bishop was present, and consequently none of the rite had to be deferred, and there was no need for episcopal 'confirmation' at a later date.

The information about confirmation in southern Gaul supplied by the councils of Riez, Orange, and Arles, and by Salvian and Gennadius, is rather overshadowed by that found in a Whitsun sermon which was destined to be much quoted in later centuries. Although the preacher, formerly known as Pseudo-Eusebius of Emesa, could not for a long time be identified, it is now generally accepted that he was in fact Faustus of Riez, a bishop in southern Gaul in the later fifth century and a prominent exponent of the doctrine of grace which has been labelled Semi-Pelagian.[17]

Since this sermon was delivered when Faustus was bishop of Riez, it must be dated after the third council of Arles (c. 449–461), because at that time he was abbot of Lérins. The text of the sermon was 'In those days, says the Lord, I will pour out of my Spirit upon all flesh' which, being probably from the lections for Pentecost, indicates that the sermon was preached at that feast.

Faustus' main purpose in his sermon was not to give a full exposition of the doctrine of confirmation as such, but to relate the grace of confirmation with the grace of baptism, and to show why those who had been baptized still needed to be confirmed by the bishop. The sermon began thus:

Let us mark the riches of the supreme goodness. What now, in the confirmation of neophytes, the imposition of the hand confers on each, the descent of the Holy Spirit on the congregation of the believers then conveyed to all. But because we have said that the laying on of the hand and confirmation are able to give something to him who has already been born again in Christ, perhaps somebody thinks to himself, 'What can it profit me after the mystery of baptism to have the ministration of some one to confirm me?' So far as I can see, we have not obtained everything at the font, if after the font we yet need something extra of a new kind. That is not so, beloved brothers; listen to me.[18]

The point raised here is different from that raised in the second canon of the council of Orange. There it was a question of ensuring that there was only one chrismation during the process of initiation, and that that one chrismation took place at baptism, not at the subsequent laying on of the bishop's hand. Here it is a matter of finding a compelling reason for having the episcopal hand-laying at all. The words which Faustus put into the mouth of an imaginary questioner suggest that there were those in southern Gaul who thought that the presbyteral baptism and anointing constituted a full initiation, and saw no point in the ministration of the bishop. We may wonder whether they believed the chrismation to confer the Holy Spirit.

Secondly, in these opening words of his sermon Faustus showed that confirmation consisted in a hand-laying only, received some time after baptism. Moreover, this sermon was almost certainly preached in the bishop's own church in Riez itself, because Van Buchem (pp. 119f) has adduced evidence to show that the bishop was required to officiate in his own church at Pentecost. For instance, the council of Agde in 506 ordered the clergy on certain great festivals, including Pentecost, to assist at the eucharist only in the see church or in the parish churches.[19] Again, the council of Clermont en Auvergne required the clergy to celebrate some great festivals, including Pentecost, with their bishop in the see church[20]; and the council of Orleans in 551 forbade the bishops to observe certain feasts in the country. Evidently, therefore, at the festival of Pentecost bishops were expected to celebrate the eucharist in the see city; furthermore, since its text came from one of the eucharistic lections for Pentecost, it seems highly probable that Faustus preached his sermon at the eucharist at Pentecost in Riez. In addition, since the sermon was concerned with the importance of the bishop's hand-laying and its relation to baptism, it may reasonably be supposed that shortly before he preached that sermon Faustus had administered confirmation, and that in his see church.

We do not know who were the persons on whom Faustus laid his hand on the occasion of his sermon. As Faustus' argument implies an interval of time between the hand-laying and the baptism, they cannot have been baptized on the same day. Perhaps they were persons who lived a little way from Riez and had been baptized and anointed by their parish priests some time previously. Nor does it follow that, because on this occasion Faustus confirmed at Pentecost, he never confirmed at other times also

Faustus' sermon is of interest for five reasons. First, it represents, so far as we know, the first serious attempt to work out a theology of initiation based upon a disintegrated rite. The Fathers before him and others after him founded their doctrine on the assumption that in principle baptism and 'confirmation', normally administered together, formed a single and coherent whole. Hence, if they expressed the view that the Holy Spirit was given in that part of the baptismal complex now known as confirmation, they were not *ipso facto* denying that he was given in baptism. Faustus, however, faced with a situation where baptism and confirmation were commonly separated in time, was obliged to explain what confirmation by itself conferred. This problem has remained with the churches of the West ever since.

Secondly, from the time of Faustus in the later fifth century it becomes permissible to use the term 'confirmation' in its present liturgical sense. Up to this time to use this word of the ceremonies which followed baptism in water is something of an anachronism; and it obscures the organic unity which the Western rites of initiation originally possessed.

Thirdly, this rite of confirmation was unusual in that it consisted in a single act of hand-laying without any anointing. The Roman rite as found in Hippolytus and the *Gelasian Sacramentary*, while including the imposition of the hand among the post-baptismal ceremonies, laid greater emphasis on the sealing of the forehead with chrism which accompanied it. The practice of confirming by hand-laying only was peculiar to southern Gaul, and came to an end there at the latest by the closing years of the eighth century when Charlemagne ordered the use of the Roman rite throughout his empire.[21] This had the effect of undoing the decision taken at Orange that there should be only one chrismation in initiation, because the Roman rite included two unctions after baptism, the first by a presbyter and the second by a bishop. Since, however, the Roman rite required the presence of a bishop to perform the hand-laying and second anointing, Charlemagne's order caused throughout his dominions the same separation of confirmation from baptism that we have seen in southern Gaul over three hundred years before.

Fourthly, in view of the later tendency to interpret confirmation solely in terms of strengthening, it is important to notice the meaning which Faustus attributed to the word. There are two places in his sermon where it is quite evident that for him 'to confirm' was not synonymous with 'to strengthen'. First, when he wished to say that after baptism we are strengthened, he used a different word, *roboramur*. Secondly, when he said that a baptized person who died in a state of innocence but unconfirmed was confirmed by death, 'confirmed' cannot possibly mean 'strengthened'. The meaning must be that the baptism which could not be completed or consummated in the normal way by confirmation was completed by death. Leo I wrote in 458 that, when persons whose only baptism had been in a heretical sect wished to be received into the Catholic Church, they were to be confirmed only with the invocation of the Holy Spirit through the laying on of hands, meaning that they were not to be baptized again, but their imperfect baptism was to be perfected by hand-laying and the invocation of the Holy Spirit; so their membership of the Catholic Church would be established and sealed.[22] Similarly the episcopal confirmation mentioned in canon 2 of the council of Orange refers to that part of the initiatory rite which had to be omitted when presbyters baptized in the absence of a bishop: the subsequent confirmation supplied what was lacking, completing what was otherwise a deficient initiation. So in the fifth century, when the words *confirmare* and *confirmatio* first came into use in connection with initiation, confirmation meant not just strengthening but completing, perfecting, or consummating.

Fifthly, in the middle ages when confirmation emerged as a sacrament in its own right, detached from baptism, Faustus' doctrine of confirmation was found useful by medieval theologians because it took such a situation into account. But it is strange how this came about. In the middle of the ninth century Pseudo-Isidore, the anonymous compiler of the *False Decretals*, took parts of Faustus' sermon and attributed them to Melchiades and Urban I, popes who lived before the peace of the church, one of whom was believed to have perished in the persecution in the early fourth century. Taken in by the deception, many of the leading authorities in the middle ages quoted Melchiades or Urban, when in fact they were quoting Faustus, believing that this teaching about confirmation came from the remote past, from the highest authority in Rome, even from the pen of a holy martyr. It is doubtful whether Faustus' sermon would have become so famous if all the time the real identity of the preacher had been known.

10 *The Present in the Light of the Past*

A study of confirmation in the age of the Fathers is not of purely antiquarian interest, but is extremely relevant to the debate about Christian initiation that is going on, especially in Anglican circles, today.

In the first place it is quite clear what confirmation originally was not—it had nothing to do with personal confession of the faith by those who had been too young to do this at their baptism: it was not an act of self-commitment.

In Hippolytus' *Apostolic Tradition*, 21, there is a rubric: 'they shall baptize the little children first. And if they can answer for themselves, let them answer. But if they cannot, let the parents answer or someone from their family.' So when it came to the renunciation of Satan and the replies to the baptismal interrogations, the sponsors spoke on behalf of those children who were too young to speak for themselves, and the latter were considered to have renounced Satan and confessed the faith through those who presented them. There is no trace in the *Apostolic Tradition* of a requirement that these children when old enough should do in person what they had done through their proxies at their baptism.

Or again, in the *Gelasian Sacramentary*, the rubrics of which assume that the candidates are infants, there is found the well known ceremony of the *traditio symboli*, in which on a day shortly before Holy Week the candidates were assembled in church to have the creed delivered to them. On the morning of Holy Saturday came the *redditio symboli*, when a priest exorcized the infant candidates, touched their nostrils and ears with spittle, and their breast and back with exorcized oil; addressing each candidate by name, he asked, 'Dost thou renounce Satan? . . . And all his works? . . . And all his pomps?' And each candidate replied through his sponsor, 'I renounce.' Then the priest, laying his hand on their heads, recited the creed.[1] An adult candidate would have said the creed himself, showing that he had assimilated that which had been delivered to him at the *traditio symboli*. But the infants showed that in theory they too had learnt the creed when the priest said it on their behalf. Thus infant candidates confessed the faith before the church through their sponsors. No more than the *Apostolic Tradition* does the *Gelasian Sacramentary* provide an opportunity for these infants, when old enough, to confess their faith in person before the congregation.

It is quite plain that the infants were committed at their baptism. Neither scripture nor early tradition knew of a baptism without commitment. Hence if any service of personal commitment and commissioning were drawn up for adolescents or adults who had been baptized in infancy, and obscured the fact of commitment in baptism itself, this would represent a departure from primitive practice and also from the New Testament.

Nevertheless a rite of personal commitment such as those in the Reformed tradition envisage by confirmation, is a pastoral and theological necessity in the case of all baptized in infancy. But such a rite is not derived from and has nothing in common with the rite which began to be called confirmation in the days of Faustus of Riez.

The sixteenth-century Reformers required those baptized in infancy as they grew older to learn a catechism and to make a public confession of their faith before the church before they could be admitted to communion.[2] This was a great gain because it restored one element that had been lacking from Christian initiation since the introduction of infant baptism. But they regarded this personal confession of the faith as confirmation in its pure and original form,[3] whereas the evidence from the early church proves conclusively that there was then no such confirmation as this.

In the Prayer Book of 1662 the personal affirmation of faith comes at the beginning of the confirmation service, when the bishop invites the candidates, who have already learnt the catechism, to ratify and confirm the promises made in their name at their baptism. This is confirmation as the Reformers understood it. There follows at once the laying on of the bishop's hand with prayer that the candidates may be strengthened with the Holy Spirit of sevenfold grace. This is the traditional confirmation of early times, but with one notable alteration in that the prayer asks not that the Holy Spirit may be sent down upon the candidates, as in the traditional confirmation prayer of the West, but that they may be strengthened by the Spirit whom they have already received in baptism.

At the end of the confirmation service of 1662 comes the well-known rubric forbidding any to be admitted to communion until they have been confirmed or are ready and desirous to be confirmed. The purpose of the rubric was to ensure that ignorant and ill-instructed persons were not given communion. It had the effect of fencing the altar against children who were too young to learn the catechism and older persons who through negligence had not been taught it. In the age of the Fathers, however, the altar was not fenced against any baptized persons, unless they were under ecclesiastical discipline.

Thus the Prayer Book places the personal affirmation of faith with the bishop's hand-laying and before communion, so preserving the ancient sequence of baptism, confirmation, communion. But it does not define the age at which children may be presumed to be eligible for confirmation and so for communion also. Jewel[4] said that children at their confirmation yielded a reason of their faith openly before the whole congregation: 'They professed they would so believe, that they would live and die in that faith.' That is, for Jewel confirmation was a mature profession of faith and an act of lifelong commitment to our Lord. Commenting on the confirmation rubric, Cosin[5] wrote: 'Many can say their catechism, and are confirmed at seven years old; should it be then in the power of the curate to admit them also to the Communion? *Non credo*: but this shows that they should not be confirmed so young as they used to be, but when they are of perfect age, and ready to be admitted to the Holy Communion, which is between fourteen and sixteen years of age.' Now the fact remains that the confession of faith which was the necessary preliminary to baptism in the New Testament was a responsible and mature confession of faith: and such a confession of faith is necessary to the fullness of Christian initiation. Hence if the intention of confirmation is to supply what is lacking in the baptism of infants, then it cannot properly be given to children until they have reached the age of responsibility. Those who have this point in mind can reasonably argue that nobody should be confirmed before the age of seventeen. But those who regard confirmation as a sacramental means of grace naturally feel that this would deprive children for too long of the strengthening gift of the Holy Spirit. The best solution to this problem is to recognize that the conferring of the gift of the Holy Spirit and the mature profession of faith, which together constitute confirmation in the Prayer Book, are in fact two different things, and do not necessarily have to be administered together. Then the laying on of hands with prayer could take place at a very early age, so making possible the giving of communion to children at a very early age, while the making of an act of lifelong commitment can be deferred to an age when it is truly meaningful.

In the time of the Fathers this problem did not arise, because confirmation then meant one thing and not two: it was the moment in the rite of initiation when the Holy Spirit was given to the candidates. Now, in having one moment with which the giving of the Holy Spirit was specially associated, these early rites were true to scripture, inasmuch as the New Testament shows knowledge of one moment, often not specified, when Christians came to receive the Holy Spirit. Thus there are eight places where St Paul refers more or less plainly to the fact that christians have received the Spirit, yet without throwing any light on the circumstances in which this gift was imparted to them. These are 1 Thess. 4.8, 2 Thess. 2.13, Gal. 3.5, 1 Cor. 6.19, 11.23, Phil. 1.19. In addition there are five further passages where St Paul, using a verb in the aorist tense (four times mistranslated in AV), shows that the Spirit had been received on some particular occasion in the past. These are Gal. 3.2, 1 Cor. 2.12, 2 Cor. 5.5, Rom. 5.5, 8.15. A comparison of Gal. 3.26f with Gal. 4.4–6 enables us to identify this occasion as baptism, because adoption to sonship in the first passage is connected with baptism and in the second with reception of the Holy Spirit. But from this no firm conclusion can be reached as to the content of the rite of baptism.

There are also three passages where St Paul treats his readers as persons who have been sealed by the Spirit. These are 2 Cor. 1.22, Eph. 1.13 and 4.30. In these three instances St Paul used verbs in the aorist tense, twice mistranslated in AV, showing that he was alluding to an event in his readers' past experience. Although he did not say at that event was, we may assume that it was the occasion of their baptism.

Similarly in the Acts of the Apostles there is seen to be one moment when new converts received the Holy Spirit, whether apart from any sacramental act (10.44), or at baptism (2.38–41), or at the laying on of hands after baptism (8.17, 19.6).

Now the early rites of initiation had recourse to the biblical acts of hand-laying and anointing to signify this one moment. But as in scripture this moment was intimately connected, if not identical, with baptism, so in the early rites the hand-laying or anointing which was held to confer the Holy Spirit were an integral part of the rite of baptism. The Holy Spirit was given in baptism and the hand-laying or anointing which accompanied the baptism gave visible and sacramental expression to this fact. It could be said that the Holy Spirit was given in the hand-laying or unction without implying that he was not given in baptism.

Hence the Church in the early centuries did not have to face the problem which has arisen in the West, now that confirmation is there separated from baptism by an appreciable interval of time. When that happened, there was no escaping the question, 'What is the grace which baptism and confirmation respectively confer?' If the Church continued to say that the Holy Spirit was given in confirmation, did this mean that he was not given in baptism? and could it be said that he was not given in baptism without departing from scripture? The Western church is faced with a dilemma. The more one links the gift of the Holy Spirit with confirmation, the more one seems to detract from baptism: and conversely the more one associates the gift of the Holy Spirit with baptism, the more one seems to detract from confirmation.

In modern discussion of this question it has often been said that the Holy Spirit is given in baptism and further graces of the Spirit are given in confirmation. But whether the Holy Spirit can be received without his further graces has been challenged by Davies.[6] Certainly in the traditional confirmation prayer of the West it is the Holy Spirit with his sevenfold graces who is invoked upon the candidates at their confirmation. Moreover Schmemann[7] has shown that the Eastern formula at the chrismation, 'The seal of the gift of the Holy Spirit', uses the word 'gift' in the singular. The seal does not convey gifts of the Holy Spirit but the Spirit himself: it is the personal Pentecost of the initiate who receives as gift him whom only Christ has by nature.

Some, in trying to distinguish between the work of the Spirit in baptism and his work in confirmation, have spoken of internal and external operations of the Spirit. But the objection to this line of thought is that spatial terms are inappropriate when it is a question of defining the relationship of God the Holy Spirit, who is infinite, with the human soul. Others have not always avoided the error of speaking in quantitative terms of man's reception of the Spirit, so much given in baptism and more given in confirmation. This too is a wrong way of thinking about the relationship of the Holy Spirit with the human soul. Others have said that the Holy Spirit is given in baptism, and there is no further giving of him in confirmation, because the latter is mainly an act of personal profession of the faith with a solemn blessing.

This problem is the price which has to be paid for the separation in time of confirmation from baptism. In the age of the Fathers it did not exist. The Holy Spirit was given once in Christian initiation, at the hand-laying or anointing with chrism immediately after the actual baptism. In the *Gelasian Sacramentary*, for instance, the Holy Spirit with his sevenfold graces was given to the initiates at the episcopal chrismation which was the concluding ceremony of the rite of baptism. This was the one moment in the rite in this Sacramentary where attention was focussed on the giving of the Spirit to the candidates themselves, although he had previously been invoked upon the water so becoming the agent by whom the blessings received at the font were conveyed.[8]

When the New Testament writers spoke about receiving the Holy Spirit, they had in mind that gift of the Spirit which was outpoured upon the church at Pentecost. When the Fathers spoke of receiving the Holy Spirit in Christian initiation it was to this Pentecostal gift of the Spirit that they referred. It is this same Pentecostal gift of the Spirit which the ancient rites of initiation for the most part ascribed to the hand-laying or anointing which took place during the rite of baptism. Even after the rite of initiation had begun to break up in southern Gaul in the fifth century, Faustus of Riez still identified the gift conferred in confirmation with the gift first bestowed at Pentecost.[9]

In modern Anglican discussion of this subject an important date is 1880, when there appeared a booklet *What is the Distinctive Grace of Confirmation?* written by Fr F. W. Puller, S.S.J.E., who had made a study of confirmation in the patristic period. 'Are we to understand,' Puller asked, 'as some people would persuade us, that this "reception, or partaking, of the Holy Ghost" merely means the increase of a gift already imparted in baptism; so that through confirmation is poured forth, in a fuller measure, that same indwelling presence of the Spirit which the baptized Christian already possesses? Or are we to understand that confirmation sets up in the soul a new relation to the Holy Ghost, which it had not before; so that, although in baptism the Holy Ghost operates and works on the soul by his purifying, consecrating, regenerating influence, yet he does not impart his indwelling presence until he is given in a new way by the laying on of hands?'[10]

Of these two alternatives Puller pleaded for the latter:

Do you mean to deny, they would ask, that baptism conveys a gift of the Holy Ghost to the soul? I should answer, That depends on what you mean by a gift of the Holy Ghost. If you mean *the* gift of his indwelling presence, I do deny it, because I hold that that is the peculiar effect of confirmation. If you mean that in baptism the Holy Ghost works on the soul, purges it from sin, begets it again into the supernatural Christian life, makes it a child of God, a member of Christ, and an inheritor of the kingdom of heaven, then in that sense I admit it entirely. In baptism the Holy Ghost pours down gifts of grace, which, as coming from him, may be called gifts of the Spirit; but in confirmation he imparts, not merely gifts of grace, but himself. In baptism the Holy Ghost refashions the person, whom he is regenerating, into a holy temple, meet to be the dwelling place of God: and then, in confirmation, the Shekinah, the tabernacling presence of God's glory, comes to take possession of the shrine which has been prepared for him.[11]

This will be recognized as an attempt to maintain the patristic doctrine of confirmation even when confirmation is a separate rite usually received many years after baptism.

In 1883 J. B. Parker, curate of Chislehurst, read to a junior clergy society a paper in which he expressed sympathy with the views of Puller, although he freely conceded that the preponderating opinion was that the Holy Spirit was given for the first time in baptism and a fuller measure of his presence was imparted in confirmation.[12] In 1891 Dr A. J. Mason published a well known full-length work on this subject, *The Relation of Confirmation to Baptism*, in which he also contended that *the* gift of the Holy Spirit was not received until confirmation, and that (p. 414) 'notwithstanding all previous operations of the Holy Ghost upon the soul, the baptized but unconfirmed believer may, unless the Divine action departs from its ordinary course, be truly said not to have received the Holy Ghost.' It is, he said (p. 478), the gift of the indwelling of the personal Spirit of God himself which is vouchsafed to us in confirmation.

But while he said as much as this of confirmation, Mason was very far from denying that baptism by itself without confirmation bestowed great spiritual blessings:

> If we may judge by the natural symbolism of that sacrament, as well as by the plainest words of scripture, it conveys the washing from sin. As surely, by virtue of grafting us into the body of Christ, it conveys to us the participation of his risen human life, and even of his divine nature. And all this is most certainly the work of his Holy Spirit. The new relationship formed by baptism between us and Christ must needs form a new relationship between us and that Holy Spirit. In a sense we 'receive' him then,—receive him in a different way from anything that could have been predicted of us before, although the penitence and faith which led us to baptism were breathed into our souls by him. His grace acting upon us through and before confirmation is not merely a prevenient grace, or one that acts upon us from without. It is a habitual grace which enters into the very composition of our being (p. 455).

Clearly, although they have frequently been accused of doing so, neither Puller nor Mason reduced Christian baptism to the level of the baptism of John. If it conveyed the great blessings of regeneration and remission of sins and incorporation into Christ, it cannot be regarded as a purely negative rite awaiting its positive fulfilment in confirmation. Nor is it a mere water rite. The expression 'water baptism', which has appeared in some recent discussion about initiation, is highly misleading, because it suggests that there is a Spirit-baptism in which the Holy Spirit is fully active and a water-baptism from which he is absent. Neither Puller nor Mason nor the Fathers believed in the possibility of a water-baptism in which the Holy Spirit is inoperative. It is only necessary to read what the Fathers from Tertullian[13] onwards wrote about the blessing of the font to see that such a suggestion is utterly untenable.

A similar view of confirmation to that held by Puller and Mason was expounded by bishop A. C. A. Hall of Vermont in his *Confirmation*, published in 1900. F. H. Chase, bishop of Ely, in his *Confirmation in the Apostolic Age*, published in 1909, defended the view that confirmation was an apostolic rite which included anointing as well as hand-laying, and which made a child a partaker of the Holy Spirit, strengthening the child of God by the Father's gift of the Father's Spirit.

The first criticism of the Puller–Mason thesis came in a much quoted sermon by professor W. Bright of Oxford, and published in 1892 in *Morality in Doctrine*, in which he said:

> It is hard to see how the recipient of baptism as such could be a child of God, yet destitute of that 'assurance of sonship' which comes from the Spirit of adoption: could be 'in' Christ, yet not 'in' the Holy Spirit: could be incorporated into the body mystical, yet not really 'inhabited' by the 'giver of life', who is the very informing and vitalizing principle of that body.[14]

Now Bright's criticism applies with devastating effect to the views of Puller and Mason when they tried to interpret the grace of confirmation in terms of the patristic teaching long after the pastoral practice of the Fathers had been abandoned, and confirmation was separated in time from baptism. As Quick pertinently observed, 'a theory which declares that confirmation marks the first gift of the indwelling Spirit, and a practice which places confirmation a dozen years or more after baptism, point, when taken together, to conclusions which are intolerable.'[15]

Now, although Bright and Quick and those who follow them have exposed a fatal weakness in the attempts of Puller and Mason to maintain the patristic doctrine of initiation in the situation which prevails in the West today, their argument does not apply to the undivided rite of initiation which was normal in the primitive church. The teeth of Bright's criticism are drawn when confirmation is received a few minutes after baptism, because then the question of being in Christ but not also in the Spirit does not arise. Hence Davies[16] could well ask whether the Puller–Mason theory would be acceptable if baptism and confirmation were once again to be united. Indeed Puller and Mason both contemplated the possibility of such a return to primitive practice, Puller preferring baptism and confirmation to be received together in infancy,[17] and Mason (p. 480n) at years of discretion. Quick,[18] too, appreciated that, if the primitive doctrine ought to be restored, 'the logical consequence seems to be that we should join together in time the two rites of baptism and confirmation.' Bicknell[19] held that the letter of scripture supported the view that the indwelling Spirit is given in confirmation, 'but it is most difficult to see how we can be members of Christ by baptism, unless he dwells in us through the indwelling Spirit ... Scripture does not deal with the question. The separation of the two parts of a single sacrament is unscriptural, and the best solution is to see that it ceases to exist at the earliest opportunity.'

A full-scale criticism of the Puller–Mason thesis came in 1897 with the appearance of *The Doctrine of Confirmation* by Dr A. T. Wirgman, who tried to prove from scripture and the Fathers that baptism confers *the* Holy Spirit and confirmation confers 'Holy Spirit', that is to say, baptism imparts the personal indwelling of the Spirit, while confirmation supplies subsequent gifts of spiritual endowment. The weakness of his case arises from the extreme difficulty of proving that the meaning of 'Spirit' is affected in this way by the presence or absence of the definite article before it; furthermore a study of the Greek Fathers shows conclusively that they were unaware of any difference of meaning in the word 'Spirit' if it was, or was not, preceded by the definite article.

A further reply to Puller and Mason was made by Dr Darwell Stone, who maintained in his *Holy Baptism*, published in 1899, that the New Testament, the Fathers, and the Book of Common Prayer all taught that the Holy Spirit personally indwells those who have been baptized, even if they are as yet unconfirmed, and that in confirmation he comes upon them with special confirmation gifts. Although he conceded that the views of Puller and Mason had been received with no little approval, Stone's own view was more widely held in the Church of England at that time, and still enjoys considerable support.

Then there came something of a lull in the debate. Indeed it is noteworthy that the Report, *Doctrine in the Church of England*, issued in 1938, devoted only three of its two hundred and fifty pages to confirmation, and dealt with the subject under discussion in a single paragraph.

The Revised Prayer Book of 1928 claimed in the introduction to the confirmation service that the church in its ministering of confirmation followed the examples of the apostles. It then quoted Acts 8.5–17, inferring from this that scripture taught that a special gift of the Holy Spirit was bestowed through laying on of hands with prayer: the congregation was then invited to pray to almighty God that he would strengthen with his Holy Spirit in confirmation those who in baptism were made his children. Among the occasional prayers in this book was a prayer for confirmation candidates with this petition that God would make ready the hearts and minds of his servants who were seeking the gift of the Holy Spirit through the laying on of hands.

The gift of the Spirit in confirmation is treated as a strengthening gift of the Spirit, because at the end of the infant baptism service the godparents are charged to see that their godchild comes to be confirmed, so that strengthened with the gift of the Holy Spirit he may come to the holy communion. The reading of Acts 8.15ff in the introduction does not necessarily imply that the Holy Spirit was not received in baptism; indeed the baptism service of 1928 retains the 1662 prayer which asks, 'Give thy Holy Spirit to this infant that he 'may be born again . . .'

The debate was resumed in 1944 when a joint committee of the Convocations of Canterbury and York produced its report, *Confirmation Today*, in which the authors stated that the gift of the Spirit was not to be thought of as if it were deferred until confirmation had been received, but that in confirmation there was a further outpouring of his divine power, completing what he had done at baptism; the committee further suggested that confirmation could be regarded as the ordination of the laity, and that it need not necessarily precede first communion.

This Report was severely criticized by Dr L. S. Thornton, C.R., who in an address given in 1945 rejected the notion that confirmation is the ordination of the laity, and claimed that it conferred the seal of the Spirit. Hence he has been said to belong to the Puller–Mason school. He expounded his views about confirmation at much greater length in his *Confirmation: its Place in the Baptismal Mystery*, published in 1953.

The Report was also criticized by Dr K. E. Kirk, bishop of Oxford, in his diocesan magazine for November and December 1944. Having in mind the traditional confirmation prayer of the West, he asserted that baptism confers sacramental remission and regeneration, while confirmation bestows the Holy Spirit. This led him to claim that it is confirmation rather than baptism which admits to the Church, and that unconfirmed persons have not yet received the Holy Spirit sacramentally, or within the ambit of the Church's ordinances, although the possibility of uncovenanted operations of the Spirit are by no means excluded.

Kirk's articles were in turn criticized by professor A. M. Ramsey, as he then was, in the September 1945 issue of *Theology*. He cited the well-known words of Bright which we have quoted already, and also some words of Beveridge:

As baptizing necessarily implies the use of water, so our being made thereby disciples of Christ as necessarily implies our partaking of his Spirit; for all that are baptized, and so made the disciples of Christ, are thereby made the members of his body, and are said to be baptized into Christ. But they who are in Christ members of his body must needs partake of the Spirit that is in him their head.

So Ramsey could see no hope of Kirk's views gaining any wider support, unless the Church of England were to reunite baptism and confirmation, either by reintroducing infant confirmation or by postponing baptism.

Although he recognized that there was a case for questioning the developments in the Western practice of initiation, and for giving serious attention to the primitive pattern, Ramsey ended by resisting this possible course of action on the ground that the Western development is not entirely a distortion.

The apostolic practice was the admission of adults to the Church and their anointing with the Holy Spirit in the closely linked rites of baptism and confirmation, *through faith*. Infant baptism is right because the Church is a family; but the retaining of the other part of the apostolic fact at an age of discretion (or even at an age more mature) is right because of the words *through faith*, and the implications of the words for heart and mind and will. Our Western practice seeks to reproduce in its own way the totality of the apostolic fact; and if it fails to do so wholly, did the patristic way succeed in doing so wholly and does the Eastern way succeed?

This criticism of the patristic and Eastern manner of initiation, when it is used for infants, is justified because, when infants have been baptized, confirmed, and communicated, they have received all the privileges of church membership, and have apparently been fully initiated, without ever having confessed their faith in person. That is, they have not experienced all that the New Testament means by baptism. Hence we may agree with Ramsey that there is some advantage in the Anglican practice of having two foci rather than only one—baptism in infancy and confirmation at a later age.

But in this context Ramsey was thinking of confirmation primarily as a personal profession of faith. The point which he rightly made can be met even if the laying on of hands with prayer is reunited with baptism, so long as there is a subsequent rite in which those who have been baptized and received the laying on of hands in infancy can, when old enough, make a mature profession of their faith. Moreover if the present practice is maintained, we are still left with the theological problem concerning the giving of the Holy Spirit.

Dr A. R. Vidler, while editor of *Theology*, in the Sept. 1945 issue of that journal agreed that if the present separation of confirmation from baptism is defensible, Ramsey had found the best defence for it, but was not himself so confident that a re-examination of our Western theology and practice would lead us to say No to the plea for a recovery of the primitive pattern of initiation.

No one person in recent years has done more to stimulate discussion about confirmation than Dom Gregory Dix, who, in a lecture in Oxford first published in 1946 under the title *The Theology of Confirmation in Relation to Baptism*, maintained that confirmation was a rite derived from the New Testament, and consisting in a sealing with chrism, the outward sign of the sealing of the Spirit unto the day of redemption. In his insistence that confirmation is the baptism of the Spirit Dix may be said to belong to the Puller–Mason–Thornton school of thought, although some of his ideas would not have been shared by them. However, he advocated a revision of the Church's doctrine of confirmation without a revision of its present practice. But Dix's doctrine of confirmation requires that there be no interval of time between confirmation and baptism; otherwise it becomes subject to the devastating criticism of Bright.

A theological commission appointed by the archbishops of Canterbury and York, and having Dix for one of its members, issued in 1948 *The Theology of Christian Initiation*, in which the authors asserted that full Christian initiation should be thought of as a process beginning with a request for baptism and ending with first communion, and that confirmation is still the *sphragis*, not only a strengthening of Christian warfare but first a sealing unto the day of redemption.

There was a big swing of the pendulum when in 1951 professor G. W. H. Lampe published his *Seal of the Spirit*. Setting out to establish that the seal of the Spirit is given in baptism, the author argued that confirmation is a post-apostolic rite for strengthening those baptized in infancy with the Holy Ghost the Comforter; and he insisted that, since membership in Christ is bestowed sacramentally by faith in baptism, therefore as a consequence baptism mediates the indwelling presence of the Spirit who indwelt Christ. That is to say, whatever spiritual blessings confirmation may confer, all the blessings of initiation are conferred by baptism itself.

The final report of the Joint Committee of the Convocations, entitled *Baptism and Confirmation Today*, and published in 1955, included a majority and a minority report. In the former the view taken was that professor Lampe's book provided a useful antithesis to the Mason–Dix–Thornton case, and that the Prayer Book services of baptism could claim justification in the New Testament for their doctrine that the Spirit is bestowed in baptism. Critical of the views of Lampe, and much more sympathetic towards those of Mason and Dix, the minority report concluded that in the apostolic age the neophyte received, first, the remission of sins by the washing of regeneration; and secondly, the renewing of the Holy Spirit by the laying on of hands together with anointing and the sign of the cross; and thirdly, completed his initiation in the eucharist.

In 1971 a Commission appointed by the archbishops of Canterbury and York, and having the bishop of Ely for its chairman, issued a report under the title *Christian Initiation: Birth and Growth in the Christian Society*. It declared its conviction that all the blessings of initiation, including the gift of the Holy Spirit, are received in baptism in a single sacramental moment, and found no firm evidence for the existence of confirmation before the time of Irenaeus in the late second century. Since it regarded confirmation as primarily a service of commitment and commissioning, it saw no reason to insist on confirmation before first communion. It recommended that the church should make explicit its recognition that baptism is the full and complete rite of Christian initiation.

Since then it has become evident that the recommendations of this latest Anglican commission are acceptable only to a section—perhaps a large section—of the Church of England, to which belongs canon E. C. Whitaker, who in 1975 published a booklet with the title *Sacramental Initiation Complete in Baptism*.

The Ely Commission has failed to settle the Anglican debate about confirmation because it has come down too heavily on one side. It has aroused opposition from many who adhere to the belief that confirmation is a sacramental rite conveying an objective gift of the Holy Spirit, and necessary to the fullness of initiation. While no participants in the debate would deny that the Holy Spirit is present and active in baptism, opinion is divided as to how far confirmation may be said to confer the gift of the Holy Spirit. It is possible so to associate the giving of the Spirit with baptism as in the opinion of others to leave too little room for a giving of the Spirit in confirmation. Conversely it is possible so to associate the giving of the Spirit with confirmation as to seem to others to leave too little room for the work of the Holy Spirit in baptism. Moreover those who emphasize the giving of the Spirit in confirmation naturally advocate that children receive this grace at an early age, and before first communion, while those who see the rite as mainly an act of personal commitment just as naturally wish confirmation to be received at a later age. Plainly, the problem about the right age for confirmation cannot be settled only on grounds of practical expediency without regard to what confirmation essentially is.

Since agreement in the Church of England about the meaning of confirmation is not yet in sight, the several points of view or varieties of emphasis must continue to co-exist within the same church. In 1974 a way was discovered by which the various schools of thought could co-exist more happily, when the General Synod of the Church of England accepted the principle that full sacramental participation within the church might precede a mature profession of faith. This would lead to a re-ordering of traditional Anglican practice in one or other of two ways, either by permitting baptized children to receive communion before confirmation, or by dividing the 1662 rite of confirmation into two parts so that the hand-laying with prayer—possibly accompanied by anointing—was reunited with baptism, as in ancient times, and the affirmation of baptismal promises was deferred to a later time, possibly many years after first communion.

The first alternative does not offer a satisfactory solution, because the gift of the Spirit which many ascribe to confirmation has a strongly initiatory character and must precede first communion, which is the climax of initiation. Secondly, since baptism and confirmation would still be separated in time, nothing would have been done to ease the theological problem about the moment when the Holy Spirit is given to the initiates.

The second alternative is greatly to be preferred. It would turn baptism into a rite which included hand-laying and perhaps also anointing. There would be no disagreement as to whether those baptized by this rite had or had not, or had not fully, received the Holy Spirit. Those who believe that the Holy Spirit is given in baptism would ascribe the actual giving of the Spirit to the moment of baptism itself, and regard the ensuing hand-laying and anointing not as sacramental acts but as explicatory symbols of the grace just bestowed at baptism. Those who believe the hand-laying and anointing to be sacramental acts signifying and effecting the giving of the Holy Spirit would not be denying that the Holy Spirit is given in baptism, but associating that gift with a very slightly later moment in the one rite of baptism. This would considerably narrow, though it would not entirely close, the gap between the different schools of thought.

But in 1976 the General Synod of the Church of England refused to adopt either of the above alternatives, contenting itself with giving permission to bishops to exercise their discretion more widely in regard to the age for confirmation. This decision cannot be regarded as satisfactory, and is unlikely to be the conclusion of the matter. Since baptism and confirmation would still be separate in time, the problem about the grace conferred by baptism and confirmation respectively would remain. Secondly, if as a result children were confirmed at a much younger age than at present, the renewal of baptismal promises would lose in meaning. Children of seven years are capable of receiving the gift of the Holy Spirit, but cannot properly be asked at that age to make an act of lifelong commitment.

Since this latest decision of the General Synod cannot have brought a permanent solution to the problems which we have been discussing, we may consider again the proposal to reunite the laying on of hands with baptism, and so return much nearer to the practice of the ancient Fathers. In this connection there is food for thought in the statement of the Ely Commission: 'So long as the series of rites remained a single complex, administered at one service, it was possible for the theology of initiation to interpret the complex as a whole, merely associating particular elements in it with particular aspects of baptism. Thus, even when the coming of the indwelling Spirit was especially linked with the post-baptismal part of the rite, this still remained a part of the baptismal complex; there was no suggestion that the candidate might be baptized and yet still not possess the Spirit.'[20] These words hold out the hope that, if baptism and confirmation were once more a single complex, those who agree with the Commission and those who are strongly opposed to it could live together more easily.

As we have seen, the thought of reuniting baptism and confirmation is not new. Puller, Mason, and Vidler were all sympathetic towards such a step. More recently, Mitchell (p. 175) has observed that those rites 'which have separated baptism and confirmation have lost their hold on the unity of the rite and thereby introduced manifold theological and pastoral problems.' More recently still, Fairweather remarked that the proposal to restore the patristic pattern of initiation 'retains the sacramental gesture of confirmation as part of the total sacramental sign of initiation, without separating confirmation from baptism, and therefore without introducing the puzzling (and perhaps insoluble) Western problem of the theological interpretation of confirmation as a separate sacrament.'[21] Commenting on the disagreement within the Church of England about the nature of the gift received through the laying of hands, Richardson wrote that in the case of adults, who could receive baptism and laying on of hands together, the problem hardly arose: but it became more acute when baptism in infancy was separated from confirmation by a number of years. 'Even so,' he concluded, 'the problem is an unreal one: it has been created by the unbiblical disjunction of the total act of Christian initiation into two separate acts, or separate sacraments. When this disjunction occurs in theology as well as in time, there is no solution for a problem which is entirely of artificial manufacture.'[22]

It is not only in England that serious proposals have been made for the putting together of baptism and confirmation. In 1970 the Liturgical Commission of the Episcopal Church in the United States published *Prayer Book Studies 18*, in which it was claimed that a unification of the rite would avoid 'both the practical disadvantages of delaying confirmation and the theological problem of attributing to confirmation separately some necessary aspects of Christian initiation which belong to the very beginning of our Christian life.'[23] A unified rite of baptism appeared in the *Draft Proposed Book of Common Prayer* presented to the General Convention of the Episcopal Church in 1976. When all the candidates have been baptized the bishop, or a priest, in full sight of the congregation prays over them: 'Heavenly Father, we thank you that by water and the Holy Spirit you have bestowed upon these your servants the forgiveness of sins, and have raised them to the new life of grace. Sustain them, O Lord, in your Holy Spirit . . .' Then the bishop or priest lays his hand on each person's head, and signs his forehead with the cross, using chrism if desired, and saying, '*N*., you are sealed by the Holy Spirit in baptism and marked as Christ's own for ever.' When all have been baptized, the celebrant says, 'Let us welcome the newly baptized.'[24] Thus it is made abundantly clear that the sealing with the Spirit and the hand-laying are to be regarded as part of baptism.

In 1974 the Worship and Doctrine Committee of the Anglican Church in Canada observed that confirmation had come to mean two things for Anglicans. First, it was the completion of the process of Christian initiation begun in baptism, implying some gift of the Holy

Spirit; secondly, it was a renewal of the baptismal confession of faith by those now able to answer for themselves.

> Baptism and confirmation (in the first sense) are theologically two complementary aspects of a single action of Christian initiation through which a person is re-born of water and the Spirit for the forgiveness of sins, conformed to Christ in his death and resurrection, gifted and sealed with the Holy Spirit as the pledge of eternal life, and so incorporated into the church which is the body of Christ and temple of the Holy Spirit. Confirmation in the second sense (renewal of baptismal vows) is not an essential part of this initiation act . . .

So the Committee proposed that these two aspects of confirmation be separated, the first part expressed through the laying on of hands being re-united with baptism as a single act of Christian initiation for both infants and adults, following the practice of the primitive church, and the second part, the renewal of baptismal vows, being retained as a separate service of commitment for mature Christians.

In 1971 a Commission on Christian Initiation in its report to the Episcopal Synod of the Church of South Africa recommended that the sacrament of Christian initiation, now divided into holy baptism and confirmation, should be reunited, and should be administered by the bishop, or by a priest with the bishop's authority, either to adults or to the infants of believing parents.

Thus in a number of Anglican provinces there has been seriously proposed a return to the practice of the Fathers by reuniting the sacramental part of confirmation with baptism. It remains to be seen how soon any province will adopt for permanent use such a reintegrated rite of Christian initiation. A study of confirmation in the age of the Fathers has shown what confirmation essentially is, and what it is not, has exposed some problems created by the changed practice of the medieval West, and has shown the way forward now.

Notes

CHAPTER 1

1. *La Didaché, Instruction des Apôtres*, Paris 1958, pp. 359, 365.
2. *The Church and the Ministry*, London 1936, p. 252.
3. 'The Seal in the Second Century', in *Theology*, Jan. 1948, p. 9.
4. 'Second-Century Teaching on Holy Baptism', in *Theology*, March 1947, p. 88.
5. *Ep.* 46.6.
6. See also *Mand.* 3.1.1, 5.1.2, 10.1.2, *Sim.* 5.7.1, 9.24.2,4.
7. *Sim.* 5.7.1.
8. 16.8ff.
9. 11.11.
10. *The Apostolic Fathers*, London 1893, p. 280.
11. 9.8f.
12. W. Schneemelcher, *Acts of Paul*, in *New Testament Apocrypha*, ed. E. Hennecke, II, London 1965, p. 360.
13. ibid. p. 364.
14. ibid. p. 365.
15. ibid. pp. 386f.
16. M. R. James (ed.), *The Apocryphal New Testament*, Oxford 1926, p. 292.
17. C. Schmidt, *Acta Pauli*, 1904, pp. 31ff.
18. Schneemelcher, op. cit. p. 285.
19. O. Perler, *Méliton de Sardes, Sur la Pâque et Fragments*, SC 127, Paris 1966, p. 68.
20. ibid. p. 96.
21. ibid. pp. 66, 68.
22. art. cit. p. 10.
23. See Perler, op. cit. pp. 144f.
24. 'The Emergence and the Form of a Rite of Initiation in the Church', in *Theology*, June 1972, p. 308.
25. See E. Haenchen, *Acts of the Apostles*, Oxford 1971, p. 51.
26. 59. R. McL. Wilson, *The Gospel of Philip*, London 1962, p. 40. See also sections 101 and 109.
27. ibid. pp. 49f.
28. ibid. p. 43.
29. ibid. pp. 3, 15.
30. *Sacramental Initiation Complete in Baptism*, Bramcote 1975, p. 26.

31. E. Evans (ed.): Tertullian, *adv. Marcionem*, Oxford 1972, p. xviii.
32. ibid. p. 37.
33. ibid. p. 79.
34. ibid. p. 241.
35. op. cit. 4.5.
36. *Syntagma, apud* Epiphanius *Haer.* 42.
37. J. Daniélou and H. Marrou, *The Christian Centuries*, I, 1964, p. 97.
38. *The Making of a Christian*, 1964, pp. 122f.
39. *Apol.* 1.65.
40. art. cit. p. 88.
41. art. cit. p. 9.
42. *Histoire des Dogmes*, V, Paris 1936, p. 186.
43. *Allegory and Event*, London 1939, pp. 312ff.
44. *Liturgy and Worship*, London 1931, p. 447.
45. 'Christian Initiation', in *CQR*, Jan.–March 1957, pp. 28f.
46. 'L'Introduction du Catéchuménat à Rome', in *Recherches de Théologie ancienne et mediévale*, Louvain 1938, pp. 129–54.
47. 'Baptism: the Liturgical Pattern', in *CQR*, Oct.–Dec. 1956, p. 399.
48. 29. See Dix, art. cit. p. 10.
49. art. cit. pp. 9f.
50. 'Justin Martyr and Confirmation', in *Theology*. April 1948, p. 134.
51. *The Holy Spirit and Modern Thought*, London 1953, p. 95.
52. art. cit. p. 88.
53. art. cit. p. 138.
54. ibid. pp. 135f.
55. 'Was there a Complementary Rite of Initiation in the First Two Centuries?', in *Theology*, April 1972, pp. 196f.
56. See Moreton, art. cit. p. 309.
57. art. cit. p. 137.
58. 'Justin Martyr and Confirmation—A Note', in *Theology*, Dec. 1952, pp. 458f.
59. ibid. p. 459.
60. *Confirmation: Its Place in the Baptismal Mystery*, p. 38.
61. ibid. pp. 49f.
62. ibid. p. 51.
63. J. Armitage Robinson (ed.), St Irenaeus, *The Demonstration of the Apostolic Preaching*, London 1920, p. 72.
64. ibid. p. 191.
65. ibid. pp. 92f.
66. *Theological Studies*, Woodstock, June 1953, p. 277.
67. Mason pp. 111f.
68. op. cit. pp. 56f.
69. *Christian Worship*, London 1927, p. 336.
70. Mason pp. 115f.
71. *Confirmation or the Laying on of Hands*, p. 19.
72. See Mitchell p. 12.
73. Mason pp. 113f.
74. *Water and the Spirit*, London 1967, p. 72.
75. 'Confirmation in the Early Centuries', in *The Churchman*, June 1963, p. 88.

76. op. cit. p. 18.
77. 'Seal in the Second Century', p. 9.
78. *L'Imposition des Mains et les Rites Connexes*, Wetteren 1925, p. 287.
79. *JTS*, 1911, pp. 1ff.
80. 4.7f; ed. Bernard p. 48.
81. *ad Autolycum* 1.12; Mason p. 330.
82. op. cit. pp. 325f.
83. *Institutiones Theologicae de Sacr. Eccles.* I, p. 266.
84. *De Baptismo et Confirmatione*, Paris 1922, pp. 102, 181.
85. op. cit. p. 353n.
86. *The Origin and Evolution of the Christian Church*, London 1948, pp. 129f.
87. op. cit. pp. 313f.

CHAPTER 2

1. *de Bapt.* 1; E. Evans, *Tertullian's Homily on Baptism*, London 1964, p. 5.
2. See Refoulé & Drouzy (ed.), Tertullien, *Traité de Baptême*, SC 35, Paris 1956, pp. 10f.
3. *de Bapt.* 7; Evans p. 17.
4. Tertullian; *de Baptismo*, Rome 1933, p. 12.
5. *Tertulliani Opera, Corpus Christianorum*, Turnholti 1954, p. 282.
6. op. cit. p. 76.
7. *de Trin.* 2.14.
8. *de Eccles. Offic.* 2.26. See Refoulé op. cit. p. 41, P. Dabin, *Le Sacerdoce Royal des fidèles dans la tradition ancienne et moderne*, Paris 1950, J. Lécuyer, 'Essai sur le sacerdoce des fidèles chez les Pères', in *Maison Dieu*, no. 27, pp. 27–50.
9. 'La Consignation à Carthage et à Rome', in *RSR* 1911, p. 352.
10. *de Bapt.* 8; Evans pp. 17, 19.
11. ibid. 17; Evans p. 35.
12. *de Res. Carnis* 8.
13. *de Cor.* 3.
14. *adv. Marcionem* 3.22. See Refuolé, op. cit. pp. 41f, J. Daniélou, *Bible et Liturgie*, Paris 1958, pp. 76ff.
15. *de Bapt.* 4; Evans p. 11.
16. Evans p. 15.
17. See E. C. Ratcliff, 'The Relation of Confirmation to Baptism in the Early Roman and Byzantine Liturgies', in *Theology*, Oct. 1946, pp. 291f.
18. See Didymus, *de Trin.* 2.7.6, J. M. Lupton (ed.), Tertullian, *de Baptismo*, Cambridge 1908, pp. 15f.
19. art. cit. p. 292.
20. Evans p. 31.
21. op. cit. pp. 122f.
22. *Theology of Confirmation in Relation to Baptism*, London 1953, p. 17.
23. *Holy Baptism*, London 1901, pp. 75f.
24. *Ep.* 70.2.
25. *Ep.* 73.6.
26. *Ep. ad Dem.* 22.
27. *Ep.* 69.15.
28. *Ep.* 64.2.

29. *Ep.* 69.1.
30. *Ep.* 69.3.
31. *Ep.* 69.8.
32. *Ep.* 73.1.
33. *Ep.* 69.2.
34. *Ep.* 72.1.
35. *Ep.* 63.8.
36. op. cit. p. 234.
37. *Serm.* 324.
38. apud Eusebius *H.E.* 6.43.
39. *Ep.* 74.5.
40. *Ep.* 194.11. See also Clement Alex. *Prophet. Eclog.* 12.
41. *Ep.* 74.7.
42. See *Serm.* 229 and 272.
43. *Serm.* 227. See also *Enarrat. in Ps.* 44.19.
44. *de Trin.* 15.46.
45. *de Bapt. c. Donat.* 3.16.21. See also *Retract.* 1.13.7.
46. *de Bapt. c. Donat.* 5.20.28.
47. *CQR,* Jan. 1898, p. 372.
48. *de Bapt. c. Donat.* 5.20.28.
49. *in Ep. Joan. Tract.* 6.10.
50. *Serm.* 178.7.
51. *Serm.* 210.2.
52. Above p. 45.
53. *de Bapt. c. Donat.* 3.16.21.
54. *Revue Bénédictine,* 1948, pp. 177ff.
55. ibid. p. 208.
56. Below p. 58.

CHAPTER 3

1. See B. Botte, *La Tradition Apostolique de saint Hippolyte,* Münster 1963, pp. IX–XXVIII, G. Dix, *The Treatise on the Apostolic Tradition of St Hippolytus of Rome,* London 1968, pp. b–k, xi–xliv.
2. ed. Botte pp. 50f.
3. ibid. pp. 52–5.
4. *Hippolytus, The Apostolic Tradition,* Cambridge 1934, p. 93.
5. op. cit. p. 38.
6. 'Christian Initiation', in *CQR,* Jan.–March 1957, pp. 23–7.
7. op. cit. pp. XXXVII, 53n.
8. *Theological Studies,* June 1953, pp. 277ff.
9. below p. 93.
10. *Ep.* 1.6.
11. *Serm de Bapt.* 6.
12. *de Sacramentis* 2.24.
13. *de Mysteriis* 6.30.
14. *de Sacr.* 3.2.8.
15. *St Ambrose On the Sacraments and On the Mysteries,* London 1950, p. 25.
16. See J. B. Umberg, 'Confirmatione baptismus perficitur', in *Ephemerides*

Theologicae Lovanienses, Oct. 1924, pp. 525ff, J. D. C. Fisher, *Christian Initiation: Baptism in the Medieval West*, London 1965, pp. 35f.

17. L. C. Mohlberg, *Liber Sacramentorum Romanae Aeclesiae Ordinis anni circuli*, Rome 1958, p. 74, ET in Whitaker p. 188.
18. *Le Sacramentaire Gélasien*, Tournai 1959, pp. 155–76.
19. G. Morin, 'Sermones Sancti Augustini', *Miscellanea Agostiniana*, I, Rome 1930, p. 490.
20. *Serm.* 249.3.
21. *de Sacr.* 3.2.8.
22. *Ep. ad Him.* 2.
23. *Ep.* 25.3.
24. *Comm. in Matt.* 15.10.
25. above pp. 15ff.
26. above pp. 53ff.
27. L. A. Van Buchem, *L'Homélie Pseudo-Eusébienne de Pentecôte*, Nijmegen 1967, p. 61.

CHAPTER 4

1. *Paedagogus* 1.6.
2. op. cit. pp. 316f.
3. *Quis Dives Salvetur?* 39.
4. op. cit. p. 316.
5. below pp. 121f.
6. *Stromateis* 2.3.
7. op. cit. p. 153.
8. *Quis Dives Salvetur?* 42.
9. op. cit. p. 317.
10. *Principles of Sacramental Theology*, London 1956, p. 162.
11. *Excerpt. Theodot.* 86; Leeming p. 165.
12. *Paed.* 2.8.
13. *Hom. in Rom.* 5.8.
14. *Excerpt. Theodot.* 22.
15. *adv. Haer.* 31.2.
16. op. cit. p. 479.
17. *in Lev. Hom.* 6.2.
18. *de Principiis* 2.10.7.
19. *Exhort, ad Martyrium* 30.
20. *Hom. 5.5 in Ex.*
21. *in Joan.* 6.17.
22. op. cit. p. 320.
23. *in Rom.* 5.8.
24. *Selecta in Ezek.* 16.
25. *in Lev. Hom.* 8.11.
26. *in Joan.* 3.5.
27. ibid. 6.17.
28. *in Joshua Hom.* 4.1.
29. Evidence of the *disciplina arcani*.
30. op. cit. p. 323.
31. op. cit. pp. 506–11.

32. op. cit. pp. XIV–XVII; and *Bulletin de Théologie Ancienne et Médiévale*, Janv.–Juin 1960, pp. 375ff.

33. *JTS*, April 1960, pp. 164ff.

34. Dix, *The Apostolic Tradition*, pp. g–h.

35. *Les Canons d'Hippolyte*, Paris 1966, pp. 318–21, 329ff.

36. ibid. pp. 382ff.

37. We have used the ET by Whitaker, pp. 83, 85.

38. B. Botte, 'L'Eucologe de Sérapion est-il authentique?', in *Oriens Christianus*, 48 (1964), pp. 50–56.

39. *Hom.* 17.1.

40. ibid.

41. *Hom.* 4.6.

42. *Ep. ad Sarapionem* 1.23.

43. ibid. 4.4.

44. ibid. 4.9.

45. ibid. 4.10.

46. ibid. 1.4.

47. *de Trin.* 2.6.

48. ibid.

49. *in Is.* 3.1.

50. *in Joan.* 3.5.

51. *in Is.* 4.2.

52. *in Luc.* 22.8.

CHAPTER 5

1. See E. C. Ratcliff, 'The Relation of Confirmation to Baptism in the Early Roman and Byzantine Liturgies', in *Theology*, Oct. 1946, p. 293.

2. *Cat.* 3.4.

3. *Procat.* 2.

4. *Cat.* 18.32.

5. *Cat.* 18.33.

6. *Cat.* 13.36.

7. ibid. See also *Cat.* 15.22.

8. *Cat.* 17.36.

9. *Cat.* 5.6.

10. *Cat.* 14.25.

11. Whitaker p. 82.

12. *Cat.* 18.33.

13. 'The Old Syrian Baptismal Tradition and its Resettlement under the influence of Jerusalem', in *Studies in Church History*, II, 1965, pp. 32–6.

CHAPTER 6

1. art. in *L'Orient Syrien*, 1956, pp. 239–54.

2. *The Offices of Baptism and Confirmation*, Cambridge 1914, p. 31.

3. 'The Significance of the Pre-Baptismal Seal in St John Chrysostom', in *Studia Patristica*, VI, 1962, p. 90.

4. *The Liturgical Homilies of Narsai*, Cambridge 1909, pp. xliii–xlix.

5. *Confirmation or the Laying on of Hands*, I, London 1934, pp. 31–4.

6. *Baptism in the Demonstrations of Aphraates the Persian Sage*, Washington 1945, pp. 108–23.

7. ed. G. Bornkamm in *New Testament Apocrypha*, ed. W. Schneemelcher, ET, London 1965, p. 456.

8. ibid. pp. 437f.

9. ibid. p. 470.

10. ibid. pp. 506f.

11. ibid. p. 512.

12. ibid. pp. 525f.

13. op. cit. pp. 31f.

14. 'The Old Syrian Baptismal Tradition', in *Studies in Church History*, II, 1965, p. 26.

15. op. cit. pp. xvi f. See also his 'Unction in the Syrian Baptismal Rite', in *CQR*, April–June 1961, p. 178.

16. *Exorcism and the Healing of the Sick*, London 1931, p. 55.

17. Whitaker p. 187.

18. ibid. p. 19.

19. ibid. p. 22.

20. ibid. p. 23.

21. R. H. Connolly, *The Liturgical Homilies of Narsai*, p. xliv.

22. E-P. Siman, *L'Expérience de l'Esprit par l'Église d'après la Tradition Syrienne d'Antioche*, Paris 1971, p. 75.

23. Connolly op. cit. p. xlvi.

24. R. H. Connolly, *Didascalia Apostolorum*, Oxford 1929, p. 2.

25. 2.32.

26. *Greek Baptismal Terminology*, Nijmegen 1962, pp. 312, 360f. For a criticism of Ysebaert's theory see Whitaker pp. xixf.

27. op. cit. p. 147n.

28. Whitaker p. 30.

29. art. cit. p. 26.

30. ed. G. W. Horner, London 1904, p. 163.

31. below p. 94.

32. 3.12.

33. 6.21.

34. ibid. Connolly p. 246.

35. *Hymni in Fest. Epiph.*, 3.17; ET in *Select Library of Nicene & Post-Nicene Fathers*, XIII, Oxford 1898.

36. 4.1.

37. 7.2.

38. 3.9.

39. 3.13.

40. 3.16.

41. 1.6.

42. 6.1f.

43. op. cit. p. 86.

44. ibid. pp. 105f.

45. ibid. p. 106.

46. quoted by Siman p. 106.

47. below pp. 111, 116f.

48. Duncan op. cit. pp. 5f.
49. *Dem.* 12 *de Paschate.*
50. *Dem.* 23.
51. *Dem.* 4.
52. *Dem.* 6 *de Monachis.*
53. Connolly, *Liturgical Homilies of Narsai*, p. 40.
54. ibid.
55. ibid. pp. 41f.
56. ibid. p. 42.
57. op. cit. p. 31.
58. art. cit. p. 177.
59. Connolly, pp. 48f.
60. ibid. p. 50.
61. ibid. p. 55.
62. ibid. pp. 58f.
63. art. cit. p. 177.
64. *Hom.* 22; Connolly pp. 42f.
65. *de Bapt.* 4.
66. Connolly pp. 43, 45.
67. 3.16; Whitaker p. 30.
68. 7.42; Whitaker p. 33.
69. 7.44.
70. 'Le Baptême dans l'Église Syrien', in *L'Orient Syrien*, Paris 1956, p. 138.

CHAPTER 7

1. Harkins p. 169, Whitaker p. 37.
2. Harkins p. 51.
3. ibid. pp. 169, 52.
4. ibid. pp. 49f.
5. See also *ad Illum. Cat.* 1.2.
6. pp. 140f.
7. ibid. p. 58.
8. *de Cor.* 3.
9. *adv. Jud.* 8.
10. *Hom. 12.7 in 1 Cor.*
11. *Hom. 13.1 in Phil.*
12. *de Res. Carnis* 8.
13. *Cat. Myst.* 3.5, 7.
14. Harkins p. 169.
15. ibid. p. 164.
16. ibid. p. 52.
17. *Hom. 12.2 in Matt.*
18. *in Gen. Hom.* 40.4.
19. *Cat.* 3.5; Wenger p. 153.
20. Harkins p. 164.
21. ibid. p. 52.
22. ibid. p. 171.
23. *Hom. 86.4 in Joan.*
24. Harkins p. 164.

25. ibid. p. 53.
26. op. cit. pp. 99f.
27. See *ad Illum. Cat.* 1.1, *Hom. 40.2 in 1 Cor.*, Harkins p. 166, Finn op. cit. p. 35.
28. Series 1, vol. 12.
29. Harkins p. 53.
30. op. cit. pp. 105f.
31. See Tonneau and Devréesse, op. cit. p. xvi.
32. *Hom. 18.2 in Act.*
33. ibid. 40.2.
34. 19.2.
35. Yarnold, op. cit. pp. 176, 189.
36. Mingana p. 35, Yarnold p. 176, Whitaker p. 46.
37. op. cit. pp. xv, xvi.
38. ibid. pp. 31ff.
39. ibid. p. 33.
40. ibid. p. 46.
41. ibid.
42. ibid. p. 47.
43. ibid. p. 55.
44. ibid. p. 58.
45. ibid. pp. 53f.
46. ibid. p. 68.
47. art. cit. p. 144.
48. op. cit. p. 31.
49. Yarnold p. 246.
50. ibid. p. 247.
51. ibid. p. 254.
52. ibid. pp. 209f.
53. op. cit. p. xvi.
54. *Patrology*, Edinburgh & London 1960, p. 372.
55. op. cit. p. 209.
56. op. cit. pp. 78, 88.
57. op. cit. pp. 208f.
58. 'Studies in the Early History of the Syrian Orthodox Baptismal Liturgy', in *JTS*, April 1972, p. 24.
59. Yarnold p. 202.
60. *in Cant.* 1.2; Mason p. 374.
61. in 2 Cor. 1.21.
62. *Hom. in Act.* 1.
63. *Haeret. Fab. Compend.* 5.18.

CHAPTER 8

1. *The Testaments of the Twelve Patriarchs*, 1953, p. 128.
2. *Ante-Nicene Christian Fathers*, vol. 8, p. 14; Siman p. 74.
3. 'Entry into Membership of the Early Church', in *JTS*, Jan–April 1947, pp. 59ff.
4. op. cit. p. 74.

5. See J. Irmscher, 'The Pseudo-Clementines', in *New Testament Apocrypha*, vol. 2, p. 533.

6. *Ante-Nicene Fathers*, vol. 8, p. 132.

7. 'Seal in the Second Century', p. 10.

8. H. Duensing, 'Epistula Apostolorum', in *New Testament Apocrypha*, vol. 1, p. 220.

9. art. cit. pp. 26–9.

10. 'Chrismation prébaptismale et Divinité de l'Esprit chez Grégoire de Nysse', in *Recherches de Science Religieuse*, April–Juin 1968, p. 190.

11. *The Pelican Guide to Modern Theology*, vol. 2, 1969, p. 160.

12. Yebamoth 47a, ed. I. Epstein, London 1936, pp. 310–13, F. Gavin, *The Jewish Antecedents of the Christian Sacraments*, London 1928, pp. 33–6.

13. 'L'Origine de l'Institution du Baptême pour les Prosélytes', in *Revue des Études juives*, Paris 1934, pp. 50–7.

14. *Baptism in the New Testament*, London 1962, pp. 18–25.

15. art. cit. pp. 7f, and *Confirmation or the Laying on of Hands* (*Theology Occasional Paper*), pp. 10–13, Manson, art. cit. p. 30.

16. op. cit. pp. 18–25.

17. But see Couratin, op. cit. p. 158.

18. art. cit. p. 26.

19. art. 'Confirmation', in *A Catholic Dictionary of Theology*, 1966, p. 90.

20. Mansi 2.571.

21. op. cit. p. 511.

22. P.G. 3.404; trans. J. Parker, London 1899, p. 87.

23. op. cit. p. 90.

24. art. cit. pp. 246f.

25. *Liturgical Homilies of Narsai*, p. xlix.

26. art. cit. p. 248.

27. 'San Juan Crisosotomo y la Confirmation', in *Orbis Catholicus*, Barcelona Nov. 1958, pp. 385ff.

28. op. cit. p. 87.

CHAPTER 9

1. *Apostol. Trad.* 30.

2. Eusebius, *H.E.* 6.43.

3. Ps-Cyprian, *de Rebapt.* 3.

4. *Dial. c. Lucif.* 9.

5. Mansi 2.12,14.

6. *Ep. ad Him.* 3.

7. *Ep. ad Victric.* 9.

8. *Ep. ad Sen.* 4.

9. C. Munier, *Concilia Galliae*, Turnhout 1963, pp. 66ff.

10. See P. de Puniet, 'La Liturgie Baptismale en Gaule avant Charlemagne', in *Recherches de Science Religieuse*, vol. 2, 1911, pp. 350–83, 'Onction et Confirmation', in *Révue d'Histoire Ecclésiastique*, vol. 13, 1912, pp. 467–76, P. Galtier, 'La Consignation à Carthage et à Rome', ibid. pp. 257–301, 'La Consignation dans les Églises d'Occident', ibid. pp. 450–66, D. van den Eynde, 'La deuxième canon du Concile d'Orange sur la Chrismation', in

Recherches de Théologie ancienne et médiévale, vol. 2, 1939, pp. 97–109, A Chavasse, 'La deuxième canon du Concile d'Orange de 441', in *Mélanges E.Podechard*, Lyon 1945, pp. 103–20, Ysebaert, op. cit. pp. 289, 302f, 387, Mitchell pp. 125f, Van Buchem, pp. 95–110.

11. Munier p. 202.
12. ibid. p. 131.
13. ibid. p. 133.
14. *de Gubernatione Dei* 3.2.
15. ibid. 66.
16. *de Eccles. Dogm.* 74.
17. See A. Souter, 'Observations on the Pseudo-Eusebian Collection of Gallican Sermons', in *JTS*, vol. 41, 1940, p. 47, G. Morin, in *ZNTW*, vol. 34, 1935, pp. 92–115, B. Leeming, 'The False Decretals, Faustus of Riez and the Pseudo-Eusebius', in *Studia Patristica*, vol. 2, part 2, Oxford 1955, pp. 125ff.
18. Van Buchem pp. 61f, Mason p. 192.
19. Munier pp. 202f.
20. *c.* 15.
21. *MGH, Cap. Legum Franc.* I p. 64; *capit.* of 789, *c.* 23.
22. *Ep.* 159.7.

CHAPTER 10

1. ed. Mohlberg n.419.
2. See J. D. C. Fisher, *Christian Initiation: The Reformation Period*, London 1970, pp. 173–260.
3. ibid. pp. 175, 182, 194, 232, 235, 258–60.
4. *A Treatise of the Sacraments*, Parker Soc.II p. 1125.
5. *On Confirmation or Laying on of Hands*, Parker Soc. V, p. 488.
6. *The Spirit, the Church and the Sacraments*, London 1954, pp. 4–8.
7. *Of Water and the Spirit*, London 1976, pp. 78f.
8. nn. 446–50, ed. Mohlberg pp. 73f.
9. Van Buchem p. 40.
10. op. cit. p. 11.
11. ibid. p. 24.
12. *Confirmation*, London 1883, pp. 5f.
13. *de Bapt.* 4.
14. op. cit. p. 91.
15. *The Christian Sacraments*, London 1936, p. 184.
16. op. cit. p. 193.
17. op. cit. p. 39.
18. op. cit. p. 183.
19. *A Theological Introduction to the Thirty Nine Articles*, London 1947, p. 478n.
20. p. 33.
21. *Partners in Mission*, London 1973, pp. 45f.
22. *A Dictionary of Christian Theology*, p. 171.
23. p. 19.
24. p. 310.

Bibliography

(a) Main Works

AUDET, J. P., *La Didaché, Instruction des Apôtres*, Paris 1958.
BÉNOIT, A., *Le Baptême Chrétien au Second Siècle*, Paris 1953.
BERNARD, J. H., *The Odes of Solomon*, Cambridge 1912.
BICKNELL, E. J., *A Theological Introduction to the Thirty Nine Articles*, London 1947.
BOHEN, M., *The Mystery of Confirmation*, London 1966.
BONNER, C., *Melito of Sardis, On the Passover*, London 1940.
BOTTE, B., *La Tradition Apostolique de saint Hippolyte*, Münster 1963.
BRIGHT, W., *Morality in Doctrine*, London 1892.
BROWN, H., *Justin Martyr's Dialogue with Trypho the Jew*, Cambridge 1846.
BUCHANAN, C. O. (ed.), *Evangelical Essays on Church and Sacraments*, London 1972.
CHADWICK, H., *Saint Ambrose On the Sacraments*, London 1960.
CHAVASSE, A., *Le Sacramentaire Gélasien (Vaticanus Reginensis 316)*, Tournai 1959.
CONNOLLY, R. H., *Didascalia Apostolorum*, Oxford 1929.
——— *The Liturgical Homilies of Narsai*, Cambridge 1909.
COPPENS, J., *L'Imposition des Mains et les Rites Connexes*, Wetteren 1925.
COQUIN, R-G., *Les Canons d'Hippolyte*, Paris 1966.
CREHAN, J. H., *Early Christian Baptism and the Creed*, London 1956.
CRICHTON, J. D., *Christian Celebration: The Sacraments*, London 1975.
CULLY, K. B. (ed.), *Confirmation, History, Doctrine and Practice*, Greenwich 1962.
CROSS, F. L., *St Cyril of Jerusalem's Lectures on the Christian Sacraments*, London 1951.
DABIN, P., *Le Sacerdoce Royal des fidèles dans la tradition ancienne et moderne*, Paris 1956.
D'ALÈS, A., *De Baptismo et Confirmatione*, Paris 1927.
——— *Tertulliani de Baptismo*, Rome 1933.
DANIÉLOU, J., *Bible et Liturgie*, Paris 1958.
DANIÉLOU, J. and MARROU, H., *The Christian Centuries*, I, 1964.
DANIÉLOU, J., COURATIN, A. H. and KENT, J., *The Pelican Guide to Modern Theology*, II, 1969.
DAVIES, J. G., *The Spirit, the Church and the Sacraments*, London 1954.
DAVIS, C., *The Making of a Christian*, 1966.
DEWAR, L., *The Holy Spirit and Modern Thought*, London 1959.

DIX, G., *The Theology of Confirmation in relation to Baptism*, London 1953.
—— *The Shape of the Liturgy*, London 1945.
—— (ed. H. Chadwick), *The Apostolic Tradition of St Hippolytus of Rome*, London 1968.
DUCHESNE, L., *Origines du Culte Chrétien*, Paris 1920.
DUNCAN, E. J., *Baptism in the Demonstrations of Aphraates the Persian Sage*, Washington 1945.
EVANS, E., *Tertullian's Homily on Baptism*, Oxford 1964.
—— *Tertullian adversus Marcionem*, Oxford 1972.
FINN, T. M., *The Liturgy of Baptism in the Baptismal Instructions of St John Chrysostom*, Washington 1967.
FISHER, J. D. C., *Christian Initiation: Baptism in the medieval West*, London 1965.
—— *Christian Initiation: The Reformation Period*, London 1970.
FLEMINGTON, W. F., *The New Testament Doctrine of Baptism*, London 1948.
FUNK, F. X., *Didascalia et Constitutiones Apostolorum*, Paderborn 1905.
GAVIN, F., *The Jewish Antecedents of the Christian Sacraments*, London 1928.
GILMORE, A. (ed.), *Christian Baptism*, London 1960.
GORE, C. (ed. C. H. Turner), *The Church and the Ministry*, London 1936.
HALL, A. C. A., *Confirmation*, London 1915.
HANSSENS, J. M., *La Liturgie d'Hippolyte*, Rome 1959.
HANSON, R. P. C., *Allegory and Event*, London 1959.
HARKINS, P. W., *St John Chrysostom, Baptismal Instructions, Ancient Christian Writers* 31, Westminster & London 1963.
HARRIS, J. RENDEL, *The Odes of Solomon*, London 1909.
HARVEY, W. W., *Irenaeus c. Haereses*, Cambridge 1857.
HENNECKE, E. (ed.), *New Testament Apocrypha*, ET R. McL. Wilson, London 1963, vol. 2 London 1965.
HORNER, G. W., *Statutes of the Apostles*, London 1904.
HUBERT, F., *Die Strassburger Liturgischen Ordnungen in Zeitalter der Reformation*, Göttingen 1900.
JALLAND, T. G., *The Origin and Evolution of the Christian Church*, London 1948.
JAMES, M. R., *The Apocryphal New Testament*, Oxford 1926.
JAUBERT, C. A., *Clément de Rome, Epître aux Corinthiens*, SC 167, Paris 1971.
JOLY, R., *Hermas, Le Pasteur*, SC 53, Paris 1968.
KIDD, B. J., *Documents Illustrative of the History of the Church*, 2 vols. London 1933.
KLIJN, A. F. J., *The Acts of Thomas*, Leiden 1962.
KRAFT, R. A. and PRIGENT, P., *Epître de Barnabé*, SC 172, Paris 1971.
LAMPE, G. W. H., *The Seal of the Spirit*, London 1967.
LAMY, T. J., *Sancti Ephraem Syri Hymni et Sermones*, Malines 1882.
LEEMING, B., *Principles of Sacramental Theology*, London 1956.
LIGHTFOOT, J. B., *The Apostolic Fathers*, London 1893.
LOWTHER CLARKE, W. K. (ed.), *Liturgy and Worship*, London 1931.
LUYKX, B. and SCHEYVEN, D., *La Confirmation, Doctrine et Pastorale*, Bruges 1958.
MACLEAN, A. J., in *Confirmation or the Laying on of Hands*, London 1934.
MAERTENS, T., *Histoire et Pastorale du Rituel du Catéchuménat et de Baptême*, Bruges 1962.
MARSH, H. G., *The Origin and Significance of the New Testament Baptism*, Manchester 1941.

MASON, A. J., *The Relation of Confirmation to Baptism*, London 1893.
MINGANA, A., *Woodbrooke Studies 6*, Cambridge 1933.
MITCHELL, L. L., *Baptismal Anointing*, London 1966.
MOHLBERG, L. C., *Liber Sacramentorum Romanae Aeclesiae Ordinis anni circuli (Sacramentarium Gelasianum)*, Rome 1958.
MOODY, D., *Baptism: Foundation for Christian Unity*, Philadelphia 1967.
MORIN, G., *Sancti Augustini Sermones, Miscellanea Agostiniana*, Rome 1930.
MOSS, B. S. (ed.), *Crisis for Baptism*, London 1965.
MUNIER, C., *Concilia Galliae A. 314–A.506*, Turnhout 1963.
NEUNHEUSER, B., *Baptism and Confirmation*, ET J. J. Hughes, London 1964.
O'DWYER, M., *Confirmation*, Dublin 1915.
OTTO, J. C. T., *Corpus Apologetarum*, Jena 1947.
PALMER, P. F., *Sacraments and Worship*, London 1957.
PERLER, O., *Méliton de Sardes, Sur la Pâque et Fragments*, SC 123, Paris 1966.
PERRY, M. (ed.), *Crisis for Confirmation*, London 1967.
PITRA, J. B., *Analecta Sacra*, vol. 2, 1876.
POCKNEE, C. E., *The Rites of Christian Initiation*, London 1962.
—— *Water and the Spirit*, London 1967.
POHLE, J. and PREUSS, A., *The Sacraments, A Dogmatic Treatise*, St. Louis and London 1946.
POURRAT, P., *Theology of the Sacraments*, St Louis & London 1930.
PULLER, F. W., *What is the Distinctive Grace of Confirmation?*, London 1880.
QUICK, O. C., *The Christian Sacraments*, London 1936.
REFOULÉ, R. F. and DROUZY, M., *Tertullien, Traité du Baptême*, SC 35, Paris 1952.
RICHARDS, G. C., *Baptism and Confirmation*, London 1942.
ROBINSON, J. ARMITAGE, *St Irenaeus, The Demonstration of the Apostolic Preaching*, London 1920.
SCHMEMANN, A., *Of Water and the Spirit*, London 1976.
SEHLING, E., *Die Evangelischen Kirchenordnungen des XVI. Jahrhunderts*, Leipzig 1902 etc.
SIMAN, E-P., *L'Expérience de l'Esprit par l'Église d'après la Tradition Syrienne d'Antioche*, Paris 1971.
STONE, D., *Holy Baptism*, London 1901.
THOMPSON, T. and SRAWLEY, J. H., *St. Ambrose On the Sacraments and On the Mysteries*, London 1950.
THORNTON, L. S., *Confirmation, Its Place in the Baptismal Mystery*, London 1953.
THOMPSON, T., *The Offices of Baptism and Confirmation*, Cambridge 1914.
THURIAN, M., *La Confirmation, Consécration des Laïcs*, Neuchâtel 1957.
TONNEAU, R. and DEVRÉESSE, R., *Homélies Catéchétiques de Théodore de Mopsueste*, Citta del Vaticano 1949.
VAN BUCHEM, L. A., *L'Homélie Pseudo-Eusébienne de Pentecôte*, Nijmegen 1967.
VILLIEN, A., *The History and Liturgy of the Sacraments*, London 1932.
WAINWRIGHT, G., *Christian Initiation*, London 1969.
WARREN, F. E., *Liturgy of the Ante-Nicene Church*, London 1897.
WENGER, A., *Huit Catéchèses Baptismales Inédites*, SC 50, Paris 1957.
WHITAKER, E. C., *Documents of the Baptismal Liturgy*, London 1970.
—— *The Baptismal Liturgy*, London 1965.
WHITE, R. E. O., *The Biblical Doctrine of Initiation*, London 1960.

WILMART, A., *Analecta Reginensia*, Citta del Vaticano 1933.
WILSON, R. McL., *The Gospel of Philip*, London 1962.
WIRGMAN, A. T., *The Doctrine of Confirmation*, London 1897.
WOOLLEY, R. M., *Exorcism and the Healing of the Sick*, London 1931.
WOTHERSPOON, H. J., *Religious Values in the Sacraments*, Edinburgh 1928.
WRIGHT, W., *Apocryphal Acts of the Apostles*, London 1871.
YARNOLD, E., *The Awe-Inspiring Rites of Initiation*, Slough 1971.
YSEBAERT, J., *Greek Baptismal Terminology*, Nijmegen 1962.

(b) Shorter Works and Articles

ATKINSON, J., 'Confirmation: the Teaching of the Anglican Divines', in *The Churchman*, June 1963, pp. 92–9.
Baptism and Confirmation, Latimer Monograph 2, Abingdon 1967.
Baptism and Confirmation Today, Final Report of the Joint Committee on Baptism, Confirmation and Holy Communion, London 1955.
Baptism Today, Second Interim Report of the Joint Committee on Baptism, Confirmation and Holy Communion, London 1949.
BAREILLE, G., 'La Confirmation d'après les Pères Grecs et Latins', in *Dictionnaire de Théologie Catholique*, III, 1908, cols. 1026–58.
BECK, E., 'Le Baptême chez Saint Ephrem', in *L'Orient Syrien*, I, Paris 1956.
BECKWITH, R. T., 'The Age of admission to Communion', in *The Churchman*, Spring 1971, pp. 13–31.
BISHOP, W. C., 'The African Rite', in *JTS*, Jan. 1912, pp. 250–77.
BOTTE, B., 'Le Baptême dans l'Église Syrienne', in *L'Orient Syrien*, I, Paris 1956, pp. 137–55.
BOUYER, L., 'La Signification de la Confirmation', in *La Vie Spirituelle Suppl.*, May 1954, pp. 167–79.
BROCK, S., 'Studies in the Early History of the Syrian Orthodox Baptismal Liturgy', in *JTS*. April 1972, pp. 16–64.
BYWORTH, C. H. B., *Conversion, Confirmation and Commitment*, Bramcote 1972.
CAMELOT, Th., 'Sur la Théologie de la Confirmation', in *Revue des Sciences Philosophiques et Théologiques*, Paris 1954, pp. 637–57.
CARRINGTON, P., 'Confirmation and St. Justin', in *Theology*, Dec. 1949, pp. 448–52.
CHAVASSE, A., 'L'Initiation à Rome dans l'Antiquité et le Haut Moyen Age', in *Communion Solennelle et Profession de Foi*, Paris 1952, pp. 13–45.
CLARK, N. and JASPER, R. C. D., *Initiation and Eucharist*, London 1972.
Confirmation Today, Report of the Joint Committee of the Convocations of Canterbury and York, London 1944.
COPPENS, J., 'Confirmation', in *Dictionnaire de la Bible, Suppl. 2*, Paris 1934, cols. 121–45.
COURATIN, A. H., 'Baptism, the Liturgical Pattern', in *CQR*, Oct.–Dec. 1956.
—— 'Justin Martyr and Confirmation – A Note', in *Theology*, Dec. 1952, pp. 458ff.
CREHAN, J. H., 'Confirmation', in *A Catholic Dictionary of Theology*, 1966.
—— 'The Sealing at Confirmation', in *Theological Studies*, Woodstock, June 1953, pp. 273–9.

DANIÉLOU, J., 'Baptême, Pâque, Eucharistie', in *Communion Solennelle et Profession de Foi*, Paris 1952, pp. 117–33.

DAVIES, J. G., 'The Disintegration of the Christian Initiation Rite', in *Theology*, Nov. 1947, pp. 407–12.

DE CATANZARO, C. J., 'The Gospel according to Philip', in *JTS*, April 1962, pp. 35–71.

DE PUNIET, P., 'La Liturgie Baptismale en Gaule avant Charlemagne', in *RSR*, vol. 2 (1911), pp. 383–411.

—— 'Onction et Confirmation', in *RHE* vol. 13 (1912) pp. 450–66.

—— 'Confirmation', in *Dictionnaire d'Archaeologie Chrétienne et de Liturgie*, vol. 3 (1914) cols. 2532ff.

DIX, G., *'Confirmation or the Laying on of Hands'*, Theology Occasional Paper, London 1936.

—— 'The Seal in the Second Century', in *Theology*, Jan. 1948, pp. 7–12.

FAIRWEATHER, E., 'Memorandum on Confirmation: the Basic Issue', in *Partners in Mission*, Dublin 1973, pp. 44ff.

FISHER, J. D. C., 'The Consecration of Water in the Early Rites of Baptism', in *Studia Patristica*, vol. 2, Berlin 1957, pp. 41–6.

—— *Confirmation and the Ely Report*, London 1971.

—— *'Confirmation and Commitment'*, in *The Anglican Catholic*, Spring 1973, pp. 4–7.

—— 'A Critique of Prayer Book Studies 26', in *The Anglican Catholic*, Summer 1974, pp. 2–6.

GALTIER, P., 'La Consignation à Carthage et à Rome', in *RSR*, 1911.

—— 'La Consignation dans les Églises d'Occident', in *RHE*, vol. 13 (1912), pp. 261–301, 467–76.

HANSON, A. T., 'Was there a Complementary Rite of Initiation in the First Two Centuries?', in *Theology*, April 1972, pp. 190–7.

HICKINBOTHAM, J. P., 'Confirmation in the Early Centuries', in *The Churchman*, June 1963, pp. 84–91.

—— 'The Sacrament of Baptism and its Relation to Confirmation', in *Baptism and Confirmation*, London, pp. 21–30.

Holy Baptism with the Laying on of Hands, Prayer Book Studies *18*, New York 1970.

Holy Baptism, Prayer Book Studies *26*, New York 1973.

HUGHES, P. E., 'Confirmation in the Church Today', in *The Churchman*, June 1960, pp. 84–9.

—— 'Confirmation: Recent Theological Trends', in *The Churchman*, June 1963, pp. 100–13.

KIRK, K. E., Criticism of the Report of the Joint Committee of the Convocations of Canterbury and York, *Oxford Diocesan Magazine*, Nov. and Dec. 1944.

LAMBOT, C., 'L'Écrit Attribué à S. Augustin Adversus Fulgentium Donatistam', in *Révue Bénédictine*, 1948, pp. 177–209.

LAMPE, G. W. H., 'The Holy Spirit and Baptism', in *The Churchman*, Dec. 1952, pp. 198–208.

—— 'Baptisma in the New Testament', in *Scottish Journal of Theology*, vol. 5 (1952), pp. 163–74.

—— 'Theological Issues in the Baptism–Confirmation Controversy', in *The Modern Churchman*, July 1957, pp. 15–28.

LAWTON, W., 'Confirmation in the Light of Prayer Book Revision', in *The Churchman*, Sept. 1963, pp. 185–96.

LÉCUYER, J., 'La Confirmation chez les Pères', in *Maison Dieu*, no. 56 (1958), pp. 23–52.

—— 'San Juan Crisotomo y la Confirmacion', in *Orbis Catholicus*, Barcelona Nov. 1958.

LEEMING, B., 'The False Decretals, Faustus of Riez and the Pseudo-Eusebius', in *Studia Patristica*, vol. 2, Oxford 1955, pp. 122–40.

LOCKTON, W., 'The Age for Confirmation', in *CQR*, April 1925, pp. 27–64.

MANSON, T. W., 'Entry into Membership of the Early Church', in *JTS*, Jan.–April 1947, pp. 25–32.

MITCHELL, L. L., 'The Baptism Rite in Chrysostom', in *Anglican Theological Review*, vol. 43 (1961).

MORETON, M., 'Groundwork for Initiation', in *Theology*, Nov. 1971, pp. 522–9.

—— 'The Emergence and the Forms of a Rite of Initiation in the Church', in *Theology*, June 1972.

MORRIS, A. E., 'Confirmation and South India', in *Theology*, Jan. 1930, pp. 28–40 and Feb. 1930, pp. 71–6.

NEUNHEUSER, B., 'De Consecratione aquae baptismalis', in *Ephemerides Liturgicae*, vol. 44 (1930), pp. 194–207, 258–81, 369–412.

OULTON, J. E. L., 'Second Century Teaching on Holy Baptism', in *Theology*, March 1947, pp. 86–91.

POCKNEE, C. E., 'Confirmation in the Anglican Tradition', in *CQR*, Jan.–March 1966, pp. 71–6.

—— 'The Matter and Form of Confirmation', in *CQR*, April–June 1966, pp. 236–42.

—— *The Rites of Christian Initiation*, London 1962.

RAES, A., 'Où se trouve la Confirmation dans le Rite Syro-Oriental?', in *L'Orient Syrien*, vol. 1 (1966), pp. 239–54.

RAMSEY, A. M., 'The Doctrine of Confirmation', in *Theology*, Sept. 1945, pp. 193–201.

RATCLIFF, E. C., 'Justin Martyr and Confirmation', in *Theology*, April 1945, pp. 133–9.

—— 'The Relation of Confirmation to Baptism in the Early Roman and Byzantine Liturgies', in *Theology*, Sept. and Oct. 1946, pp. 258–65, 290–5.

—— 'The Old Syrian Baptismal Tradition and its Resettlement under the influence of Jerusalem in the Fourth Century', in *Studies in Church History*, vol. 2 (1965), pp. 19–37.

RAWLINSON, A. E. J., *Christian Initiation*, London 1947.

SLADDEN, J. C., 'Baptism and the Gift of the Holy Spirit', in *CQR*, July–Sept. 1948, pp. 220–45.

SOUTER, A., 'Observations on the Pseudo-Eusebian Collection of Gallican Sermons', in *JTS*, vol. 41 (1940).

STONE, D., in *CQR*, Jan. 1898, pp. 358–81 (review of F. W. Puller, A. J. Mason, and A. T. Wirgman).

—— 'The Age for Confirmation', in *CQR*, Oct. 1886, pp. 52–83.

TAYLOR, F. J., 'The History of Confirmation in the Christian Church', in *Baptism and Confirmation*, London 1945, pp. 35–44.

The Theology of Christian Initiation, Report of the Theological Commission, London 1948.

THORNTON, L. S., 'Baptism and Confirmation in Current Controversy', in *C.R.* June 1952, pp. 1–7.

—— 'The Holy Spirit in Christian Initiation', in *Eastern Churches Quarterly*, vol. 7, suppl. 1948, pp. 53–69.

—— *Confirmation Today*, 1946.

TINDALL, F. C., *Christian Initiation*, Lyminster 1951.

UMBERG, J. B., 'Confirmatione baptismus perficitur', in *Ephemerides Theologicae Lovanienses*, Oct. 1924, pp. 505–15.

VAN DEN EYNDE, D., 'Le Deuxième Canon du Concile d'Orange de 441 sur la chrismation', in *Recherches de Théologie Ancienne et Médiévale*, vol. 2 (1939).

VIDLER, A. R., Editorials in *Theology*, Jan. 1945, p. 1, April 1945, p. 73, Sept. 1945, p. 193.

VISCHER, L., *Ye are Baptized*, Geneva 1954.

WHITAKER, E. C., 'Unction in the Syrian Baptismal Rite', in *CQR*, April–June 1961, pp. 176–87.

—— *Sacramental Initiation Complete in Baptism*, Bramcote 1975.

WILSON, W. G., 'Christian Initiation', in *CQR*, Jan.–March 1957, pp. 21–38.

ZEITLIN, S., 'L'Origine de l'Institution du Baptème pour les Prosélytes', in *Révue des Études juives*, Paris 1934.

Index